JOURNAL FOR THE STUDY OF THE NEW TESTAMENT
SUPPLEMENT SERIES
114

Executive Editor
Stanley E. Porter

Sheffield Academic Press
Sheffield

Argument and Theology in 1 Peter

The Origins of Christian Paraenesis

Lauri Thurén

Journal for the Study of the New Testament
Supplement Series 114

Published by
Sheffield Academic Press Ltd
Mansion House
19 Kingfield Road
Sheffield, S11 9AS
England

Typeset by Sheffield Academic Press
and
Printed on acid-free paper in Great Britain
by Bookcraft
Midsomer Norton, Somerset

British Library Cataloguing in Publication Data

A catalogue record for this book is available
from the British Library

ISBN 1-85075-546-9

CONTENTS

ABBREVIATIONS

AB	Anchor Bible
AnBib	Analecta biblica
Bauer-Aland	W. Bauer, K. Aland and B. Aland, *Wörterbuch zum Neuen Testament*
BDR	F. Blass, A. Debrunner and F. Rehkopf, *Grammatik des neutestamentlichen Griechisch*
Bib	*Biblica*
BibB	Biblische Beiträge
BNTC	Black's New Testament Commentaries
BR	E. Bornemann, and E. Risch, *Griechische Grammatik*
BTB	*Biblical Theology Bulletin*
ConBNT	Coniectanea biblica, Old Testament
EKKNT	Evangelisch-katholischer Kommentar zum Neuen Testament
EWNT	*Exegetisches Wörterbuch zum Neuen Testament*
ExpTim	*Expository Times*
HNT	Handbuch zum Neuen Testament
HTKNT	Herders theologischer Kommentar zum Neuen Testament
JBL	*Journal of Biblical Literature*
JETS	*Journal of the Evangelical Theological Society*
JSNTSup	*Journal for the Study of the New Testament*, Supplement Series
JTS	*Journal of Theological Studies*
LD	Lectio divina
MeyerK	H.A.W. Meyer (ed.), Kritisch-exegetischer Kommentar über das Neue Testament
NABPRSSS	National Association of Baptist Professors of Religion, Special Studies Series
NCB	New Century Bible
Neot	*Neotestamentica*
NICNT	New International Commentary on the New Testament
NovT	*Novum Testamentum*
NovTSup	*Novum Testamentum*, Supplements
NTD	Das Neue Testament Deutsch
NTS	*New Testament Studies*
RHPR	*Revue d'historie et de philosophie religieuses*
SB	Sources bibliques

SBLDS	SBL Dissertation Series
SBLMS	SBL Monograph Series
SBS	Stuttgarter Bibelstudien
SCBO	Scriptorum Classicorum Bibliotheca Oxoniensis
SNTSS	Society for New Testament Studies Special Studies
SUNT	Studien zur Umwelt des Neuen Testaments
Teubner	Bibiotheca Scriptorum Graecorum et Romanorum Teubneriana
TRu	*Theologische Rundschau*
ThWNT	G. Kittel and G. Friedrich (eds.), *Theologisches Wörterbuch zum Neuen Testament*
TTki	Tidsskrift for teologi og kirke
TynBul	*Tyndale Bulletin*
WA	M. Luther, *Kritische Gesamtausgabe* (= 'Weimar' edition)
WBC	Word Biblical Commentary
WUNT	Wissenschaftliche Untersuchungen zum Neuen Testament
ZNW	*Zeitschrift für die neutestamentliche Wissenschaft*

Part I

INTRODUCTION

Chapter 1

THE PROBLEM: EARLY CHRISTIAN PARAENESIS AND 1 PETER

1. *The Aim of the Study*

The growing interest in moral rules among the Christians of the late first century is often seen as a symptom of a degradation of unique Christian ideas. This meant that the revolutionary teaching of Jesus and the Pauline justification by faith were gradually replaced by an emphasis on good works and ethics borrowed from the surrounding Hellenistic and Jewish culture.[1] Other scholars, however, still claim that the *paraenesis*[2] should be seen as an original and essential part of Early Christian doctrine and life (Schrage 1982: 1, 16-20).

In the discussion it is important to mention the possible unique characteristics of Christian paraenesis and the actual function of the exhortations given to the congregations. Despite lively debate the scholars have hitherto reached one basic result: in the rules for thought and behaviour there is little which is original or exceptional.[3] Similar or corresponding teaching can be found in contemporary philosophical and religious texts.

The essence of the practical moral teaching may, however, not be found in commands but in the motivation.[4] It is possible that the very

---

1. Preisker 1949: 195-219; Sanders 1986: 67ff. He discerns a 'movement toward an unreflected ethics that is indistinguishable from good citizenship' (1986: 88). Donelson (1986: 198, 200) characterizes the Pastoral Epistles and 1 Peter as 'primarily an exhortation to ethical behavior', which also means an ethical view of Christianity and thus a diversion from original Paulinism. Schulz (1987: 614-20) speaks of 'die Moralisierung des Heils'. Marxsen correspondingly characterizes the ethics in Matthew as a 'Rückfall in pharisäische Ethik' (1989: 216).

2. For a definition, see Chapter 1 §2.b.

3. For discussion, see Piper 1979: 101-102; *Semeia* 50 (1990). An exception to the rule according to Piper is the command to love your enemy (1979: 63-65). See also Marxsen 1989: 189-94. Concerning 1 Peter see already van Unnik 1954/55: 107.

4. For discussion of the terms 'motivation', 'persuasion', 'argumentation' etc., see Chapter 2 §3.a.

way whereby the requirements are motivated reveals the actual nature of the Early Christian paraenesis.[5] Thus a thorough investigation of the motivation of the paraenesis is needed. We must ask, what kind of argumentation was used in order to support the commands, how they were designed to shape and modify the first Christians' attitudes and beliefs, and how they were thereby motivated to think and act in a certain way.

The answers are hard to find, since the New Testament texts were not theoretical ethical treatises, but usually written to actual congregations, which lived in various situations and had specific problems. When attempting to influence real people an author cannot present all his ideas in a theoretical and balanced way throughout the text; he has to fit his message to his audience (see below Chapter 2 §1). This means that the nature of these texts is rhetorical. A superficial comparison of different texts, or a synthesis of diverse expressions with little reference to their argumentative situations, easily leads to a biased result.[6] Therefore this study focuses on one particular text.

The First Letter of Peter builds on general Christian traditions to a greater extent than, for example, the Pauline letters. It is generally seen as bound to tradition, where the author's individual theology is less dominant (Lohse 1954: 85; van Unnik 1954/55: 92; Piper 1980: 218). As a circular letter sent to a large, although definite, area (Thurén 1990: 81-83), it has a rather general, 'catholic' nature. Therefore the letter can be seen with some justice as representative of at least one type of ordinary faith in its original milieu, which probably was Rome (see Selwyn 1947: 60-61; Schelkle 1970: 11; Goppelt 1978: 66; cf. also Thiede 1986: 532-38). Thereby a study of the grounds for the commands in 1 Peter can in principle shed new light on the character of the paraenesis in one form of Early Christianity, provided that the effects of the rhetorical

---

5.   Thus e.g. Marxsen 1989. According to him the decisive factor is the Christological motivation. If the ethics of a text are not clearly combined with Pauline or pre-Pauline Christology, they cannot be called real Christian ethics (1989: 201-203) (Matthew, 2 Thessalonians, James and the Pastoral Epistles are examples for such a decline: see 1989: 216, 223, 229, 220). Marxsen's perspective, however, is very narrow since he only picks up a single theme in the motivation. The approach is also theoretical and dogmatic since it does not focus on the actual function of Christological statements in their immediate rhetorical situations. Lategan (1990: 327) has a more realistic view.

6.   This, I believe, is the fundamental problem with long presentations of New Testament ethics, such as most of the works mentioned above.

situations of the letter can be taken into account.

This book attempts to explain how the paraenesis is motivated in 1 Peter. An ideological analysis of this rhetorical text will be executed with a specific technique. By identifying the motivating expressions, and analysing their function in their argumentative context, and by comparing the roles which different themes play in the structures of argumentation in the whole Letter, I seek to reconstruct an ideological structure beyond the text and its particular situation, and thereby reach a sound and cogent picture of the author's thinking as it can be observed here. Such a view then provides us with a basis for wider inferences about the nature of the Early Christian paraenesis and ethics.

The main task leads to two inherent objectives, which may even have some independent value. First, the necessary detailed investigation of the argumentation in 1 Peter may also facilitate the understanding of many themes and problematic expressions in that text. Secondly, in order to carry out the main task, a suitable approach for argumentation analysis must be devised, which may be applied even to other texts.

Thus, this book is not only another study of 1 Peter, but a survey on paraenesis in general, including a methodological discussion about argumentation analysis.

This first chapter of Part I, Introduction, presents a brief overview of the studies of 1 Peter. I shall review some trends in the scholarship and show that the current situation in the research of the Letter even as such requires an exhaustive investigation of the motivating themes therein.

Chapter 2 presents a method for analysing the argumentation. First, the theory and current trends in argumentation analysis are discussed; for those readers who are familiar with the recent development, a cursory reading of this section may suffice. Second, a viable model for identifying ideological structures is proposed. The discussion stays on a rather general level and may thus be applicable even to other types of texts.

In Part II, Analysis, the method is applied to 1 Peter and the actual text is analysed.

In Part III, Synthesis, the general ideological structure of the motivation in 1 Peter is delineated, and finally some conclusions concerning the Early Christian paraenesis are offered.

2. *The Research on 1 Peter*

Introduction

The First Letter of Peter is a puzzling text. Despite its background comprised of scattered traditions,[7] its hazy historical situation (see below), its inclusion of several different themes,[8] and its many obscure or ambiguous expressions and ways of thought (see further Thurén 1990: 4-29), it nevertheless appears to have a clear message, a warm pastoral tone[9] and an exquisite command of language and rhetorical techniques (Thurén 1990: 175-76).

The scholars do not agree, however, on what that message actually is, and what is the *theology* or *ideology*[10] behind the text. The complex background and appearance of the text have prompted many possible ways of understanding it; even the use of a great number of methods has led to different questions, augmenting thereby the plurality of interpretation. The scholars have arrived at several, even opposite results when explaining individual themes in the text, the author's goals, his ethics and theology.

In a recent dissertation, I sought to show that in order to perceive the message of the author, we have to understand his use of ambiguous expressions. A rhetorical perspective proved to be the only viable means

7. There is a consensus among the scholars that 1 Peter is to a great extent bound to different traditions (e.g. Lohse 1954: 85; van Unnik 1954/55: 92; Vanhoye 1979: 97-128; Piper 1980: 218). It contains material from the Old Testament, Jewish and Early Christian tradition (see Goppelt 1978: 55-56), but is also influenced by the Hellenistic popular philosophy (see Goppelt 1978: 168-73). This material further appears in varying literary forms, e.g. liturgical sections and catalogical paraeneses.

8. E.g. the themes of the exodus, baptism, Christology, eschatology, ethical exhortation, mission etc. A characteristic feature for 1 Peter is that many such themes appear throughout the text and play so important a role that several of them have been assessed as *the* theme of the letter (see below).

9. This can be said, despite the rather theoretical character of the text: no particular problems are mentioned and the author's person appears clearly only in the beginning (1.1) and end (5.1) of the text.

10. I distinguish between features on the *text* level (including syntactic, semantic and pragmatic aspects) and features on the *ideological* level. To the latter I assign *general sets of ideas*, which do not directly belong to the actual communication or interaction between the author and the addressees, but which exist beyond the text and influence it. Theology is seen as a specific type of ideology: general sets of ideas concerning issues about God and religion.

to this end. The letter is written by an unidentified author at an unknown time to several congregations not familiar to us; therefore their historical situations cannot be identified with precision (for detailed discussion, see Thurén 1990: 30-38). However, the use of modern rhetorics and a search for the encoded situation(s) in the text proved enlightening. It turned out that the ambiguities are often due to the author's rhetorical strategy, by which he attempts to meet the addressees' different and delicate problems: the conscious use of ambiguity enables him to appeal in a single text to different types of audience and overcome their negative expectations (Thurén 1990: 175).

It also became apparent that a rhetorical perspective would facilitate the understanding of other problematic expressions in the text, and that especially the idea of deliberate ambiguity as a rhetorical device would greatly assist the study of issues on a higher, ideological level, such as the ethics and theology of the author (see Thurén 1990: 26-27, 185-86). This book is an effort to proceed in that direction.

The study of the motivation of paraenesis in 1 Peter is however prompted not so much by the possibilities offered by the new approach as by the current situation in the research of the Letter.

a. *The Cultic Interpretation*

In studying the text of 1 Peter there have been two possibilities: to focus on particular themes while disregarding others, or to seek a common denominator to the different themes and attempt to create a general picture of the Letter.[11] The first choice is traditional: such themes as the universal priesthood (in 1 Pet. 2.5; for discussion, see Brox 1979: 108-10) or Christ's proclamation in Hades (1 Pet. 3.19; for discussion, see Brox 1979: 182-89; Goppelt 1978: 250-54) have been culled from the text.

In the era of the History of Religions School at the beginning of this century, the scholars chose the alternative, and saw baptism as the central theme of the whole text. According to this cultic interpretation, 1 Peter was a baptismal homily or liturgy, and particular sections of the text were interpreted by using this hypothesis.[12] The text in fact includes

11. This according to Balch (1981: 14) is something characteristic of 1 Peter. Martin (1992a: 1-40, 277-84) presents a history of the compositional analyses of 1 Peter, dividing the studies into six groups. However, his principle of classification combines formal and contentual aspects, and is thereby artificial.

12. R. Perdelwitz compared 1 Peter with mystery religions and claimed that 1.3–4.11 is a baptismal homily (1911: 19) and 1.1-2; 4.12–5.14 a later exhortatory

many allusions to baptism (such as 3.21 and 1.3, 23; 2.2), but the problem is that they are limited to its first part (thus Lohse 1954: 70). A greater part of the text discusses, for example, the question of unjust suffering, rules for the social life, internal relations in the congregation, and so on—issues that have no clear connection to baptism.[13] The baptismal interpretation also overlooks some epistolary and rhetorical features in the text (see Thurén 1990: 89 n. 2).

b. *The General Paraenetic Interpretation*
The arrival of form criticism meant a turn in the study of 1 Peter, or 'die neuen Wege'.[14] Already in 1931 M. Dibelius criticized the earlier research and characterized 1 Peter as a typical paraenesis,[15] which resulted in a new approach to the Letter. After E.G. Selwyn's commentary in 1947[16] the paraenetic view became generally

---

sermon (1911: 26). The idea was developed by W. Bornemann, according to whom 1 Peter is a baptismal homily based on Ps. 34 and written by Silvanus (Bornemann 1919/1920). H. Preisker attempted to reconstruct a whole service on the basis of 1 Peter: 1.3–4.11 would be a baptismal service and 4.12-15 a liturgy for the whole congregation (Windisch and Preisker 1951[3]: 156-61; originally Windisch 1911). The cultic interpretation culminated in F.L. Cross's article (1957[2], originally published in 1954), in which he accepted Preisker's thesis about the baptismal liturgy, but attempted to do justice to the many references to suffering in the text, which were not suited to a baptismal feast. According to Cross, the text deals with a baptism at Passover because of a popular etymological connection between πάσχω and πάσχα (1957: 12-17). In 1963/64 he gained further support from A.R.C. Leaney (238-51). The most recent representive of the theory, M.-E. Boismard (1961), claimed that the text at least includes some fragments of an earlier baptismal liturgy.

13. For more criticism of the cultic interpretation, see e.g. Thornton 1961; Manke 1976: 9-11; Hill 1976: 181-82; Goppelt 1978: 84-85.

14. The term was first used by Lohse (1954: 71). See also Nauck 1955: 68.

15. Dibelius 1931. As a ground for his thesis Dibelius referred to the central position of the household code, which is difficult to combine with a baptismal view of the whole text.

16. Selwyn did not criticize the baptismal interpretation severcly, but he showed that Perdelwitz's relation of thoughts in 1 Peter to mystery religions is not viable (1947: 305-11; cf. also the interpretation of νῦν on p. 41). Instead he directs attention to traditional Christian material, based on A. Seeberg's (1903) and P. Carrington's (1940) studies, and finds among other material catechetical elements (Selwyn 1947: 17-24, 459-61), from which he attempts to reconstruct an Early Christian catechism (1947: 389).

accepted.[17] Before proceeding, a brief discussion of the term is necessary.

The word 'paraenesis' often carries a somewhat vague significance.[18] It is useful to start from a definition, according to which paraenesis refers to a literary genre, consisting of various practical moral instructions aimed at changing the audience's behaviour (cf. Stowers 1986: 91; Malherbe 1986: 124; Perdue 1990: 6; Gammie 1990: 70). Such paraenesis appeared throughout the Near East,[19] and was commonly used as a device for social formation and control.[20]

Attempts at a narrower definition, for example, a distinction between paraenesis, *protrepsis* and *paraklesis*, have proven difficult.[21] Such definitions remain idiosyncratic, since they cannot comply with the vague ancient usage of the terms. It is also difficult to classify the existing texts, since they seldom have such a homogeneous form and message.[22]

On the contrary, the definition must be even broader. It is questionable whether paraenesis can be restricted to texts aimed at changing behaviour—often it rather has a confirming function (Stowers 1986: 92-93). In terms of ancient rhetoric, paraenesis is usually epideictic, not

17. Lohse (1954: 68) provides a good review of the study of 1 Peter in the late 1940s and early 1950s. The paraenetical view of 1 Peter has since become widely accepted (see e.g. Berger 1984: 133).

18. Already Dibelius, the first great scholar of paraenesis, used the word about a single section in a text (1921: 4: 'Die Mandata des Hermas enthalten also ausgeführte P.'), as referring to a whole book (*ibid.*: 'Wir dürften also den Jakobus-"brief" als P. bezeichnen'), or about a specific form of tradition (*ibid.*: 'Denn die urchristliche P...'). The usage in modern scholarship is equally vague. E.g. Goppelt used the word paraenesis when referring to an exhortation (1978: 21), a short collection of exhortations (1978: 155), a specific type of exhortation (1978: 113, 196), or exhortation as a collective term (1978: 163).

19. A good presentation is provided by Perdue (1990).

20. Perdue 1990: 7-9. According to him, paraenesis was commonly aimed at a conservative conformation to the rules of the society (1990: 24-26), but could even have a critical role vis-à-vis the existing rules (1990: 26-27). It was typical in liminal settings such as baptism or death (1990: 19).

21. See Gammie's critique of Stowers (Gammie 1990: 43), his own attempt (1990: 47), and Robbins's critique thereof and the presentation of Berger's system (1990: 262-63; cf. Berger 1984: 117-220).

22. Thus e.g. Attridge (1990: 212-14) concerning the application of Gammie's criteria on Hebrews.

deliberative.[23] This means intensifying and reinforcing existing values rather than creating new ones.

This, in turn, makes it difficult in practice to distinguish between moral instruction aimed at affecting behaviour, and instruction aimed at affecting values and convictions. The assessment is arduous already concerning single statements, and we should be even more hesitant when defining the function or goal of the whole paraenesis: the use of paraenesis in social control is but one possibility.[24]

Thus, I use the term 'paraenesis' as referring to a universal genre consisting of exhortation and admonition, aimed at affecting the audience's attitudes and behaviour.

After Dibelius and Selwyn, a more conscious attempt at a paraenetic interpretation of 1 Peter was made by E. Lohse in 1953.[25] Although skeptical of Selwyn's hypothesis about an Early Christian catechism behind 1 Peter (Lohse 1954: 71-72), Lohse approves his thesis concerning the Letter's general paraenetic nature.[26] According to him the paraenesis is usually motivated by references to the will of God or to his acts, but states that 'the ultimate and actual rationale that 1 Peter offers for the ethical admonitions, however, is of a christological nature'.[27] The paraenesis is based on the Christological kerygma, which together with the eschatological hope is aimed at producing good works (1954: 89). Lohse sees the admonitions in 1 Peter mainly as ethical (1954: 86), although he also uses a somewhat obscure expression

23. Thus also Attridge 1990: 214, confirmed by Robbins 1990: 270-71; cf. also Quinn 1990: 197. Even Berger has a class called 'postconversionale Mahnrede' (1984: 130-35), although among 'symbuleutische Gattungen'. In a wide sense of the word, an epideictic text is aimed at reinforcing existing values and behaviour (see Thurén 1990: 72). Carter claims that epideictic rhetoric affects the audience by means 'beyond instrumental language' (1991: 232). We could say that epideictic is the rhetoric of rhetoric!

24. The goal may be e.g. changes in behaviour as such, or intensification of religious convictions, which then materialize in new conduct. The function of the paraenesis may even be only to serve the ethos of the author, as it presents the author as a man of high ethical standards (concerning Romans, see Botha 1991: 142-43; concerning Galatians, see Kraftchick 1985: 271-72).

25. The article was published one year later.

26. This view is based on comparison with other material in the New Testament.

27. Lohse 1954: 86: 'Die letzte und eigentliche Begründung aber, die der 1 Petr für die etischen Ermahnungen bietet, ist christologischer Art'. The translation is by J. Steely.

'Leidensparänese'.[28] Lohse's survey is far from complete—he neglects many types of motivating expression in the text[29]—yet his view of the dominant position of Christology in the motivation of paraenesis has strongly influenced subsequent research.[30]

In the same year, 1953, W.C. van Unnik also studied 1 Peter as a paraenesis.[31] Even he saw the admonitions mainly as ethical, and stated that 'they correspond to the highest standard of a decent man or woman in the ancient world... No special "Christian", but truly human, ethics are demanded' (1954/55: 107). The essential difference from the Gentile surroundings is found in the motivation (1954/55: 108), which van Unnik examines more closely, and finds more themes: (a) the end is at hand; (b) the addressees are set free by Christ, (c) from the vain life and the desire of the Gentiles; (d) they belong to God; (e) God is the Judge who has set certain conditions for their lives; (f) to suffer with Christ also means sharing his glory. A missionary ground (g) is found also: the addressees should so live that the Gentiles may glorify God in the day of Visitation (1954/55: 106). Although van Unnik calls this presentation 'systematic', he nevertheless does not expatiate on the motivating themes' relation to each other. He does, for example, mention expressions which mean that the addressees should do good since God will judge them according to each person's work (1954/55: 106), but simultaneously claims that 'these good works have no place in the process of salvation' (1954/55: 107).

An opposite interpretation of the motivation is presented by Preisker,[32] who sees the doctrine of retaliation, the idea of punishment and reward, as the most important factor in the Early Christian ethics in general, and so also in 1 Peter. The fear of the vindication and hope for

28. Lohse 1954: 81. If the term refers to advice and consolation given in a difficult situation, it may not be characterized as a set of purely ethical rules.

29. Even those grounds which Lohse mentions (the holiness and vengeance of God) are not compared with the Christological theme. He only states that the latter is the actual one (1954: 86).

30. It has, according to Piper (1980: 213), become a commonplace. Cf. also Schrage 1982: 256.

31. Van Unnik 1954/55. The two articles were completed almost simultaneously: Lohse 1.9.1953; van Unnik 9.9.1953.

32. Preisker 1949. Although Preisker's new version of Windisch's commentary (Windisch and Preisker 1951³) can be included among the 'old ways' of research, he discusses the same questions as Lohse and van Unnik in the above-mentioned book *Das Ethos des Urchristentums* (1949).

reward are aimed at motivating the Christians for good works (1949: 197). This new perspective, wholly incompatible with Lohse's and van Unnik's view, was unfortunately defectively documented in the text of 1 Peter, mainly because Preisker's book is a general presentation of the New Testament ethics in their entirety.

Summarizing the form-critical 'New Ways', it can be said, that by changing the comparative material from mystery religions to the New Testament the scholars were able to see 1 Peter as a representative for Early Christian paraenesis instead of being a cultic baptismal sermon. The principal function of the Letter was regarded as being to encourage the Christians under a persecution; however, the scholars' chief interest focused on the origin of the material in the text (cf. Lohse 1954: 72; Nauck 1955: 68). The main merit of the 'New Ways' was to place 1 Peter in its general paraenetic milieu, which, in contrast to the cultic interpretation, which was bound to a specific situation, was certainly in accordance with the heterogeneity of the text. However, the goals and methods of this trend also generated certain problems for the under-standing of the text. It was not read from its own premises or in view of its special character: while Preisker interpreted 1 Peter in connection with other Catholic epistles, Pastoral epistles, Acts, 1 Clement, and so on (1949: 195 n. 1; so also Grundmann 1938: 552), Lohse used Pauline ideas and expressions when studying 1 Peter without reflecting the issue.[33] The main object for the studies consisted in exhortations and admonitions, but their *origin*, not their function in the text.[34] The greatest discrepancy is however to be seen in the question of the *motivation of the paraenesis*.

33. When trying to see a difference between Paul and 1 Peter Lohse (1954: 82) says that according to 1 Peter, 'In baptism the Christian has died with Christ...'—a Pauline expression which does not occur in 1 Peter!—(89) '...through Christ's atoning death we have died to sin, in order to live unto righteousness...' added with a misleading reference to 2.24 where 1 Peter certainly has a pattern similar to Paul, but instead of ἀποθάνοντες (cf. Rom. 6–7) uses a less mystical expression ἀπο-γενόμενοι. H. Goldstein provides another warning example in his book *Paulinische Gemeinde im ersten Petrusbrief* (1975). These types of interpretations may be due to an effort to show that 1 Peter is a pseudo-pauline text (cf. Kosala 1985: 1). For further criticism against a Pauline tendency in the research of 1 Peter see Elliott 1976: 243.

34. Usually they are seen as being of an extra-Christian origin (see van Unnik 1954/55: 107), while some scholars also find specifically Christian features (Brandt 1953: 14; Piper 1979: 101-102).

In the interpretation of the motivation two main lines can be discerned: first, a view that I call 'positive'[35]: the motivation is based on the Christological kerygma, and good works have no significance for the addressees' salvation; secondly, a view that I call 'negative': fear of punishment and hope for a reward are aimed at motivating the addressees to good behaviour. These two views have not been contrasted because of a superficial approach to the material. Advocates for both views have neglected factors pointing in the opposite direction.

After Lohse and van Unnik the research in the 'New Ways' provided some important knowledge about particular themes in the text, but the basic situation concerning the motivation of paraenesis did not change: opposing themes were not compared with each other, which resulted in one-sided interpretations of the motivation, and thereby also of the Letter as whole. Several different grounds for motivation were studied, however, and the hypothesis about the purely 'positive' character of the motivation gained more support.

For example, W. Brandt examined the missionary motivation claiming that the Christians' good life serves as a commentary on the word proclaimed (1953: 25), the goal of which is that God is praised (1953: 14). W. Nauck stated in an article entitled 'Freude im Leiden' that joy over the reward the addressees have already obtained in Christ gives a reason for their perseverance in the midst of suffering (1955: 76-77). J.H. Elliott and F. Danker studied, from two different perspectives, the meaning of the honorary titles originally used about Israel, which are now applied to the addressees (Elliott 1966; Danker 1967). G. Delling emphasized the importance of dogmatic expressions about 'Christusgeschehen in Kreuz'[36] and the new existence of the addressees as Christians. These themes together lead according to Delling into an 'eschatological' hope.[37] Expressions about the fear of God or his Judgment were not discussed, although Delling also included a short overview of the motivation in the Letter (1973: 112). The 'negative' interpretation was poorly represented: only J.R. Michaels, when studying the eschatological motivation for unjust suffering, argued that the wrath of God is the ultimate rationale (1966: 401).

Despite the wide acceptance of these 'positive' interpretations of the

---

35. This is a technical term and does not reflect any priority of the interpretations.

36. Delling 1973: 101, 105—hardly a Petrine expression.

37. Delling even makes a distinction between 'endeschatologisch' and 'zukunftseschatologisch' 1973: 101, 104.

motivation, attempts to explain how, for example, the Christological 'Kerygma' or God's 'Heilshandeln' sought to prompt good behaviour were short and obscure.[38] At the same time, the scholars after Lohse took two steps backwards: while the cultic interpretation was rejected, the new idea of the paraenetic character of the Letter was not used in order to create an alternative total view thereof. Instead, the scholars began anew to study separate ideas in the text, with a focus on parallels in other texts, and on their origin (cf. e.g. van Unnik 1954/55; Coutts 1956/57; Best 1969/70), while paying little attention to their role in the context.

c. *New Perspectives*

After a period of stagnation, J.H. Elliott's characterization of 1 Peter as a 'step child' in New Testament exegesis (1976), and two large commentaries in the late seventies by L. Goppelt (posthumously in 1978) and N. Brox (1979; 2nd edn 1986), meant a certain renaissance in the studies of the Letter.[39] Many useful surveys in particular themes have been made,[40] which however prove no essential difference from the 'New Ways' research.

F. Neugebauer, for example, claims that the Christians' good works are motivated by their hope in God (1979: 73; cf. also Wendland 1970: 102) and their new freedom (Neugebauer 1979: 85). Neugebauer also notices the idea of fear of God, but only by stating that in 2.17 the author distinguishes between φοβέομαι and τιμάω, of which the stronger is connected with God.[41] D. Balch claims that the function of the 'Household Code' is missionary and apologetic (1981; so also J. Holdsworth 1978). T.P. Osborne studies the example of Christ in 2.21-25, which according to him is the motivating factor in the section (1983). Osborne also claims that the motif of 'God's judgment' serves only as a positive counterpart to the Gentiles' 'reproach, insult or reviling'

---

38. E.g. Brandt (1953: 16) says, 'Für unsere Thema mag der Hinweis genügen, dass noch eimal ganz stark heraustritt: Das neue Sein und das neue Tun der Christen sind durch Gottes Tun in Christus begründet und sind allein auf Gott gerichtet'. Cf. also Delling 1973: 112!

39. In Scandinavia, B. Olsson's excellent commentary (1982) also provoked interest in 1 Peter. Recently several commentaries have gathered the new knowledge on the letter: Michaels 1988; Davids 1990; Knoch 1990; Marshall 1990.

40. For an exhaustive catalogue until 1982, see Sylva 1982.

41. Neugebauer 1979: 85. However, in 3.2 the wives are told to show φόβος to their husbands.

(1983: 389): it is only aimed at increasing the addressees' faith in God. E. Richard stresses the dual function of Christology: soteriological statements simultaneously present Christ as a model for the addressees (Richard 1986; cf. also Elliott 1985). But Richard concludes his article by referring to rhetorics and states that the 'logic and argument (logos) [of the author] would require considerable analysis' (Richard 1986: 139).

There are, however, clear signs of discontent with the form-critical scholarship, which ended by discussing only details. Attempts have been made to achieve a new total view of the Letter with new methods: 1 Peter has become a test-field of new exegetical methods.[42]

The new approaches have provided us with additional aspects in the text, neglected by former research, and emphasizing its originality and specific goals. They have usually disregarded the paraenetical total view of the nature of the letter, however without providing any convincing alternative. Therefore they seldom cast new light on the theology or ideology behind the whole text.[43]

Elliott[44] and Balch (1986), for example, apply sociological models for 1 Peter which yield opposite results (see Thurén 1990: 36-37). Calloud and Genuyt analyse the text with Greimas's structuralist model (1982). The pattern fits neatly in the text but I have difficulty in finding many new solutions for understanding the problematic sections in 1 Peter.[45] Rousseau (1986) applies a 'multidimensional' method to the text including various old and modern approaches. Schutter (1989) studies the way in which the Old Testament is used in 1 Peter (cf. also Green 1990); here he applies a modern literary-critical approach. He claims *inter alia* that due to the pastoral tone in the Letter, no direct conclusions about the theology of the author can be drawn from the statements in the text. My dissertation utilizes modern and ancient rhetoric and epistolography (Thurén 1990).

However, in some studies the interest has returned to the paraenesis as a whole, and to its motivation. These have avoided some of

42. Such approaches as structuralism, sociological exegesis, text-linguistics, rhetorics, epistolography and modern literary criticism have been applied to the text.

43. Here, of course, I must regard my own rhetorical approach as an exception. But even in this study only the message of the author, rather than his theology, is examined.

44. Elliott 1981 and 1986. For a thorough and well-grounded criticism, see Feldmeier 1992.

45. However, even as affirming old results, a new well-reflected approach can be valuable.

the weaknesses of the earlier scholarship.

H. Manke and W. Schrage can be mentioned as representives of the 'positive' line of interpretation. Manke discusses the Christology and the idea of suffering and glory in 1 Peter (1976). He also briefly clarifies the meaning of these themes for the paraenesis in the Letter (1976: 233-46). Contrary to earlier research, he concentrates in 1 Peter alone. Speaking of a paraenetic 'Grundtenor' in the letter (1976: 233), Manke finds several types of motivating theme.[46] Contrary to van Unnik, for example, he also attempts to show how these themes function in the motivation.[47] Unfortunately, the result corresponds to what every scholar who has studied a particular theme in 1 Peter usually claims about his own topic: 'Die Christologie ist nun das massgebende Moment, das die paränetischen Aussagen motivieren hilft'.[48] This can be said, since several other central themes are in practice overlooked.[49] W. Schrage discusses the motivation of paraenesis in 1 Peter, and even provides the first systematic classification of the ideas used therein.[50] His system, however, represents only the 'positive' line and, typically enough, disregards among other things expressions about God's Judgment.

F.-R. Prostmeier also seeks a holistic view of the Letter. Like Elliott and Balch, he applies a sociological approach (Prostmeier 1990). While ignoring the 'negative' aspect, Prostmeier finds the 'Christological-soteriological' theme, based on the 'Kreuzestode [sic] Jesu', to be most important in the fourfold motivation.[51] The second theme is

46. The Old Testament, the calling God, new birth, Christ, will of God, the example of Sarah and the imminence of the end (Manke 1976: 236-37).

47. E.g. the use of Christology serves to emphasize the 'Einmaligkeit, Grösse und Ernsthaftkeit' of the addressees' situation (Manke 1976: 233) and the Old Testament quotations are intended to increase the power of the author's statements (Manke 1976: 336).

48. Manke 1976: 237. Cf. e.g. Moule's argument for the central meaning of the baptism in 1 Peter (Moule 1956/57: 4, 11).

49. E.g. about God's judgment he only says that it gives the seriousness required by the commands (Manke 1976: 237), and about the will of God that it is a 'letztlich entscheidendes Kriterium' (Manke 1976: 234).

50. Ten pages in Schrage's presentation of the New Testament ethics are devoted to 1 Peter (1982: 255-65). The motivation is classified in the following way: (1) The Christological-soteriological motifs; (2) The eschatological hope; (3) baptism and spiritual-charismatic grounds; (4) the Scriptures; (5) The example of Christ; (6) The missionary grounds.

51. Prostmeier 1990: 512-15—a typical unpetrine expression.

baptismal theology, the third 'pneumatisch-charismatische' motivation. Prostmeier's sociological approach enables him also to find a fourth, profane motivation, which refers to the expectations of the society. Thanksgiving is seen as central in the motivation (1990: 501). His short comment on the nature of the paraenesis is also interesting. According to him, the goal of the paraenesis is not to give new ethical education, but to justify existing rules which are already accepted (1990: 500).

Another fresh attempt to describe the paraenetic character of the Letter was published two years later by Troy Martin (1992a, esp. pp. 81-134). Unaware of Prostmeier, Martin arrives at similar results.[52] He too emphasizes, for example, that paraenesis concerns things already accepted by the addressees. However, since Martin only seeks the general function of the paraenesis and the formal composition of the text, disregarding its communicative and interactive functions, the study remains defective.

Moreover, Martin studies the motivation of the paraenesis (1992: 95-96). He too assesses the Christological statements (the sacrificial death and the example of Christ) as the most important. Eschatology is seen as another prominent motif, while other factors, including the will of God, the praise of God, impact on husband, and successful prayers, are less significant. This collection of the motifs is arbitrary and the 'negative' aspects are ignored.

The 'negative' line too, which was earlier rather poorly advocated, has gained new support. K.C.P. Kosala returns to the old idea of baptism as the central factor in the motivation (1985), thus invoking the line of thought previously discussed by Moule (1956) and Hill (1976), without mentioning them. Moule claimed that the letter has two main themes: baptism[53] and suffering. These are supposed to be in 'natural' connection, but how baptism actually motivates suffering remains unclear.[54] Twenty years late Hill goes one step further: 'A Christian's suffering and

---

52. His results concerning the epistolary structure of the Letter (pp. 41-80) and its double rhetorical strategy (274) also come close to my dissertation, which like Prostmeier's book was published two years earlier (Thurén 1990).

53. With the following impressive arguments: 'Who, indeed, could deny it?' (1985: 4) and 'as all are agreed' (1985: 11).

54. I have difficulties in finding support in 1 Peter for Moule's explanation: 'Suffering is connected with baptism (through Christ's baptism which meant the cross), and baptism is an epitome of the Christian doctrine of suffering. There is no context where Christian thought more naturally takes baptismal shape than the context of persecution...' (1956/57: 11).

baptism are linked because, in accepting baptism, he is affirming willingness to share in the known experience of baptized persons who were
commonly, if not constantly, treated with suspicion and hostility' (1976:
185). Hill interprets 1 Pet. 3.21 so that baptism means 'a firm response[55]
to God, a commitment to maintain before the world an upright life'
(1976: 188-89).

Now Kosala gives a more explicit explanation of the role of baptism in
the motivation. It has no saving effect[56] but gives power for a new life,
being a sign of the Christian's willingness to seek salvation, which is not
at all secure (1985: 31-32, 37, 197). The Christological expressions have
according to Kosala a similar function. The redemption only gives a
possibility of a new way of life, but does not as such lead to final
salvation (1985: 137).

Kosala has succeeded in two points better than the other scholars. He
searches seriously for a holistic interpretation of the Letter, and he coun-
ters the common 'positive' interpretation with the rare 'negative' one.
Unfortunately, Kosala does not discuss other new studies, which come
close to his topic, such as Manke and Balch (1981), although he knows
them. Important factors in the motivation, such as the ad-dressees' joy
over their new status, or the Gentiles' praise of God, are neglected.
Therefore even Kosala's results remain defective.

S. Schulz offers a detailed presentation of the motivation of paraenesis
in 1 Peter (1987: 613-32, esp. pp. 620-25). He claims that the tension
between faith and good works is totally absent from the Letter, the goal
of which is merely practical and moralistic. Old Pauline themes like
grace, baptism, cross (sic) still exist but their function has been changed
(1987: 618). For example baptism has in principle a soteriological
meaning, but in practice only makes a new life possible (1987: 623). The
Letter does not explicitly reject Pauline soteriology, but it is evident that,
contrary to Paul, to do good and to avoid bad is the decisive factor in
the Last Judgment (1987: 614-17).

Another type of the 'negative' interpretation is presented by J. Piper.[57]

---

55. In Greek ἐπερώτημα! For discussion of the word, see Chapter 5 §5.b.

56. Here Kosala reacts against a Pauline interpretation of 1 Peter.

57. In a study on 1 Pet. 3.9 Piper emphasizes that even when interpreting a
single verse, whole the text must be taken into account. First an 'hermeneutical
circle' between particular verses and the context may provide an adequate picture of
the motivation in 1 Peter (Piper 1980: 212). Piper's study 'Hope as the motivation for
love' is an extended version of pp.122-26 in his book *Love your Enemies* (1979).

He criticizes the earlier 'positive' interpretation for its failure to answer the question of *how* the Christological kerygma actually seeks to create motivation. In order to understand the character of the motivation Piper asks for *the* factor that is to guarantee that the addressees do as they are told to (1980: 213). After a short survey of the motivating expressions in the letter Piper provides a general picture of the motivation (1980: 217) and claims that the decisive factor is hope for the future given by God. When, on the other hand, love of enemy is put forward as a condition for salvation, this very stipulation becomes a crucially important factor in the whole motivation.[58]

Piper does not, however, totally succeed in his attempt to review the motivation in the Letter in a short article.[59] Central motifs such as the example of Christ or the intention of God are not examined at all. Even Piper's explanations of how hope actually should create motivation remain obscure.[60]

3. *The Situation and Guidelines for a New Study*

The situation in the research can be assessed so as to conclude that the paraenetical nature of 1 Peter is widely seen as the factor combining various ideas and traditions in the text. In the paraenesis the commands seem to be rather conventional. Thus, when seeking the specific nature of the paraenesis, the interest must be focused on the motivation. Several particular motivating themes have already been thoroughly discussed, but a proper synthesis is still lacking. Such an overview would not only yield a better picture of the motivation and thereby of the whole letter, but would also affect the interpretation of particular expressions and themes in the text. The new studies on the epistolary, literary, sociological, and especially rhetorical features in the text have provided us with new knowledge of 1 Peter and new perspectives to it,

58. This result is especially built upon an interpretation of 1 Pet. 3.9.

59. Piper admits this himself (1980: 213 n. 1).

60. He explains: 'For...we inevitably conform our behaviour to the future we desire most of all to enjoy' and describes good behaviour as 'a *natural* outgrowth of fully hoping in the future which is given and secured by the grace of God in Christ' (Piper 1980: 216-17, my italics). What the word 'natural' means is not explicated. Is the good future seen as a reward? If not, how does it motivate good behaviour? Because of unclarity at this crucial point, and because of defects in gathering the material in the letter, even Piper's explanation of 1 Pet. 3.9 remains problematic (see in more detail Chapter 5 §4.g.).

thus facilitating the characterization of the whole motivation in the Letter. Two basic requirements for a proper study of the motivation have become evident.

First, in order to obtain a sound view of particular ideas in the text a holistic picture of the letter is required. A diachronic study of different traditions and their origin does not suffice for this purpose. A synchronic approach, which focuses on the text itself instead of purely on its ideological or historical background or its consequence is also needed.[61]

Secondly, it would be misleading simply to collect similar words used in the motivation and then draw conclusions based on their content. Instead, in order to correctly interpret the separate ideas, their functions should be in focus. Since particularly the admonitory or motivating functions are common denominators for the different themes in the text, their study is important also when outlining the interaction between themes, resulting in a view on the ideology behind the whole paraenetical text.

The study of the functions calls for examination of the way in which each particular expression is designed to affect the addressee, or how in practice it should create motivation to follow an exhortation.[62] To this end, the rhetorical situations and the argumentative functions of the expressions must be taken into account.

Some of the recent studies partly satisfy the requirements presented above. But one point has always been neglected: in order to create a balanced, total picture of the motivation, all different motifs should be observed. Carelessness in this small and seemingly technical requirement appears to be a major source in a biased reading of the text in all studies

---

61. The usual over-emphasis of the role of baptism in 1 Peter is a typical example of negligence of this principle.

62. A principal lack at this point can be observed even in other research of paraenesis. E.g. F. Laub's study on the paraenetical function of the Christology in Hebrews (1980) does not ask how the Christological expressions seek to affect the addressees' behaviour. An example of a corresponding deficiency in the study of Pauline paraenesis is found in W. Schrage's book *Die konkreten Eizelgebote in der paulinischen Paränese* (1961, e.g. pp. 20, 82-83, 165). In a major study L. Nieder (1956, esp. 103-45), classifies the motivation of the Pauline paraenesis and finds several types of motifs, including God's will, judgment and salvation; Christ's example, death and redemption; Church, baptism, Spirit, and even motifs reminiscent of Stoic and popular philosophy. The specific function of each type and their interrelations remain, however, unclear. Nieder has a striking tendency to undermine the threatening aspects in the motivation.

of 1 Peter. This fact, together with the lack of an applicable method of analysing the rhetorical aspects and the structure of argumentation, has led to casual conclusions and biased results. One of the crucial issues in 1 Peter, the motivation undergirding the paraenesis, has therefore not yet been satisfactorily addressed.

From this situation emerge the objectives of this study: to provide a picture of how the paraenesis is motivated in 1 Peter, and to devise a method suitable for building up such a picture. These goals are, as has been argued earlier, significant for understanding Early Christian paraenesis and ethics.

Chapter 2

THE APPROACH: ON STUDYING THE STRUCTURE
OF ARGUMENTATION AND PERSUASION

1. *Introduction*

A basic reason for inconsistent results in characterizing the motivation in
1 Peter has been the lack of an adequate approach to the problem.
Therefore we have to start by discussing this issue. Since the situation
reflects a wider question in studying any ideological pattern in the New
Testament, this chapter may serve even further goals.

Conventional exegetical attempts to describe theological ideas or
ethics tend to suffer from negligence of one basic fact: the scholar wants
to find general concepts or doctrines in New Testament texts, but the
biblical author never intended to give a neutral, balanced presentation of
his ideology.[1] The Epistles especially were written in specific situations,
and usually to specific audiences, for the purpose of influencing the
recipients in a particular manner.[2] Knowledge of the historical situation
and of the literary genre are required (see Doty 1977: 37-38), but this
does not suffice for their understanding.

Since the author's goal has been to change or modify the addressees'
attitudes and behaviour, he could not give an unbiased picture of his
thoughts. Instead he has emphasized, even exaggerated, certain aspects.
Thus the main goal governs to a great extent the way in which different
themes and ideas are presented.

---

1. Not even Romans, which has been called Paul's description of his theology,
can be counted as such a presentation (against already Melanchthon, *Loci communes*
2.1, 7; Nygren 1944; O. Kuss 1971: 163). This rather common opinion, however,
does not mean that Paul did have a theology.

2. The Catholic Epistles may be somewhat different, since they are claimed to be
general treatises. Even if this were true, it would not mean that they lacked a certain
purpose to convince and persuade the addressees.

Paul's letters contain traces of how his search for rhetorical effectiveness led to misunderstanding from the beginning, when the addressees' expectations and the author's intentions did not coincide. Thus in 1 Cor. 5.9-13 Paul has to correct a misunderstanding concerning relations with immoral individuals.[3] 2 Pet. 3.16 deals with later misinterpretations of Paul. Such cases may serve as warnings for modern scholars against too fast, too shallow comprehension and description of the author's thoughts. If we simply focus on some conceptions in a text and then systematize them into a 'theology' or 'ethics', the result is easily dominated by some prejudice, such as our own ideological patterns.[4]

When the goal is to reconstruct any ideological or theological systems or patterns, these must be considered in their contexts—not only their historical, but especially their argumentative contexts. Two issues are of great importance.

(a) We need to discover the type of situation in which the argumentation is intended to function, that is, the rhetorical situation(s) for which the texts are written. Based on this, (b) we need to identify the statements and ideas in the text, including central, implicit thoughts, and clarify their relations in the text. These steps facilitate the understanding of the persuasive and interactive functions of those ideas, which in turn serves as a basis for a more general view of them.[5] In order to meet these requirements specific tools are needed.

As for (a), it is not possible precisely to recognize the situation of an

3. 'I have written you in my letter not to associate with sexually immoral people—not at all meaning the people of this world... in that case you would have to leave this world. But...' A sign for a corresponding feature may be the unexpected structure in Rom. 6.3-4: 'we were baptized into his death; we were buried with him... in order that, just as Christ was raised from the dead... we too may *live a new life*'. It would be more balanced to continue: '... we were made alive in Christ and raised from the dead', thus Eph. 2.5-6 (for the connection between the verses, see e.g. Schnackenburg 1991: 94-95). The missing balance suggests that Paul's original emphasis had been misread so that there will be no second resurrection (cf. 1 Cor. 15.12-13).

4. Thus J.T. Sanders, preoccupied with the idea of 1 Peter as an example of a 'horrible' ideological degeneration of Paulinism, has great difficulties with the actual text, and has to conclude that its effect is 'the opposite of what the author really intended' (Sanders 1986: 84-85).

5. Simons 1990: 10, 14. According to him, the rhetorical perspective can reveal hidden factors in the text—the use of the text as material for solving larger problems thereby becomes more reliable.

ancient text by a conventional historical analysis, since in most cases we do not know enough about the original circumstances of the author or the audience—and even if *we* knew, it is not certain that the author shared our knowledge. Instead, it is more useful to search for the type of the situation in which the text appears to be aimed to function as appeal or argument, that is, its *rhetorical situation*.[6] This can be discovered by searching not only for explicit but also for implicit material in the text.[7]

Further, the situation is not static, since the author's opening words seek to adjust the recipients' thoughts so that they can be addressed in the next part of the text in a different way. This means that the rhetorical situation or conditions for the discourse change inside the text. For instance, the beginning of a letter does not yield a neutral characterization of the author's message or view of the addressees.[8] Furthermore, it is typical that at the end of the speech the author expresses himself with less reserve, after ensuring that the addressees will not misunderstand him.[9] It is necessary to be aware of this *rhetorical dynamic* of the text.[10]

A third aspect which affects the way in which the author expresses himself consists in the *stylistic devices* he uses. If he wants to alert or shock the addressees, for example, it would be a serious mistake to treat such an expression as a neutral description of the author's theology.[11]

---

6. The term 'rhetorical situation' is usual in modern rhetorical analysis, and was first introduced by L.F. Bitzer 1968. It consists of the author's picture of the audience and of the intended effects of the text (see Thurén 1990: 70-71; Botha 1991: 188-200). In classical rhetoric these questions are treated under *inventio, status, genus* etc. (for discussion, see Thurén 1990: 71-74).

7. According to Varga (1987: 292), literary texts are meant to function even without a detailed context, and thus much can be understood without a close historical knowledge. Many of the New Testament letters can to some extent be characterized as literary texts, which makes a rhetorical analysis easier to execute. However, especially where historical knowledge is necessary but lacking, the rhetorical perspective becomes important.

8. E.g., the description of the addressees' perseverance in 1 Pet. 1.6-9 does not correspond to the exhortation to persevere in the rest of the text.

9. See Lausberg on *exordium* and *peroratio* (1960 §§266-81; 431-42).

10. Ancient rhetoric studied these questions in the *dispositio*. This means that different sections, their convincing and persuading functions, and relations to each other, are identified. See Thurén 1990: 75-77.

11. E.g., according to Nissilä (1979: 254-55) Heb. 10.26-31 (...οὐκέτι περὶ ἁμαρτιῶν ἀπολείπεται θυσία...) functions as a *deinosis*. With a static reading of the text, which ignores the rhetorical situation, the passage can easily be misinterpreted (if Nissilä's interpretation is correct).

All these three aspects can be properly surveyed with a basic rhetorical analysis.

A more complex issue is the structure of argumentation (b), which consists in identification of the important statements and ideas, including central implicit expressions and thoughts, and clarification of their relations in the text. These tasks cannot be carried out with traditional means either. Normal argumentation differs to a great extent from demonstration—people simply do not follow the rules of formal logic in their reasoning, not even scholars.[12] There are also many implicit premises and rules which are not necessarily dealt with in a formal study of a discourse. This basic recognition of the inadequacy of classical formal logic in studying practical reasoning has given impetus to new theories on argumentation, which attempt a more adequate analysis of practical reasoning.

Summing up, we can state that an accurate description of any theological, ethical or other ideological pattern or structure in the New Testament letters calls for an investigation of the rhetorical situation, disposition and use of stylistic and other technical devices. With this knowledge we can then penetrate the organization of the arguments. Only then is it possible to make a quantum leap and search for models or general patterns of thought beyond the text. This in turn may lead to a description of the motivation of the paraenesis or other theological, that is ideological, constructions, which are manifested in different ways in the actual text. To characterize the ethics of the New Testament is a still larger task: several texts have to be treated in the way described above before any sound comparison between them can be made.

I recently discussed the methodological questions inherent in the study of the rhetorical situations and strategy (Thurén 1990: 68-78). In this chapter I shall deal with the further steps in the analysis: first, the approach for analysing argumentation and persuasion, and the distinction between the two, second, the discovery of ideological structures

---

12. Even scientific reasoning can usually be considered as argumentation, not merely logical demonstration (see Weinstein 1990: 269-98; Simons 1990; Gross 1991: 283-300). The term 'argumentation' can be defined in different ways. In short, it means activity aimed at an audience in order to gain their support for or disapproval of an opinion. For detailed discussion, see Perelman 1969: 13-14; Siegert 1985: 16-22; van Eemeren, Grootendorst and Kruiger 1987: 1-7. For the relation between argumentation and persuasion, see Chapter 2 §3.b.

behind the text. The application of the methods to our specific question in 1 Peter is discussed simultaneously.

2. Theories of Argumentation

Introduction
In exegetical research, the position of the analysis of argumentation resembles that of its big sister, rhetorical criticism. The scholars who are stimulated by the development of non-theological research are becoming aware of long neglected aspects of the text. Both revitalized perspectives have their roots in Ancient Greece, which in turn easily leads to a historical fallacy: reconstructed ancient methods are regarded as the only, or at least the best, means for analysing biblical texts.[13] We do not, however, know whether the biblical writers had received proper school training in these fields so that a detailed identification of ancient techniques would be meaningful. Even if this were the case, it is often evident that modern insights can offer more adequate tools for research.

According to the alternative, rhetorical features in the New Testament are seen as general human communication, and should be analysed with the best means available, whether ancient or modern. When the goal is to understand the text, rather than identify historical features therein, this perspective is feasible.

In general rhetoric, the choice between the alternatives depends on the goal pursued, and a combination is often advisable. When analysing argumentation, the situation may be different.

In the following pages the roots and current stage of argumentation analysis will be briefly discussed. This serves as a basis for sketching a method for our study in 1 Peter.

---

13. See Thurén 1990: 47-52. Rhetoric is always partly bound to the current culture, but Miller remarks that already the social contexts of the classical ancient rhetoric and biblical rhetoric were rather different (Miller 1989). Consequently I have theoretical doubts about Mitchell's remarkable rhetorical analysis of 1 Corinthians, which claims to be historical (Mitchell 1991, esp. pp. 6-11); therefore only ancient concepts are used, and the system is based on ancient texts. Non-theological specialists in classical rhetoric or modern rhetoric have a much broader view of rhetorical criticism than exegetes on the 'Betzian' line. See e.g. Classen 1988; Vickers 1988; Geissner 1987: 111; Wenzel 1987b, with an ironical comment on exegetes on p. 103.

a. *The Classical Background*

Ancient rhetoric, dialectic and logic are widely seen as the most important predecessors of modern theories of argumentation.[14] The main sources are Greek authors, especially Aristotle,[15] whereas the Romans were mostly interested in practical rhetoric.

According to Aristotle, for example, logic focuses on the certainty, dialectic on the acceptability, and rhetoric on the cogency for the audience—so that the last one includes the others.[16] Rhetoric was seen as searching for universal means of persuasion, in other words it was valid in politics as well as in science (Fuhrmann 1987: 7-14; van Eemeren, Grootendorst and Kruiger 1987: 70). The main differences from logic (by which Aristotle means deductive and inductive syllogisms) were the importance of the audience, situation, ethos and pathos. In Roman rhetoric, which is not so much concerned with the theory of argumentation as the practice of persuasion, these factors are stressed even more (van Eemeren, Grootendorst and Kruiger 1987: 77).

Particularly the recognition of the relevance of the audience and the situation for argumentation, and the interactive dimension of ancient theories, for example, the effect of the audience's feedback on the author's presentation,[17] have been important for the development of modern theories of argumentation. Compared with formal logic, which can also be counted as a predecessor of these theories, the importance of the audience and the situation can be seen as a central distinctive aspect, whereby the theories of argumentation strive for a more adequate way of analysing practical reasoning.

However, just as the general rhetoric degenerated step by step into a study of stylistics and of some technical devices (Perelman 1982: 4; Thurén 1991: 41-42), the analysis of argumentation also suffered from a similar development: it was reduced to dialectic and formal logic, which consequently diminished its relevance to the study of ordinary texts, including the Bible (Moss 1986: 7).

14. Van Eemeren, Grootendorst and Kruiger provide us with an illustrative presentation of the ancient development of argumentation theory (1987: 55-78; see also Wenzel 1987b: 101-102.)

15. For the increasing role, and even misuse, of Aristotle in modern argumentation analysis, see Warnick 1989, Braet 1992 and the whole of volume 6:3 of *Argumentation* (1992).

16. In accordance with van Eemeren, Grootendorst and Kruiger 1987: 59.

17. Braet 1987. This fact is not fully recognized by van Eemeren, Grootendorst and Kruiger (1987).

When describing the history of the study of Pauline argumentation, beginning from the Church Fathers, F. Siegert demonstrates how little work has been done in this field. In the Middle Ages some humanists were still interested in biblical argumentation, but just as rhetoric declined in the following centuries, so only a few scholars continued to focus on argumentation in the New Testament.[18]

In connection with the recent revival of rhetorical studies in exegetical research, some attempts have been made to analyse argumentation in the Bible by using ancient rhetoric.

In 1976 W. Viertel employed exclusively ancient questions and terminology. However, as Siegert rightly observes, such a theoretical basis is very narrow (1985: 5 n. 1). Unfortunately, Siegert offers little justification for his remark.[19]

Another major effort to analyse argumentation in the New Testament is made by L.R. Donelson (1986), a student of one of the founding exegetes of rhetorical criticism in our times, H.D. Betz. Donelson claims that the use of modern patterns, such as theories of language, in analysing and criticizing ancient documents necessarily leads to misreading (1986: 3). This indirect argument is the only ground Donelson gives for his solution, which is to regard Aristotle's (and some other ancient authors') works as the only basis for analysing ancient texts (1986: 3), or, more specifically, 'the most fruitful [system] for unpacking the logic in the Pastorals'—no other methods are even discussed,[20] and even Aristotle's rhetoric is used selectively.[21]

Despite a promise to 'unpack the logic' of the texts, Donelson is

---

18. Siegert 1985: 5-12. For a corresponding phenomenon in general studies of argumentation, see Moss 1986: 5-8.

19. Siegert 1985: 5 n. 1: 'Die Versuche... die "Struktur der Argumente des Paulus" durch syllogismen darzustellen, sind künstlich und teilweise albern.'

20. Donelson however admits that it is unlikely that the author of the Pastorals had any direct knowledge of Aristotle's *Rhetoric* (1986: 71) and that Aristotle's system 'is imposed from outside of the text' (1986: 72).

21. Despite noticing the role of *ethos* and *pathos* in rhetoric (1986: 75), and even counting some important factors in argumentation, such as the active role of the audience as the judge of a speech, the significance of the argumentation field by indicating Aristotle's claim, that the same arguments are not valid in ethics and physics (1986: 76), Donelson does not utilize these aspects in his analysis. For the use and misuse of Aristotle in modern argumentation analysis, see Warnick 1989 and *Argumentation* 6:3 (1992).

usually content to identify different techniques here and there in the Pastorals.[22] By so doing he manages to save the reputation of the logic in those texts. Contrary to expectations they prove to be carefully constructed according to Aristotelian principles or contemporary customs.[23] However, since no long section of the texts nor the *structure* of the argumentation as a whole are analysed, let alone their communicative or interactive functions, the result remains irrelevant to the goal of Donelson's book: his theses on the nature of the paraenesis and ethics in the Pastorals are based on loose statements, and the results difficult to approve.[24]

Donelson's study of argumentation, based on exclusively ancient material, is strikingly analogous to the current trend to make rhetorical analyses by using only ancient terminology. Although ancient terminology can and even should be used in several cases, and a great many 'modern' inventions can be found already in classical rhetoric,[25] the crucial question is, whether ancient theories of argumentation are an ideal, or even the most adequate, way of studying argumentation even in ancient texts. Even if ancient ways of thinking differed to some extent from modern discourse, and although many ancient concepts are irreplaceable due to their familiarity, one should ask whether a great deal of the discourse is not common to all human communication, and whether some modern aspects could not be more adequate in describing it.

An interesting statement reveals the problem of concentrating exclusively on ancient conceptions: 'The peculiar method of argumentation found in the Pastorals could help us understand the logic and style of modern political and ethical debate... Aristotle's *Rhetoric* would provide fruitful categories from which to begin such a discussion' (Donelson

22. This is easy to explain, since according to Wenzel (1987b: 108) 'the *only* way to unpack the argument is to put it in the totality of its actual *rhetorical* context' (his italics).

23. Donelson 1986: 199. He also claims to have managed to 'remove the onus of... nonsense from arguments in the Pastorals' (1986: 79)!

24. In Donelson's study, the rare analyses of the logical structure of argumentation are unfortunately based on distorted quotations and a simple enthymematic form of Aristotelian logic. 1 Tim. 4.7-8 is a striking example. Donelson's approach indicates that the motivation for training oneself to *eusebeia* should arise from willingness to earn salvation, while respect for the existing text and a study according to the principles presented below leads to an opposite result: the ground for motivation is knowledge or experience that God has saved Timothy.

25. E.g. the model for analysis presented by Simons (1976: 300-14) neatly corresponds to the ancient aspects in creating a speech.

1986: 4, 288-94). Donelson is following right strategy, but he is only inventing old things. From the late fifties there has been a whole 'independent philosophical discipline' (Berk 1979: 190) doing exactly what he suggests, namely, the modern theories of argumentation.

b. *Modern Theories*
Introduction. More studies have been published in the field of argumentation analysis within the past few decades than in some hundred years before.[26] It is reasonable to assume that this rapidly developing new branch can also contribute to the study of biblical texts.

Two important treatises were published in 1958: *The Uses of Argument* by S.E. Toulmin, and *La nouvelle rhétorique* by C. Perelman and L. Olbrechts-Tyteca.[27] They both share the basic theoretical view that ordinary argumentation cannot be adequately analysed with traditional, logical methods, since there is a quantum leap from logical demonstration to practical reasoning.[28] Not only the logical structure of the explicit argumentation, but especially the function of the arguments in the situation are crucial for understanding and evaluating the argumentation. The non-verbal aspects of the argumentation are at least as important as the verbal ones (cf. Siegert 1985: 91). This shift from formal logic to argumentation analysis corresponds to the 'rhetorical turn' in general philosophy (Barilli 1989; Simons 1990; see also Simons 1976: 32; Fisher 1987; Thurén 1991: 41-42).

Both Perelman and Toulmin have been influential in the development of theories and models for analysing argumentation, and many scholars still take one of them as their theoretical or practical basis.

---

26. See e.g. van Eemeren, Grootendorst and Kruiger 1987: 108-13. For the history of argumentation theory see Cox and Willard 1982: xiii-xxv. For the current discussion, see e.g. issues of *Argumentation* 1987– and papers of the conferences in Amsterdam 1986 (van Eemeren, Grootendorst, Blair and Willard 1987) and 1990 (van Eemeren, Grootendorst, Blair and Willard 1991).

27. Quoted here according to the English translation ('The New Rhetoric') as Perelman 1969.

28. Toulmin 1958: 1-10; Perelman 1969: 1-14. Harman (1986) and Cherniak (1986) offer modern philosophical support for Toulmin's and Perelman's view on argumentation. For more on the relation between argumentation and formal logic, see Walton 1989, Johnstone 1989, and several other articles in *Argumentation* 3:1 (1989).

Perelman's The New Rhetoric

In the first part of *The New Rhetoric* Perelman highlights the inadequacy of classical formal logic in describing practical argumentation, and finds Aristotle's rhetorical principles as a more suitable basis for such an analysis (1969: 1-51). His main reason is that practical argumentation does not just neutrally describe the facts or demonstrate the conclusions, but seeks to convince or persuade a certain audience. Instead of reproducing Aristotle, Perelman only takes some renewed insights and attempts to design an inductive modern version of rhetoric.[29] I shall give some examples.

According to Perelman, the role of the audience in argumentation means that the technique used and success achieved depend on the receivers (1969: 17-19; Zappel 1986: 217; van Eemeren, Grootendorst and Kruiger 1987: 211). Instead of an empirical audience, Perelman operates with a sophisticated model of particular, universal and ideal audiences, all of which are in fact created by the author designing a speech (1969: 19-23). By using this typology Perelman endeavours to identify the nature of argumentation. When particular audience is addressed, the argumentation can be called persuasion, whereas the presence of a universal audience is a sign that the author's purpose is to convince (for discussion, see below Chapter 2 §3.a).

An analysis of argumentation must also take account of the author's rhetorical strategy. According to Perelman the point of departure in argumentation must consist of a 'meeting of minds' between the author and the audience; thus the author must start from the premises and expectations of the audience before he or she can lead the addressees to assent to new ideas (1969: 14-17). Perelman also uses a modified version of the Aristotelian distinction between the three genres of speech[30] as the general frame of reference in argumentation (1969: 47-51).

In the second part of his book, Perelman describes argumentation by presenting a possible classification of several types of argumentative technique, with a general division into associative and dissociative types of argument (1969: 190-91; Arnold 1986: 42; van Eemeren, Grootendorst and Kruiger 1987: 209). However, the first part, the

---

29. One reason for this is that, according to Perelman, rhetoric was dead at the time of Enlightenment, and cannot easily be revived (1982: 4).

30. I.e. the expected reactions of the audience: forensic, deliberative and epideictic.

general discussion of the principles of argumentation, has been more significant for the research.

Perelman's theory of argumentation has later been explained and clarified in many articles and books (see van Eemeren, Grootendorst and Kruiger 1987: 293-94). Its importance has not been limited simply to launching a worldwide interest in argumentation; it has also contributed to the renewed interest in rhetoric in general, as a fresh philosophical perspective, even among biblical scholars. W. Wuellner, for example, has used Perelman's theoretical viewpoints in several articles (Wuellner 1979; 1986; cf. also Jewett 1986; Wire 1990), and F. Siegert drew chiefly on the second part of his book by searching for corresponding techniques of argumentation in LXX and in Romans (1985).

However, severe criticism has been levelled against two principal aspects.

First, not all scholars have accepted Perelman's distinction between logic as a formal, and argumentation as a rhetorical, aspect of reasoning. Since the soundness of argumentation depends on its effect on the audience, and not on its logical structure, the whole theory has been seen as 'mere rhetoric' in the pejorative sense of the word (Berk 1979: 198; van Eemeren, Grootendorst and Kruiger 1987: 220, 255-59).

Against this objection it can be stated that Perelman's aim is not to judge but to analyse and describe practical reasoning. Since there are certain conventions in argumentative strategies and techniques, it is reasonable to search for tools to study them. The criticism at this point can be traced back to the basic gap between rhetoric and logic, which however has narrowed in recent years.[31]

The second, more crucial objection does not concern the theory itself, but its application as a 'new rhetoric'. Despite the rhetorical features in Perelman's theory, it deals only with cognitive argumentation, not persuasion. In persuasion, convincing techniques and strategies, which Perelman mainly examines, do not suffice; the critical factors are, according to classical rhetoric, *ethos* and *pathos* (see below Chapter 2 §3.a). These are to a great extent ignored by Perelman.[32] Thus, for

---

31. It is commonly accepted that rhetoric can offer an important perspective to argumentation: see Makau 1986: 194, and van Eemeren, Grootendorst, Blair and Willard 1987. Cf. also Weinstein 1990.

32. Perelman even considers persuasion to be a fallacy in argumentation (1969: 111, see Huth 1975: 82-83). Psychological factors are disregarded (van Eemeren, Grootendorst and Kruiger 1987: 215), although Wenzel is right to say that it is too

analysing persuasion and motivation, Perelman's 'rhetoric' is not enough.[33]

Perelman's book has also been used for an uncritical labeling of genres and techniques.[34] When, for example, Siegert, using Perelman's classification of argumentative techniques, concludes that ancient argumentation, including Paul, well corresponds to Perelman's system, we can ask, just as with Donelson's survey, whether the result tells us more about the method than about the material studied.

In my opinion, Perelman's book is useful in two ways. (a) The general view on argumentation provides a sound basis for the scrutiny of any human reasoning, and will be used also in this study. (b) Perelman's practical application (which is not the only way of using his theories) often yields a more adequate classification of the types of argumentation than the traditional terms.

Toulmin's Analytical Model

Toulmin's theory of argumentation, also published in 1958, is less sophisticated than that of Perelman.[35] Consequently, the theory has not influenced modern argumentation analysis to the same degree as his practical model, which has proven useful in many contexts and has become more popular than Perelman's.[36] To my knowledge it has not yet been seriously applied to exegetics.

simple to label *logos* as argumentation, and *ethos* and *pathos* as psychological factors (Wenzel 1987b: 103-104).

33. Mitchell (1991: 7 n. 19) rightly states that Perelman's 'The New Rhetoric' is more concerned with argumentation than rhetoric as a whole.

34. Wenzel sees such labeling as typical for theologians dealing with rhetorical criticism (1987b: 103-104).

35. It also includes some shortcomings. See Wohlrapp 1987: 327; van Eemeren, Grootendorst and Kruiger 1987: 199-207. Their view, however, ignores Toulmin's later modification of the theory (Toulmin *et al.* 1984, first edn 1978), and, as in the case of the Perelman, the main criticism is aimed at Toulmin's 'rhetorical' view of argumentation. Freeman (1990) makes a serious effort to 'rehabilitate' Toulmin's theory into philosophy, but expands the simple method beyond its limits and is justly criticized by Henkemans (1992: 55-70). She, however, wrongly equates Toulmin's functional model with the rhetorical *epikheirema* (1992: 69 n. 16) and calls the Warrant the 'major premise'.

36. See van Eemeren *et al.* 1987: 292-93. For different uses of the model, see e.g. Ehninger and Brockriede 1966; Benoit and Lindsey 1987; Fisher 1987: 15; Wenzel 1987a: 79-80; Wohlrapp 1987; Warnick 1989; Weinstein 1990; Langsdorf 1990; Freeman 1992.

Without going deeper into Toulmin's philosophical standpoint we can say that he also sees the assessment of argumentation as dependent on particular norms instead of simply its formal logical structure (Toulmin 1958: 1-10; van Eemeren, Grootendorst and Kruiger 1987: 168). The nature of the argumentation depends on argumentation-fields: physics and ethics require different types of justification. Not only does this idea correspond to Aristotle's view of the uses of argumentation (Aristotle, *Rhetorica* 1.1358; cf. Donelson 1986: 76), but interesting similarities have also been found between Toulmin's argumentation-fields and these rhetorical genera (Benoit and Lindsey 1987).

Toulmin's treatise is mainly concerned with analysing the internal functions of argumentation (characterization by Zappel 1987: 217). According to him, each argumentation consists of certain elements, which are identified on the basis of their function.[37] They help us to describe the structure of any argumentation. Since my own forthcoming analysis will to a great extent build upon Toulmin's model, it deserves a closer look.

The *claim* (C) is the opinion put forward; it tells us the conclusion which is based on the argumentation.[38] The claim is justified by three types of argument.

The *data* (D) show the facts on which the claim is based, from which the conclusion is drawn.[39] The D includes specific information, which supports the claim in a certain situation. Usually many D's are needed to support a claim. It is also typical that a claim functions as a D for the next chain of argumentation (Toulmin *et al.* 1984: 73). The claim can never be stronger than the data on which it is based (Toulmin *et al.* 1984: 26, 37-44).

In order to show that the D's are appropriate for supporting the claim, a *warrant* (W) is needed. Contrary to the specific D, the warrant is a general rule, which indicates the relevance of the claim in the argument-ation; it guarantees that it is correct to draw a conclusion from D to C.

---

37. For a short introduction, see, e.g., Göttert 1978: 28-29. For more detailed information, see Toulmin *et al.* (1984: 29-77) and van Eemeren, Grootendorst and Kruiger (1987: 174-80).

38. Toulmin *et al.* 1984: 25, 29-32. For a further discussion of the identification of the Claim, see Toulmin *et al.* 1984: 6-7.

39. Toulmin (1958) uses the term Data. Later (1984) he has changed it to Grounds, but I find it illustrative to retain the original, since contrary to Grounds it is not easily misunderstood as a non-technical term.

The warrant is often only implicit in the text (Toulmin *et al.* 1984: 26.45-56).

These three factors are always necessary in order to make an argumentation reliable.

It is not, however, always clear that the warrant itself is acceptable or relevant in the argumentation. Then, in order to control the relevance and validity of the warrant in a specific case an extra *backing* (B) is needed. The backing expresses general information (contrary to the ground), which is implicitly included in the warrant. It is a generalization, which presents the knowledge or experience on which the particular way of supporting the claim is based, for example, historical examples, universal human needs, known experience, and so on (Toulmin *et al.* 1984: 26, 61-69).

If there are exceptions to the warrant, a *rebuttal* (R) states the circumstances under which the claim is valid, and a qualifier (Q) expresses the probability according to which the conclusion is correct (Toulmin *et al.* 1984: 81-101; cf. also Göttert 1978: 31-32).

Toulmin gives the following example (here completed with R):[40]

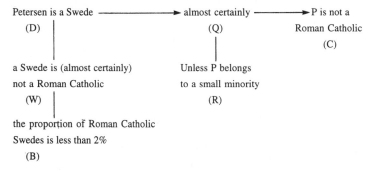

Petersen is a Swede ⟶ almost certainly ⟶ P is not a
(D) | (Q) Roman Catholic
| | (C)
a Swede is (almost certainly) Unless P belongs
not a Roman Catholic to a small minority
(W) | (R)
the proportion of Roman Catholic
Swedes is less than 2%
(B)

Note that in order to display the structure clearly, direct quotations are seldom useful. Instead, the contents of the expressions are usually given in a short or modified form. Siegert rightly states that Perelman's list of argumentative techniques in fact classifies different forms of warrants in Toulmin's system (Siegert 1985: 89; see also Freeman 1992).

The usefulness of Toulmin's model lies not only in its capacity to clarify arguments and their interrelations (cf. van Eemeren,

---

40. Toulmin 1958: 25. This example caused some hilarity at the New Testament seminar in Uppsala, Sweden, led by Professor René Kieffer, who is a Roman Catholic.

Grootendorst and Kruiger 1987: 203), but also in that it takes into account the open-endedness of argumentation.[41] This means that behind the assent to every element in the argumentation scheme, there are new, usually implicit, chains of argumentation which justify that element (Toulmin *et al.* 1984: 73-77). Thus in each argumentation there comes a certain point where something is taken for granted, which means that the argumentation becomes implicit. This also happens when the elements of the argumentation are expressed in a short or ambiguous manner, in which case a careful analysis of the explicit expressions is crucial.[42]

In a normal text even central elements may be implicit.[43] They may be taken as self-evident presuppositions (cf. Göttert 1978: 5, 29). This is due to the rhetorical nature of a normal text. If one tries to unfold as many components as possible, the text loses much of its communicative and persuasive capability. If the text is designed to affect the reader, it must be readable. When analysing a train of thought some of these elements must be identified, and this can usually be done with help of the context and the rhetorical situation. Such a reconstructed element either has to arise from the structure of the argumentation or it has to be explained elsewhere in the text, where a similar train of thought occurs.

It is even possible that in some cases the purpose of argumentation is not to justify a claim, but to make the audience—albeit unawares—assent to some implicit element in the argumentation, or to strengthen such assent in the process of accepting an argumentation that appears unobjectionable in itself, but which is built upon such a premise.

Since Toulmin's model enables the explication of the implicit factors, its use makes obscure structures of argumentation more lucid. The degree of explaining and describing argumentation and various aspects thereof, such as Q and R, is determined by the needs of the analysis, for example, which nuances are seen as important. This makes the model very flexible. Due to its purely analytical, value-free nature it also serves as a basic model, which has proven useful for different types of question.

It is worth noticing that Toulmin's model usually occurs in a modified

---

41. Wenzel (1987b: 106-107) quotes M. Scriven's metaphor: 'Arguments are like icebergs'.

42. See e.g. Huth's use of Toulmin's method (Huth 1975: 99).

43. Toulmin 1958: 14-15; Göttert 1978: 29. The problem is common in every form of argumentation analysis (see e.g. Kopperschmidt 1981: 57-62).

form. This demonstrates not only the flexibility of the model, but also its limitations. As such it can be applied only for very restricted purposes. Van Eemeren *et al.* rightly criticize many of the users of Toulmin's model of an uncritical adaptation. For example, van Eemeren *et al.* rightly claim that the model cannot be used alone in assessing the formal soundness or validity of argumentation. It does, however, offer material for such an analysis.[44]

The model reveals internal relations of arguments and their functions. It also helps to detect implicit factors in argumentation.[45] At this point, the criticism of van Eemeren *et al.* is misleading.[46]

Toulmin, however, does not take into account the finality (Zappel 1987: 217) or the rhetorical dynamics of argumentation, that is, the changing argumentative situations. The concept of 'argumentative field' is far too general for such an analysis. *Ethos* and *pathos* aspects are also difficult to study.[47] Moreover, the model is a precision tool, which involves difficulties in the scrutiny of long texts. The analysis also becomes arbitrary if in the discourse only some factors are explained.[48] Further, it gives us no direct means of validating the argumentation; it only provides a possibility of doing so by explaining the structure of argumentation. Not even Toulmin's own study of moral reasoning makes an exception at this point (Jonsen and Toulmin 1988). Instead, it clearly shows that further steps are needed.

In my opinion, Toulmin's model is very useful for analysing argumentation, provided that its narrow limits are fully recognized. In most cases it has to be enhanced with other components, which however should not be confused with the model; such additional steps should be taken

44. E.g. by revealing implicit Warrants Toulmin's model enables the reader to assess whether he can accept the W, and thus the whole argumentation. Van Eemeren *et al.* strive for logically binding soundness (cf. their criticism of Perelman above), which however is an inadequate concept in human reasoning: the crucial question is often the persuadability of the argumentation: see Wenzel 1987b: 108.

45. These two points tend to be problematic in other models of argumentation analysis: see Krabbe 1992.

46. Van Eemeren, Grootendorst and Kruiger 1987: 204-205. Their criticism of Toulmin's concept 'Warrant' is based on a misunderstanding of the term. This would have been avoided by using Toulmin's textbook (Toulmin *et al.* 1984). Weinstein (1990) also discusses their understanding of Toulmin's Warrant.

47. Such a study is attempted by Ehninger and Brockriede 1978.

48. Cf. criticism of Toulmin by Wohlrapp (1987), which, to quote Wohlrapp's own terminology, is based on 'a grave misunderstanding' of Toulmin's system.

clearly after and before the analysis (for a detailed description of my approach, see below Chapter 5, Introduction).

The Current Stage
After Perelman and Toulmin, several different approaches for analysing argumentation have been presented.

The development of modern logic, rhetorics,[49] structuralism, text-linguistics (e.g. R. Wonneberger 1976) and other analytical methods has provided the scholars with new tools and aspects for the analysis,[50] although no theory has been generally accepted. Usually the scholars from different fields deal with similar phenomena, but use different conceptions and language. Siegert illustratively reviews some branches that are important for analysing argumentation (1985: 85-107), van Eemeren *et al.* present and evaluate different major theories of argumentation (van Eemeren, Grootendorst and Kruiger 1987: 108-61) and the current stage of argumentation theory.[51] One of the most useful approaches is the application of Austin's and Searle's speech-act theory. Although not originally designed for analysing argumentation, it has been successfully applied to some types of analysis (Huth 1975; van Eemeren and Grootendorst 1984).

The appearance of *Argumentation*, a journal for studies in argumentation, and articles in rhetorical journals (*Quarterly Journal of Speech* and *Rhetorica*) demonstrate the increasing interest in this field. Recent international conferences (Amsterdam 1986 and 1990) and publications[52] have shown the plurality of methods, but also that interdisciplinary collaboration is required in order to achieve better understanding of

49. In a rhetorical approach, J. Kopperschmidt (1981: 52-53) argues that the persuasive force of argumentation is more important than its theoretical function, and focuses on the totality of the argumentation instead of separate arguments.

50. E.g., Zappel (1986: 222-23) operates with a literary theory, wanting to 'systematize textual knowledge and to rationalize the modes of its processing'. First, discursive factors, their semantic qualifications and contextual isotopies are identified, then the information is conceptualized, modulated and finally organized.

51. Van Eemeren, Grootendorst and Kruiger 1987: 260-72. Concerning their evaluation it has to be noted, that it is based on a thesis of the priority of directly judging the soundness of argumentation. Thus, they cannot evaluate theories that are designed for other purposes.

52. Examples of different approaches: Harman 1986; Cherniak 1986; Walton 1989 (see also a critical review by Krabbe 1992); Williams and Hazen 1990; Nuchelmans 1991; Henkemans 1992; van Eemeren and Grootendorst 1992.

practical reasoning. Although some scholars still believe in a 'normative theory of argumentation' (van Eemeren, Grootendorst and Kruiger 1987: 269), it has become evident at least that no single method can be acquired (see Wenzel 1987a: 73; cf. also Cox and Willard 1982: xiv), but that the central interests of the analysis influence the choice of the method.

A principal disagreement exists as regards the basic nature of argumentation. Perelman, Toulmin and the research influenced by them share, despite their differences, a common rhetorical view of argumentation: no argument is valid as such—it must be assessed with regard to its audience. In contrast, the research that is more directly influenced by formal logic indicates that the validity of argumentation must be objectively assessed.

For our needs the rhetorical line provides a better basis. First, I am not mainly interested in the soundness of the argumentation in 1 Peter (although some statements in the text will be criticized), but in the structure as such. Secondly, it is doubtful whether the soundness of argumentation in a persuasive text can ever be objectively assessed.[53]

Conclusion
After the review of the history and the present situation in the field of argumentation theories and methods we can specify the central requirements that our problem imposes on the analysis, and formulate the aspects that have to be taken into account in such an analysis.

We have seen that it cannot be predetermined which of the several modern ways of analysing argumentation is in itself the best. The choice of the tool depends on the task and the purpose (cf. Arnold 1987: 51). There is no reason to analyse something just for the sake of the analysis, as sometimes seems to be the case. Instead, since different methods focus on different aspects in argumentation, it is natural that they best serve different analytical goals.[54]

---

53. Contrary to mathematics or formal logic, the objectivity of a persuasive text can be at its best only inter-subjectivity among the designed addressees. If the argument seems valid for the audience, it serves its purpose despite formal shortcomings, and can thus be seen as 'sound'.

54. According to Zappel (1987: 219), a choice has to be made between searching for strategies of persuasion and the organizing principle behind the text. However, also when studying the structures of argumentation, a pragmatic and interactive aspect should be taken into account.

Traditionally, many scholars have been most interested in juridical argumentation. This has emphasized questions about the validity and soundness of the argumentation. In these cases, approaches that focus on the type of reasoning are most useful—not least because such a description of argumentative techniques produces different catalogues of fallacies. However, even when these models are applied, the results produce a critical question. If on the basis of them it only becomes clear that biblical writers followed precisely the ancient (Donelson) or modern (Siegert) rules of argumentation, one may wonder whether they might tell us more about the method than the subject which has been analysed.

Since our main goal is to find the ideological structure of argumentation in 1 Peter, we should not focus on the qualities of argumentative techniques employed in the Letter, but primarily see in what ways the arguments are interconnected, and identify the premises left unsaid in the argumentation; Toulmin's graphical method provides us with the most suitable basis, since it focuses more than other approaches on the structure of argumentation. In that model, the relations between arguments can be more easily controlled than in, for example, Perelman's system, where the reader must take such relations for granted. Moreover, Toulmin's model can easily be complemented by other aspects. Furthermore, it is important for our task, inasmuch as it enables a regulated explanation of implicit premises and warrants.

However, two defects must be overcome before the model can be applied to our text.

First, it suffers from the same fundamental weakness as every method for argumentation: the first stage of analysis, the identification of the argumentative expressions, remains unclear. In modern texts, this would be less serious, since we, as a part of the same culture, are well equipped for proper interpretation. In ancient texts, however, a certain controllable process of identifying at least the explicit arguments would be needed. We have already seen in Chapter 1 that the lack of such a method was one of the basic reasons for different interpretations of the argumentation in 1 Peter.

Secondly, despite its basic rhetorical nature, Toulmin's model fails to allow for the changing rhetorical situations, that is, the rhetorical dynamics and interaction in human communication.[55] Thus, it must be complemented by a more detailed analysis of the rhetorical situation and

---

55. The focus on argumentation fields may be seen as an attempt in this direction.

strategy,[56] which also means that we have to consider the author's and audience's developing expectations and goals.

But even more than for the right understanding of argumentation, a rhetorical perspective is necessary for our specific task, the study of persuasion in a paraenetic text.

3. *The Analysis of Persuasion*

a. *The Distinction between Argumentation and Persuasion*
In order to understand how the exhortations are motivated in the text, it is not enough to know how the audience is *convinced* to accept the exhortations intellectually. We must also see how it is *persuaded* to act, that is, how the author attempts to make his audience obey him. Since the terms 'argumentation', 'persuasion' and 'motivation' are used in various ways, they need first to be specified. I shall first define the difference between argumentation and persuasion, and then outline a method of motivation analysis which can be applied to our material.

Persuasion, like rhetoric, is not a value-free term (Simons 1976: 26-27). It is often used to denote activity which aims at an uncritical acceptance of something, whereas argumentation and the verb 'convince' are seen as challenges to critical interaction (see e.g. Siegert 1985: 21-22; cf. also Perelman 1969: 111 and my criticism of him [Thurén 1990: 54 n. 54]).

In order to make a more controllable distinction, Kant differentiates 'persuade' from 'convince' by using the terms 'subjective' and 'objective'.[57] But, according to Perelman, it is not possible to measure the objectivity of a presentation (1982: 34-35). Therefore, he modifies Kant's thesis and attempts to characterize the terms in a 'more technical and exact way': presentation claiming validity for a specific audience hopes to persuade, while if aimed at a universal audience, it seeks to convince (Perelman 1969: 28-31, 33-35; 1982: 17-18). This distinction may be useful in some cases, but usually remains vague, since the definition of the 'universal audience' has proven to be rather arbitrary in practice.[58]

---

56. Wenzel (1987a: 89) also sees Toulmin as a possible basis for an analysis, if complemented with rhetorical aspects.

57. Kant 1961: 645-46. It is somewhat difficult to discuss German terminology, since 'überreden' has a clearer 'negative' connotation than 'persuade'. Cf. Siegert 1985: 22.

58. For the criticism of the 'universal audience', see e.g. van Eemeren,

A third distinction is provided by Brooks and Warren. They claim that persuasion is aimed at assent, namely assent to the will of the persuader, while argumentation pertains to the search for the truth (1979: 109). In my opinion, only the first definition is feasible. The second inaccurately equates argumentation with logical demonstration, since, contrary to demonstration, argumentation always also seeks the adherence of an audience (see above Chapter 2 §2). Thus, it would be better to say that argumentation is aimed at assent to the *opinion* of the speaker, whereas persuasion seeks assent to the speaker's *will*.

Brooks and Warren also claim that the crucial distinction is that the end of argument is reached in only one way, while in case of persuasion, many ways may be used, such as *ethos* and *pathos* (Brooks and Warren 1979: 109, referring to Aristotle). But is this true? When, for example, the character of the speaker is used in order to win assent to a thesis, it also can be identified as an argument, although not always an explicit and verbal one. The *ethos* may simply represent an implicit, non-verbal argumentation:[59] 'There are many signs which indicate that the speaker is reliable, thus he is reliable, and therefore what he says is certainly true'.

The relationship becomes complicated when we notice that some forms of persuasion have little to do with even implicit argumentation (cf. e.g. the persuasive force of repetition; for rules of persuadability, see Alexandrova 1987: 271), and not all argumentation tries to persuade (J.W. Meiland 1987; Zappel 1987: 219). It would be simple to say that persuasion may include reasoning, while argumentation is built exclusively on reasoning (thus Brooks and Warren 1979: 125). But since even argumentation seeks the assent of the audience, contrary to simple formal demonstration, it also builds on many social and situational factors. Thus even such a distinction remains difficult.

Instead of these suggestions one should focus on the rhetorical[60]

Grootendorst and Kruiger 1987: 217-18; for clarifications, see Golden 1986, and above §2.b.

59. Braet (1992, esp. 316-17) criticizes the black-and-white interpretation of Aristotle's use of the three species of argument. See also Warnick 1989. Perelman (1969: 8), opposing the use of physical threat or other non-verbal means of argumentation, claims that only verbal argumentation is worth studying. This principle, however, greatly delimits the whole field. Sutton (1986) gives more examples of such misinterpretation of *ethos* and *pathos*.

60. Rhetoric is often rephrased as the study of persuasion. Our definition of persuasion, however, lets us discern a rhetorical aspect also kinds of argumentation that do not point toward action. It is more correct to say that both the argumentative and

functions of the words, since these come close to their everyday use: argumentation aims at changing or modifying the audience's thoughts, while the goal of persuasion is action.[61]

When the author exhorts the recipients, he or she aims at least on some level to impel them to act according to the exhortation. To that end, a command itself is hardly enough, nor are good arguments, but the recipients must also be persuaded to change or modify their behaviour.

In order to persuade, the author usually needs to give reasons for the change: to give such reasons, and to justify them so that the recipient's opinions are affected, is called argumentation. But an argumentation may have as its goal and result only that the recipient should see something as valid (in Latin *persuadere* + acc. *cum* inf.). It becomes *persuasion* if the goal is also to create in the recipient a volition to act in some way (in Latin *persuadere* + *ut*-clause).[62] Thus, according to Wallace, 'persuasion...has a connotation of an "ought", as opposed to the "is" of expository discourse', by which he means argumentation (Wallace 1986: 121).

To sum up, it seems meaningful to use the words 'argumentation' and 'persuasion' on two levels, which do not totally overlap. The noun 'argumentation' and the verb 'convince' mean activity aimed at gaining the audience's assent to the author's theses and opinions. The word 'persuasion' is used for the process of gaining the audience's volitional, often also intellectual, assent to the speaker's will. Finally, 'motivation' refers to the content level of this process. The speaker may (but need not) use argumentation in order to persuade the listener to comply so that the latter becomes motivated to do something.

The distinctions may be illustrated by Austin's Speech-Act theory (Austin 1976) as developed by Searle.[63] My presentation is based on a

the persuasive aspects belong to the rhetorical perspective of a text.

61. Cf. Simons's use of the word 'persuasion' (1976: 137). Van Eemeren's view on the 'normal' use of the words is slightly different (van Eemeren, Grootendorst and Kruiger 1987: 217): 'convince' is used of creating understanding, persuading of moving to a course of action. This view equates argumentation with communication, although these two have different goals. The aim of communication is understanding, while that of argumentation is an opinion. See also below.

62. Georges 1918: *s.v. persuadere*. This distinction differs from Siegert's way of understanding the two meanings of *persuadere* (Siegert 1985: 21-22).

63. Searle 1970. Searle criticizes Austin for studying verbs instead of acts, and himself attempts to classify different types of illocutionary act.

modification by van Eemeren and Grootendorst,[64] but also includes an important distinction between cognitive and volitional effects, that is, between conviction and persuasion.

Contrary to logical *demonstration*, which does not take account of the audience, and is seldom the only function of a literary text, *argumentation* focuses on the audience-oriented aspects, that is on the *communicative*, and especially the *interactive* dimension of the text. In communication the language-user wants to inform the audience of something. This, however, is usually not the only purpose of the activity. In addition, he or she seeks to produce some effect in the audience. From this interactive perspective, a discourse is seen not only as the sender's communication to the receiver, but as a bi-directional relationship. The audience's (i.e. the audience implied in the text) feedback affects the speaker's further message, which again affects the audience.

As a result of communication the reader *understands* the cognitive meaning or the propositional content of the text; in speech-act theory this is called an *illocutionary* effect of the text (Searle 1975; van Eemeren and Grootendorst 1984: 23). Thus a reader may for example learn from an encyclopedia the population of Zaire. But very few texts are purely informative, aiming only to share intellectual knowledge. The author usually also wants interaction: the reader is to *accept* the message. To this end, the text must also have a *perlocutionary* effect; the reader has to react somehow to the message.

Of the many forms of speech acts, the argumentation can have two different perlocutionary effects: readers are cognitively *convinced* when they hold a statement as true; if their behaviour is affected, they are volitionally *persuaded* (van Eemeren and Grootendorst 1984: 48), that is, they acquired *motivation*. Van Eemeren and Grootendorst also distinguish between *inherent* and *consecutive* perlocutionary effects (1984: 24): for example, to accept a request, or to acquire motivation, is an inherent effect of persuasion, while the consecutive effect of persuasion can be a change or a minor effect on the receiver's life. The following illustration shows how these terms are related to each other (1984: 25). Unlike van Eemeren and Grootendorst I include here the distinction between the *cognitive* and *volitional* effects, between conviction and persuasion.

---

64. Van Eemeren and Grootendorst 1984: 23-25. In order to apply the theory to argumentation analysis they focus on the interactive aspect of speech acts. This aspect is disregarded by Searle, who concentrates on the communicative aspect.

Dimension of activity	Sub-dimension	Speech act	Inherent effect	Consecutive effect
Demonstrative		Locution	Perceive	Perception
Communicative	Cognitive	Illocution	Understand	Knowledge
Interactive		Perlocution	Accept	
	(a) Cognitive	(a) Argumentation	(a) Conviction	(a) Opinion
	(b) Volitional	(b) Persuasion	(b) Motivation	(b) Action

An example: the text 'Close the window. It is draughty here and you may catch cold' consists of an exhorting and a motivating expression. From the cognitive perspective, that is, analysing it as argumentation, we recognize a Claim with two Data. These form a structure of argumentation. From the volitional perspective, looking at it as persuasion, we find an exhortation which is supported by two motivating expressions. These constitute a motivating structure.

Close the window	Claim		Exhortation	
It is draughty here	Data$_1$	Argumentation	Motivating expression$_1$	Motivation
You may catch a cold	Data$_2$		Motivating expression$_2$	

b. *Consequences for the Analysis*

The analysis of persuasion in an argumentative text differs from normal argumentation analysis in one aspect: we must take the volitional aspect into account.

For the persuader it is not enough to modify the receivers' opinions; it is even more important to change their attitudes toward action.[65] Thus the volitional emotional impact is crucial. Already ancient rhetoricians were well aware of this aspect (see e.g. Wallace 1986). Referring to modern psychology, Brooks and Warren explain that emotions promote the assent to the speaker's goal, because emotion always seeks both a justification and a target. After the emotion is aroused, the speaker can provide a content which defines the target for the action desired (1979: 114). They add that often the most effective approach is to operate with long-term emotional attitudes of which the receiver is only subliminally aware (1979: 114).

---

65. Thus e.g. Simons, partly building on Burke's ideas. According to him, besides appealing to the to the receiver's need for logical consistency, persuasion (although it does not have to be objectively logical) must also be able to change the receiver's attitudes as a precondition to changes in behaviour (Simons 1976: 137).

It is therefore right to say that emotion is not a less valuable or a despicable part of a person's being, but a major incentive to action, since it encompasses the values and opinions (so Moss 1986: 17). The ultimate power of persuasion lies in its capacity to affect the emotive attitudes.

The emotive aspect of persuasion can be studied with a psychological approach, but in a rhetorical analysis of argumentation it is more convenient to use as a frame of reference the ancient conceptions *ethos* and *pathos*, which do not simply focus on the emotional side of persuasion, but also include elements of argumentation,[66] occurring in all genres of speech.[67]

Summarizing, we can state that when studying persuasion, or, in other words, how exhortations are motivated, it is not enough to understand how an author obtains assent to a thesis, but we must also focus on how one attempts to effect such a volitional impact, that the addressees will act accordingly. Therefore it is necessary to add the volitional, emotional aspect to the argumentation analysis, that is, to ask what kind of emotions the author attempts to provoke in order to elicit assent to the admonition. The argumentation 'John is sleeping, don't wake him up!' can be analysed in two different ways (for a clarification of Toulmin's model, see above, chapter 2.2.b):

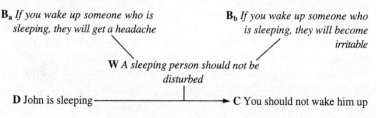

B_a *If you wake up someone who is sleeping, they will get a headache*

B_b *If you wake up someone who is sleeping, they will become irritable*

W *A sleeping person should not be disturbed*

D John is sleeping ———————————→ **C** You should not wake him up

66. See above. Cf. Wenzel, who opposes a 'psychological' study of texts (1987b: 104). Siegert (1985: 230-31) misinterprets pathos as a 'Steigerung des Ethos', which may be connected with the disregard of these aspects in his study. It is clear that when these factors are used, the role of the audience is especially important. We thus come close to Perelman's idea of the particular audience as a signal for persuasion. However, there are also emotional and moral aspects that can be thought to affect a universal audience, i.e. every rational human being.

67. It is evident that purely cognitive reasons do not suffice to change the volitional basis for the receiver's behaviour. Thus, Wallace stresses that in persuasion we have to focus especially on the *pathos* or emotive effort, and on the *ethos* or the speaker's character, which he describes as emotional and moral factors. Wallace admits, however, that those aspects need also to be seen, although to a lesser degree, in argumentation (1986: 122).

The decisive motivating factor depends on which implicit backing is chosen. In case (a) one wants to spare John a headache, that is, the factor is pity or love for him. In case (b) the idea is to avoid trouble for oneself, so the factor is love for oneself. In each case the validity of the warrant depends on the persuadee's possible willingness to save somebody from trouble, but the emotive factor is different, and these factors determine whether the persuadee obeys the persuader or not.

A specific feature in this type of text is that the C is usually not a statement but a command.[68] When studying the grounds for ethics, such differences are of great significance. However, without an adequate, controllable method for analysing the structure of argumentation, the analysis remains arbitrary.

4. *Toward a Model of Discovering Ideological Structures*

At the beginning of this chapter I stressed the needs for a rhetorical perspective and an analysis of argumentative structures, when studying specific motifs or larger ideological entities, such as the ethics or the theology of an author. Now I shall demonstrate how the ideological level can be reached in practice.

1. *Identification*

The first stage consists of clarifying how the argumentation and persuasion are designed to function on the text level.[69] With this in mind we must begin by identifying the explicit expressions used in argumentation that seek to motivate the exhortations in the text. This is problematic in the models of modern analysis of argumentation, and with a text that is both culturally and linguistically foreign to the analyst, such an identification is even more difficult. Thus, a careful semantic analysis is needed. It should begin with a definition of the logical relations that can occur between an exhortation and its motivation. Then these relations shall be identified in the text. In a case study with 1 Peter, this task has proven to be an Achilles' heel of modern exegesis.

---

68. Thus it has to be modified: e.g. 'close the window' is already formally a statement if rephrased 'you ought to close the window'. The semantic difference is not substantial, and therefore the modification may seem superfluous in actual analysis.

69. By 'text level' I mean a counterpart to the ideological level behind the text.

2. *Textual Analysis*

After recognizing the explicit material, the argumentation in the text can be analysed with the help of modern theories and with Toulmin's model, emphasizing the role of rhetorical situations, devices and strategy.[70] By taking into account the volitional perspective and emotive factors the persuasive and motivating aspect can be brought into focus. When the text has been scrutinized in this way, we can see how the expressions used in the persuasive argumentation are connected to each other, that is, we can find convincing and persuasive *structures* attached to different exhortations in various rhetorical situations in the text.

3. *Conceptualization*

When the specific functions of the expressions used in persuasive argumentation in the text are known, they can be classified according to their content into more general *motifs* and *topoi*. This means a shift in the analysis from text level to an ideological level behind the text.

One example: On text level the exhortation 'close the window' can be motivated with the expression 'you may catch cold' or 'you may become feverish'. Both phrases are manifestations of a motif 'you can fall ill', or, in more general terms, the topos 'warning for disease'. Moreover, the same topos can elsewhere be used for motivating a totally different exhortation such as 'Do not smoke'.

In all the cases the implied emotive, *persuasive* or *motivating factor* seems to be willingness to avoid disease.

4. *Ideological Analysis*

Regularities in the motifs or topoi and in their use thus yield general structures on the ideological level,[71] if we can recognize a typical function for each motif. Explanation of such a typical structure may lead to a better understanding of actual motivating structures in the text. However, there is an obvious possibility of a fallacy, if the nature of the exhortation is disregarded.

---

70. Understanding the rhetorical strategy is crucial for analyzing ambiguous forms in the text; see Thurén 1990: 39-40.

71. Just as the factors of argumentation and persuasion in a textual unit form a functional structure, the motifs in the ideological level can also constitute a structure.

A simplified illustration:

LEVEL: Text Example A	Text Example B	Text Example C	Ideological Motifs
Take this pullover	Close the window	Do not smoke	(different exhortations)
It's cold here	There is a draught in the room	—	Unhealthy conditions
You can become feverish	You can catch cold	Smoking is dangerous for your health	Warning for disease (MF_1)
Then you cannot go to the movies	X	—	Loss of entertainment (MF_2)

If the situation is identical, the model lets us see that the last component in case B (= X) plausibly corresponds to A, although it remains unsaid. Then the implied higher motivating factor (MF_2) would be the same, a specific desire to go to the movies or be entertained. However, this would hardly be true of C, although a lower motivating factor (MF_1), willingness to avoid disease, is common to all the cases. Thus, the rhetorical situation and the ideological motifs must be specifiable in order for the implication to be reliably drawn.

Identification of the functions and interrelations of the topoi yields a general picture of their structure even in larger sections in the text. By the end of the process, we may make a universal statement about the function of each motif in the whole text.

Thus, by starting from small textual units and proceeding to more general levels and to larger units, we may discover whether there is enough consistency in the persuasive argumentation, and the use of different motifs, to allow description of its qualities.

Part II

ANALYSIS: THE MOTIVATION ON THE TEXT LEVEL

Chapter 3

IDENTIFYING THE MOTIVATING EXPRESSIONS

1. *The Approach*

In an empirical study with undergraduate students, van Eemeren *et al.* showed that the most important factor in identifying argumentation consists of so-called argumentation indicators, such as 'because' or 'on the basis of' (van Eemeren 1987: 203-204). The role of the indicators is not always clear,[1] and their absence makes the identification far more difficult. In such cases contextual indication is required: in order to recognize indirect argumentation the reader needs 'some extra information' (1987: 204). Compared with modern texts, the recognition of argumentation in an ancient text sets us a specific challenge, since our knowledge of both the direct and the indirect—textual and contextual—indicators is defective. Therefore argumentation may be overlooked or misinterpreted.

Oddly enough, the same basic deficiency besets the research on 1 Peter and the motivation of its paraenesis: the scholars have arrived at opposing results at least partly because of negligence of some important factors in the motivation. In other words, the identification of argumentation has proven difficult. In 1 Peter the difficulty does not depend so much on the lack of explicit indicators, but on their problematic nature: the author has a habit of combining admonition and motivation in a peculiar way,[2] and he even likes to use semantically ambiguous expressions.[3]

---

1. Cf. Toulmin *et al.* 1984: 6-7, according to whom there is a wide spectrum from purely instrumental to purely argumentative utterances.

2. See e.g. Gyllenberg 1969: 215; Olsson 1982: 51, Thurén 1990: 184-85; Martin 1992a: 141. Ellul (1990: 17-34) manages to divide 1.3–4.11 into four proclaiming and four exhorting sections. This, however, means a grave simplification and one-sided reading of the text.

3. For the use of the ambiguous expressions as a rhetorical device in 1 Peter, see Thurén 1990: 164-76.

In the analysis it may sometimes seem superfluous to report an explicit search for the argumentation. When a command is followed by a ὅτι clause, one may think that there is a natural motivation. But even our empirical study (viz. the review of research of 1 Peter) shows that such an intuitive understanding varies significantly.[4] Thus we need a method of articulating the intuitions, with which we can execute a careful analysis of the argumentation indicators in the text.[5]

The goal in this chapter is to define the sections in 1 Peter that include explicit motivating expressions,[6] in order to identify an important part of the material for our research. The results are used in Chapter 5, and they will be demonstrated there in the Greek text. This semantic study is not comprehensive, because there are also significant implicit factors[7] in the motivation. But since the identification of the explicit expressions is easier both to execute and to control, it will be the first step, which then facilitates a study of the contextual indication, which in turn will be approached with a pragmatic method.

Thus I shall search for argumentation indicators, especially syntactic markers, which denote motivating expressions.[8] The function of such markers is seldom so clear that the text would be solely argumentative (see above): a word may have several components of meaning, only one of which serves as a marker for argumentation. Thus the strength of this function must be assessed.[9] In order to define the most plausible

---

4. This is true even when assessing words like ὅτι (see below §2.a).

5. Botha (1991: 98) is right to state that one of the merits of modern linguistics is that it can 'explicate a number of important choices which are usually made intuitively in the reading process', even when no revolutionary results are achieved.

6. By 'explicit motivating expression' I mean an utterance in the text, which seeks to persuade the addressees to obey the author's admonitions, and which is clearly expressed in the text, as opposite to 'implicit motivating expressions'.

7. An 'implicit motivating expression' here means a factor or an idea that the persuasion requires in order to be understood and effective, but which is not expressed clearly in the text. E.g. the utterance 'since this is the will of God' implies that the addressees believe in God, and that his will is of importance for them. Such implicit material will be sought in Chapter 5. An explaining expression also can be implicitly motivating.

8. Cf. Johanson 1987: 23-25. Markers and signals on a higher, pragmatic level (see Hellholm 1980: 78ff.) do not suite this type of preliminary survey, which is to be built on simple explicit factors.

9. E.g. 'Obey the law *as* a good citizen' may mean either '... since you are a good citizen' or '... following the example of good citizens'. According to Cotterell

interpretation of a vague marker, in other words to choose between the possibilities provided by a grammatical form, we need a *semantic* analysis (see Beekman and Callow 1974: 267-71). When formally identical constructions can be interpreted in totally different ways, a syntactic study of the text does not suffice (cf. 1974: 268-70). Even small nuances in the wording and the context may be important for determining the extent to which the expression is designed to motivate.[10]

We must start by defining which types of logical relations can exist between admonition and motivation; then we can search for expressions that stand in such relations to the commands.

Semantic relations that occur in argumentation are called *logical relations*, and there is a certain consensus about their main types.[11] In this study I use Beekman and Callow's classification of relations existing between cause and result:[12]

and Turner (1989: 194) only one component is usually prominent, while the rest are subsidiary or delimiting. If they are equal, little is communicated. This view can be challenged to some extent by a rhetorical study of 1 Peter: the same expression may well have several messages even for the same recipient. See Thurén 1990: 175.

10. Since my task is to study the motivation, I shall concentrate on this aspect even in polyvalent expressions. The addressees are also supposed to be motivated by some expressions, which are not logically connected to the commands (such as the expressions emphasizing the *ethos* of the author in 1.1 and 5.1). These will be discussed in connection with the pragmatic analysis of the argumentation (Chapter 5). Cf. Dressler 1973: 70-71.

11. Beekman and Callow 1974: 300 (and 290). A detailed presentation of the model can be found on pp. 301-307. This model closely resembles e.g. Nida's classification (1975: 50-51, 53-54). Later, in their lexicon, Louw and Nida use a similar system (1988: 89 G–L). Cf. also Cotterell and Turner 1989: 210-13. They closely follow the system of Beekman and Callow, but add a new category of Grounds-Exhortation. Since this, however, overlaps other categories (see Cotterell and Turner 1989: 213), I find it superfluous. Their choice seems to originate from difficulties in identifying the causal component in the conjunction εἰ.

12. Beekman and Callow study these relations mostly between 'propositions', by which they mean 'minimal semantic units consisting of a concept or a combination of concepts which communicates an Event or Relation' (1974: 273). However, they emphasize that similar relations also exist between greater semantic units (1974: 275); this makes their system applicable to our task.

CAUSE	EFFECT	CAUSE ANSWERS THE QUESTION	NATURE OF EFFECT
Reason	Result	Why this result?	definite
Means	Result	How did this result come about?	definite
Means	*Purpose*	*What action was undertaken to achieve this result?*	*desired*
Condition	Consequence	What...condition could cause the consequence to become actual?	definite
Concession	Contra-expectation	Why is the actual result unexpected?	definite, not expected
Grounds	*Conclusion*	*What fact(s) is this conclusion based on?*	*deduced*

Only in two of these relations is the effect not 'definite': Means–Purpose (MP)[13] and Grounds–Conclusion (GC)[14]. Therefore in these relations, the 'effect' can also be a command and the cause can be a motivating expression (Beekman and Callow 1974: 306-307, 303). The other relations, especially Reason–Result,[15] can also serve the motivation by connecting two factors in the reasoning, which is then attached to the command with an MP or a GC relation.[16]

If the command and the motivating expression stand in an MP relation to each other, they can be expressed: one has to do something in order to obtain/avoid something. On the syntactic level such a relation is often signified by *final* particles, and on the ideological level this is a *teleological* motivation.

A GC relation means, according to Beekman and Callow, that 'on the basis of the grounds stated, the readers are told to do or not to do something' (1974: 307), thereby signaling a *deontological* motivation. On the

13. E.g. In order to be fresh John needs to sleep. Porter (1994: 231) calls these 'purpose', 'final' or 'telic' clauses.

14. E.g. Since John is tired he wants to sleep. According to Porter (1994: 237), these are 'causal' clauses.

15. According to Porter (1994: 234), these are 'result', 'consecutive' or 'ecbatic' clauses.

16. It is often difficult to decide to which expression another expression refers. In a simple motivating case the argumentative expression is directly attached to the command. But when this is followed by an additional motivating expression, the latter can function either in parallel or in support of the first. A secondary motivating expression can be in an MP, GC or RR relation to the primary one. E.g. Let John sleep (GC) since he is tired (RR) for he has worked too hard. The choice of the motivating function of an expression can however be eventually made first on the basis of its rhetorical function (see Chapter 2 §4).

syntactic level this relation is often marked by causal signals.

We are thus looking for expressions that stand in the above-mentioned relations to commands, both of which are directed to the addressees.[17]

When examining semantic relations it is essential to observe all the grammatical and lexical signals for them (1974: 283). As examples of such markers Beekman and Callow name in Greek καί, δέ, ἀλλά, γάρ, ὅτι and ἵνα.[18] But even the contents and the context of the expressions are important: sometimes there is no clear signal for the logical relation, which is nevertheless evident.[19] For those searching for such markers traditional grammars and lexica present an etymological but semantically scattered and thus somewhat confused picture: one word is usually discussed at the time, although it may have several components of meaning. Louw and Nida are the first to provide a semantically coherent presentation: the meanings that may be presented with different words, are discussed (1988). Their lexicon, however, does not show all the possible components of the words, and when a certain component of a word is weak, the word is not discussed in that context. In the following presentation, the merits of two different lexicographic or grammatical philosophies will be combined.

I shall first study the syntactic markers, which may function as signals for motivating logical relations in 1 Peter, in order to assess the relevant component in each word.[20] This analysis makes it easier to determine the semantically polyvalent expressions, which may have many functions in the text, only one of which is motivating (such as ὡς τέκνα in 1.14; see Chapter 3 §2.e. and 5 §3.b). In such cases, it is important to know to what extent or under what circumstances such an expression is designed

17. A problematic section is 1 Pet. 1.1-12, which semantically does not contain any commands to the addressees, but which however rhetorically is aimed at motivating them (see below, Chapter 5 §2). The reasoning in this section will be studied, so that the statements about the addressees are seen as substitutes for the admonitions.

18. Beekman and Callow 1974: 269. It is of no use to study these words, since they clearly do not signify the logical relations discussed here (e.g. ὅτι *recitativum* in 1.16a). If, however, there is any sign for a possible GC, MP or RR relation, the case will be examined (e.g. ὅτι in 1.12, see below).

19. E.g. 1 Pet. 5.8. Dressler (1973: 79) states, 'Konjunktionen und andere Konnektoren sind nur äussere Ausdruck semantischer Satzverknüpfungs-relationen...' We also need other ways to identify the relevant logical relations in the text.

20. Van Rensburg (1990) provides a brief, but unfortunately incomplete, presentation of logical relations in 1 Peter (see below).

to motivate the addressees. In the next chapter I shall make, contrary to the oversimplifying tradition, a maximal interpretation of such expressions, searching for their role in the motivation, even though their primary purpose is something else. Answers to these questions also provide us with material for a deeper analysis of the meaning of the motivating expressions, when we have to decide in which way or with what power a particular expression is designed to affect the addressees.[21] After an analysis of each types of signal I shall search for corresponding motivating sections in the text.[22]

Secondly, I shall observe even such sections as do not have any clear semantic signal for a logical relation, but which on the basis of context or for rhetorical reasons can be said to stand in such a relation (see further Chapter 3 §2.g).

By combining all these expressions and sections, a catalogue of the motivating expressions in 1 Peter, which facilitates the analysis of argumentation, can be made. Nevertheless it must be complemented with implied motivating expressions and with motivation which is independent of any particular command.[23]

2. *Motivating Expressions Referring to Grounds*

Introduction

Beekman and Callow define the Grounds–Conclusion (GC) relation in the following way:

> This relation states an observation or known fact and a conclusion deduced from that observation or fact. The observation or fact represents the ground; the deduction represents the conclusion. [...] This type of relation seems to be used in two major contexts in the New Testament. The first is in arguments, when a conclusion is drawn from known facts, and stated as such. The second is when the conclusion drawn is not presented as a statement, but as a command...'[24]

21. Such a nuanced analysis of particular expressions in the letter also is important, because the style in 1 Peter is commonly seen as one of the best in the New Testament (see Selwyn 1947: 10; Reicke 1964: 70; Schelkle 1970: 13; Baltz and Schrage 1973: 63; Turner 1976: 124, 130; Goppelt 1978: 45-46 and Brox 1979: 45): there is reason to suspect that even small particles have precise functions in the text.

22. Or to be more precise, sections in 1 Peter, which because of the signal can be identified as standing in a relevant logical relation to a command or to its primary motivation will be presented.

23. Such is the emphasis on the *ethos* of the author, see above n. 10.

24. Beekman and Callow 1974: 306-307. Cf. Cotterell and Turner 1989: 211:

When the relationship between two short expressions is clearly signaled with explicit markers on the syntactic level, a *causal* meaning of these markers is required for a GC relation.[25] Therefore I discuss first, briefly, causal conjunctions, then other grammatical signs which at least partly carry this meaning, and seek among them relations which are relevant to our task.[26]

a. *Causal dependent conjunctions* ὅτι *and* διότι

ὅτι

Semantically this causal conjunction[27] is fairly straightforward. It signifies a logical relation when referring to cause or reason, and is then usually easily distinguishable from the other functions, 'that' and ὅτι *recitativum*. The ground which ὅτι gives is based on an event or fact (Louw and Nida 1988: 89.33), and usually stands in a direct causal relation to the main sentence ('because'), but also a looser connection ('since') can occur.[28]

According to some scholars the use of ὅτι to introduce a motivating statement is typical for the author of 1 Peter,[29] but also the other types of ὅτι occur (e.g. ὅτι *recitativum* in 1.16; 'that' in 1.18). The meaning is problematic twice: 1.12 and 4.1.

In 1.12 (οἷς ἀπεκαλύφθη ὅτι οὐχ ἑαυτοῖς ὑμῖν δὲ διηκόνουν αὐτά...), according to a causal interpretation of ὅτι, αὐτά would be

'One kernel offers the evidence on the basis of which the second is to be accepted'.

25. E.g. in 1 Cor. 6.2 (an example used by Beekman and Callow 1974: 307) 'and if the world shall be judged by you' the word if (εἰ) includes a causal component. See further the study of εἰ in Chapter 3 §2.g. For discussion about Cotterell's and Turner's solution, see above p. 62 n. 11.

26. The Reason–Result and Means–Result relations are signaled with the same causal markers, and can also be found in a chain of arguments (see above Chapter 2 §2.b). Beekman and Callow give the difference between these two types as being that whereas in RR the first proposition state the reason 'why', in MR it explains the means 'how' (1974: 302). For practical reasons they will be discussed in connection with the GC relation.

27. After γάρ, ὅτι (orig. neuter of ὅστις) is the most usual causal conjunction in Greek. It always opens a causal dependent clause (Bauer–Aland 1988[6] *s.v.*; Kleine 1981: 1316-17).

28. Kleine 1981: 1316-17; BDR §456,1. In the New Testament ὅτι is used on the whole in the same way as in the classical language (Kleine).

29. Selwyn 1947: 64-65. According to Dijkman, in 1 Peter ὅτι serves as an introduction formula for Jewish or Jewish-Christian catechetical material (Dijkman 1986).

subject of ἀπεκαλύφθη: the author would explain God's (*pass. div.*) revelation with an expression about the prophets' activity (thus e.g. the Finnish Bible 1938). This interpretation can be supported by the fact that ἀποκαλύπτω ὅτι in the meaning 'reveal that' never occurs in classical Greek, LXX, or elsewhere in the New Testament.[30] However, most of the modern commentators rightly translate ὅτι with 'that', since a causal interpretation would lead to problems with the preceding verse at the content level.[31] According to the common interpretation αὐτά is the object of διηκόνουν and the connection between 11 and 12 is clearer.[32]

In 4.1 (Χριστοῦ οὖν παθόντος σαρκὶ καὶ ὑμεῖς τὴν αὐτὴν ἔννοιαν ὁπλίσασθε, ὅτι ὁ παθὼν σαρκὶ πέπαυται ἁμαρτίας...) an explicative meaning has sometimes been postulated.[33] The majority of scholars, however, reject this interpretation with good alternative interpretations.[34]

In 1 Peter there are thus twelve causal ὅτι conjunctions, all of which introduce a motivating expression (most of them are primary motivating expressions). 1.16 may serve as an example: ἅγιοι ἔσεσθε, ὅτι ἐγὼ ἅγιος. Other expressions are 2.15, 21; 3.9, 12, 18; 4.1, 8, 14, 17; 5.5, 7.

διότι

διότι can introduce a causal or a consecutive sentence (Bauer–Aland *s.v.*). In the first case it can replace the causal ὅτι.[35] The word occurs

30. Thus Selwyn 1947: 137. However, according to him the expression can even be good Greek as a *hapax*.

31. The prophets wanted to know about the *time* (1.11) but they learned the *Gospel* (1.12).

32. The prophets asked for the time to which their prophecies referred, or pointed, and were told that they meant 'you', viz. the people in the last days.

33. Kelly (1969: 166-69) claims that a causal meaning is unnatural, since suffering cannot have a purgatory effect; thus the sentence must refer to Christ.

34. Goppelt (1978: 268) argues that ὅτι cannot mean 'dass', since it cannot refer to Christ. Instead, he presents the following interpretations: (a) suffering is a sign to cease from sin (so Windisch and Preisker 1951: 73); (b) suffering makes free from sin; according to Schelkle this cannot mean our own suffering (1970: 114); (c) it refers to the Pauline idea of dying to sin; (d) it does not refer to baptism, but to Rom. 6.7: the body and sin belong together. Cf. also Selwyn (1947: 209), according to whom bodily suffering has a purifying effect on the spirit. Brox (1986: 190-93) rephrases the verse: 'Leiden im Hoffnung, Freude im Leiden (192)'—according to him, ὅτι does not refer to Christ but to the Christian, who is without sins, and who must suffer, on account of being a Christian. For my solution, see Chapter 5 §4.c.

35. Schneider 1980: 812-13. A specific feature is, according to Louw and Nida

only 24 times in the New Testament (BDR §456, 1), and the usage corresponds to the classical one.

In 1 Peter διότι occurs three times: 1.16: διότι γέγραπται; see also 1.24; 2.6. According to Bauer and Aland, διότι is used as a synonym of ὅτι, but one specific feature can be discerned: it always introduces an Old Testament quotation.[36]

b. *Causal Coordinate Conjunction* γάρ

γάρ is the most usual common conjunction in Greek, indicating a somewhat looser, tenuous connection between two propositions than ὅτι.[37] When occurring after an argument it can also draw a conclusion ('thus') (Bauer–Aland *s.v.*). γάρ can also have an explanatory or confirmatory meaning, or, like δέ, carry a thought forward.[38] The usage resembles the classical one, but in the New Testament γάρ is less common than ὅτι. In the New Testament the authors use these words in an almost similar way.[39]

In 1 Peter γάρ occurs ten times.[40] Two of these do not introduce a motivating expression, but explain the activity of God (2.25; 4.6). These verses are however included in long motivating sections. The γάρ that signals motivating expressions occurs eight times. Only the first introduces a primary motivating expression with a GC relation to the command: 2.19 (τοῦτο γὰρ χάρις), 2.20, 21, 25; 3.5, 10, 17; 4.3 and 15. The last refers retrospectively to the preceding verse or even further back. The causal relation marked with γάρ is not as evident as that with ὅτι; there is often also an explanatory component.[41]

(1988: 89.26), that it focuses on instrumentality of the word to which it refers.

36. In the oldest manuscript of 1 Peter, 𝔓[72], διότι is replaced in 2.24 by ὅτι. This shows how closely the meanings of these particles in the letter have been understood.

37. Pridik 1980: 571-73; Louw and Nida 1988: 89.23. According to Porter (1994: 237), γάρ indicates only a broad causal or inferential connection.

38. Pridik 1980: 571-73; BDR §452. Denniston (1954: 58-70) makes a distinction between a 'confirmatory/causal', 'explanatory' and 'anticipatory' meaning.

39. Some authors prefer ὅτι, others γάρ (Pridik 1980: 571-73).

40. Van Rensburg does not see the word in 2.21 (1990: 292-93).

41. E.g. the Swedish translation Nya Testamentet 81 consistently leaves every γάρ untranslated.

c. *Consecutive Coordinate Conjunctions* οὖν, διό *and* ὥστε

οὖν

As a conjunction οὖν usually refers to a result or consequence ('so', 'therefore') (Bauer–Aland *s.v.*; Louw and Nida 1988: 89.50). Then it signals a causal relation between two sentences standing in a different sequence from when proper causal conjunctions are used. οὖν can carry an interrupted thought further or introduce something new (BDR §451,1). Its meaning is not always causal; it is often a general unemphasized expression.[42] It is common even in questions.[43] In the New Testament, almost half of the cases occur in the Gospel of John.[44]

In 1 Peter οὖν occurs six times. In 5.1 it introduces a sentence as a typical unemphasized transferring particle, which does not signify any logical relation.[45] Goppelt rightly claims that it would be unnatural, were the fact that the author instructs the elders (5.1) to be a consequence of a command to do good (4.19).[46]

Goppelt claims that οὖν in 5.6 is a transitionary particle just as in 5.1.[47] However, his arguments for 5.1 do not apply here.[48] 5.6 draws a conclusion from 5.5, which stands in a clear GC relation to the preceding verse: 'God gives grace to the humble. Therefore be humble...' This causal interpretation well befits in the context,[49] and corresponds to the use of οὖν in every other case in the text: it refers to an Old Testament quotation, which is introduced with ὅτι.

---

42. Porter (1994: 214-15) sees also an adversative meaning.

43. Baltz 1981: 1326-27.

44. BDR §451,1.

45. (4.19)...παρατιθέσθωσαν τὰς ψυχὰς αὐτῶν ἐν ἀγαθοποιΐᾳ, (5.1) πρεσβυτέρους οὖν ἐν ὑμῖν παρακαλῶ...

46. Goppelt 1978: 321. His other argument against a causal meaning of οὖν is not very strong: according to him οὖν cannot be causal since it is not textually certain, which would indicate that it has been interpreted as a 'weiterführend' particle (1978: 321, 4).

47. Goppelt 1978: 321 n. 4. Van Rensburg (1990: 295, 298) claims that the verse refers to 1.3ff.

48. The train of thought is not obscure, and even textually οὖν is certain.

49. Against Nauck (1958: 134-35), who interprets οὖν here (and in some other cases) in a fantastic way: 'Das οὖν pareneticum lässt den Character urchristlicher Ethik deutlich erkennen: Sie ist weder eine autonome, noch eine finale, sondern eine konsekutive Ethik; eine Ethik, die aus dem gnädigen Handeln Gottes die Folgerung im Vollzug der Lebensführung zieht'.

An οὖν signifying a motivating logical relation thus occurs five times in the Letter: 2.1,[50] 7; 4.1, 7b (πάντων δὲ τὸ τέλος ἤγγικεν. σωθρονήσατε οὖν...); 5.6.[51]

διό

Already in the classical language διό has become a conjunction (originally from a relative διό; see BDR §451,5). It signals the consequence in a way similar to οὖν but the causal meaning is more evident. Moreover the thing referred to is often self-evident ('for this very reason') (Louw and Nida 1988: 89.47). In the New Testament it is seldom used outside the Acts, the original letters of Paul and Hebrews (Schneider 1980: 811).

In 1 Peter διό occurs only once, in 1.13. There it refers to the whole of the introductory section 1.3-12 (so e.g. Goppelt 1978: 110; van Rensburg 1990: 294). It cannot be an unemphasized connecting word; it is rather a sign of a GC relation between what the author has already said and 1.13 onwards (the other limit is hard to discern).[52] Therefore we can see the whole of 1.3-12 as an argument for 1.13 and even for what follows thereafter.

ὥστε

When ὥστε introduces an independent sentence we have a clear conclusion, and the word can be translated 'therefore'. If it introduces a dependent clause with an infinitive as the main verb, the meaning is consecutive 'so that' or even final 'in order to' (BDR §391; Bauer–Aland *s.v.*; Liddell and Scott 1978: *s.v.*). It often signifies an intended or indirect purpose (Louw and Nida 1988: 89.52). The usage in the New Testament differs somewhat from the classical one (see closer BDR §391,2-3).

In 1 Peter there are two ὥστε sentences (van Rensburg [1990: 295] overlooks 1.21). In 1.21 we have a dependent clause with an infinitive, and the meaning is purely consecutive. The sentence presents the results

---

50. If the participle is interpreted as a statement, we have a Reason–Result relation.

51. Van Rensburg (1990: 294-95) argues that 2.1 and 4.1 refer to larger sections, but as 4.1 shows, this is not the case.

52. The ground, to which διό refers, is so large that it cannot be defined precisely, which sentence specifically goes together with διό. Similarly it is difficult to decide which of the three (possibly) admonishing words in 1.13 expresses the actual command, to which διό refers.

of God's activity. The only ὥστε signifying a logical GC relation is found in 4.18-19: ὥστε καὶ οἱ πάσχοντες...

d. *Prepositions with, inter alia, a Causal Meaning:* ἐν, διά *cum acc.* and κατά *cum acc.*

ἐν

The function of prepositions is related to adverbs (Porter 1994: 139), and some of them apparently serve as signals for a GC or RR relation. The most common preposition in the New Testament is ἐν. Because of its relationship to the Hebrew ב it has various meanings in the New Testament and the choice between them is often difficult to make.[53] As a marker of a logical relation ἐν resembles διά and διότι (Louw and Nida 1988: 89.26).

In 1 Peter there are altogether 51 ἐν expressions, many of which have a causal or a modal subsidiary component of meaning.

The ἐν expressions, which signify a logical relation, are chiefly found in seven places. Four of them (2.12b; 3.16b; 4.4, 14) explain the Gentiles' behaviour toward the addressees—ἐν is the only preposition used for this purpose in the text. The three remaining cases may be discussed.

In 1.5 the expression ἐν δυνάμει θεοῦ φρουρουμένους contains a clear Reason–Result relation. In the following 1.6 the expression ἐν ᾧ ἀγαλλιᾶσθε refers to the whole of 1.3-5 signifying also a RR relation.[54]

---

53. The originally local meaning of ἐν was already widened in the classical Greek, but the influence of the Hebrew ב makes the interpretation still more difficult (see Elliger 1980: 1093-96; BDR §§218-20; Zerwick 1963: 116). Bauer recognizes local, temporal and causal basic meanings (Bauer–Aland *s.v.*); Elliger adds an instrumental and a modal meaning (Elliger 1980: 1093-96), whereas the causal belongs under the modal meaning. Porter (1994: 156-59) refers to locative, distributional, spherical, temporal and instrumental meanings, the last one including manner and cause. ἐν is used also in Hebraistic expressions as a direct substitute for ב (*ibid.*).

54. Martin (1992b) argues for a future meaning of ἀγαλλιᾶσθε, which would mean that ἐν ᾧ in 1.6 refers to ἐν καιρῷ ἐσχάτῳ in 1.5. So also Goppelt (1978: 99). However, since the section describes the current situation of the addressees as a rhetorical (quasi-) *narratio*, it is more plausible that the author describes also the addressees' joy in the present tense. In that case ἐν ᾧ indicates the reason for this unnatural joy: the addressees are preserved to salvation. Cf. also Nauck 1955: 71-72. Martin refers to the communicative function of the verse against an imperative interpretation (1992b: 307-308), but the same argument contradicts the future meaning of the expression, too. In 4.13 the same expression appears as an imperative, due to another function in a modified rhetorical situation: the addressees are told to rejoice now.

A more problematic expression is found in 4.16: εἰ δὲ ὡς Χριστιανός, μὴ αἰσχυνέσθω, δοξαζέτω δὲ τὸν θεὸν <u>ἐν τῷ ὀνόματι τούτῳ</u>. The meaning of ἐν here is controversial. The expression has an instrumental basic meaning 'through this name', viz. Christian (thus Selwyn 1947: 126; Goppelt 1978: 310 n. 47; Brox 1979: 222), but it can also be understood as a modal '(by living) as a Christian'.[55] Then ἐν would correspond to ὡς in 4.16. For me the most natural solution is to compare the expression with ἐν ὀνόματι in 4.14. There the meaning of ἐν is purely causal (see Selwyn 1947: 222; Nauck 1955: 105). In that case the expression can be paraphrased 'Because you are Christians'.[56] However, the expression remains somewhat ambiguous, and attempts to delimit the meanings of the word have not been persuasive; the author seems to use a polyvalent expression on purpose in order to express different nuances simultaneously.[57]

55. Thus Selwyn 1947: 225-26. Olsson (1982: 171) sees here an idiom similar to that in Mt. 10.41-42: 'Anyone who welcomes a prophet *in the name of a prophet...*' He also states that in connection to δοξάζειν ἐν is most often modal in the New Testament.

56. Against Brox, according to whom the expression ἐν ὀνόματι Χριστοῦ in 4.14 means 'for the sake of Christ's name' and does not refer to the name of the Christians (Brox 1979: 216; so even Bauer–Aland *s.v.* ὀνειδίζω). Goppelt, however, rightly claims that the expression is a direct translation of the Hebrew לשם and interprets the expression based on ὡς Χριστιανός in 4.16 'since you belong to Christ'. Thus ἐν τῷ ὀνόματι τούτῳ in 4.16 can be understood in the same way (Goppelt 1978: 305; see also Kelly [1969: 190-91], who refers to Mt. 10.41: εἰς ὄνομα προφήτου κτλ. 'because he is a prophet').

57. The expression ἐν τῷ ὀνόματι τούτῳ is so short that it is hardly an explanatory paraphrase. Instead, the author seems to utilize the wide semantic field of the word when attempting to change the negative contents of the title 'Christian' to something positive. First, in 4.14 ἐν is purely causal, giving the reason for insult ('If you suffer because of the name of Christ', viz. because you are called 'Christians'). Second, in 4.16a the title 'Christian' has acquired a neutral, modal meaning ('If some one suffers as [ὡς] Christian'), and lastly, in 4.14b ἐν signifies a causal, instrumental and even local meaning (He shall praise God *in* this name', viz. because he belongs to the Christians and thereby to Christ). A term of abuse thereby acquires a deep theological content which is designed to motivate the addressees. When they are blamed since they are called 'Christians', they should praise God since they are 'in the name of Christ', i.e. they belong to him.

διά *cum acc.*

The originally local διά *cum acc.* is used in the New Testament mainly in order to give the ground or even the goal for an activity.[58] The later meaning does not occur in the classical Greek (BDR §222,2; Hess 1980: 712-13). It can be translated with 'because of' or 'for...sake',[59] but even a modal meaning is possible.[60] According to Porter, the causal use is related to the instrumental sense of the word (1994: 150).

In 1 Peter the combination διά *cum acc.* occurs four times. 1.20 gives the reason for God's (*pass. div.*) revelation, but in the three remaining cases (2.13, 19; 3.14) the receivers are addressed with the διά expression. In the first case διά is purely causal, signifying a GC relation between a command and a motivation (ὑποτάγητε...διὰ τὸν κύριον), whereas in the other two cases (about a causal meaning of 2.19 see Goppelt 1978: 195) also a modal subsidiary component of meaning is possible, having then the accusative instead of the correct genitive ('with a conscience bound to God', 'as righteous'), and the expressions are not directly connected to a command. This usage resembles that of ἐν in 4.14, 16.

κατά *cum acc.*

The combination κατά *cum acc.* has several meanings: it can signify local or temporal circumstances, ground or direction, and have connecting, even final meaning.[61] When giving the ground it is translated 'as a result of', 'for...sake' (Bauer–Aland *s.v.*). Then it can serve as a signal for a GC or a RR relation.[62] The usage in the New Testament corresponds to the classical one (BDR §§224-25).

In 1 Peter κατά *cum acc.* occurs eight times. Of these 1.2, 3, 17; 4.6 explain the activity of God. In three cases κατά serves as a signal for a GC relation between a command and a motivation: 1.15; 3.7a; 5.2.

58. Hess 1980: 712-13. See also Porter 1994: 148-51. An exception to this rule is in Lk. 17.11, διὰ μέσον.

59. Bauer–Aland *s.v.* In that case, according to Louw and Nida (1988: 89.26), it 'focuses on instrumentality, either of objects or events'.

60. In that case a genitive would be a correct form (thus Oepke 1935: 64-69).

61. Köhler 1981: 624-27. As a conjunction it is translated 'according to', 'like'. Porter recognizes a positional, standard, temporal and distributive meaning (1994: 162-64).

62. Louw and Nida (1988) fail to see this function of κατά; they only explain it as referring to isomorphism ('in accordance with', 1988: 89.8). Negligence of such minor semantic components is typical for their lexicon.

In 1.15 the meaning is ambiguous: first, a modal meaning 'like the Holy one' means that the addressees should keep God as their example: behave according to his norms or in a way similar to his (Selwyn 1947: 141). Secondly, a causal meaning: 'Because he is holy', meaning that the addressees should be holy since God is holy. This idea is more clearly expressed in 1.16, where we have a causal ὅτι sentence.[63] The κατά expression in 3.7 can also be interpreted either as modal or causal.[64] Even 5.2 (ἑκουσίως κατὰ θεόν) can be interpreted in both ways: a modal 'according to (the will of) God' or a causal 'for God's sake' or 'because God wants it'. The case corresponds to 4.19, which for other reasons is not a motivation.[65]

e. *Comparative Dependent Conjunctions* ὡς, καθώς *and* καθό
The choice between a command and a motivation is sometimes determined by different interpretations of the semantic signals. Such are in 1 Peter especially comparative conjunctions and participle forms. I have discussed the meaning of ὡς expressions and certain 'imperative' participle forms in my dissertation.[66] The problematic cases will be briefly presented here in the light of that study.

ὡς
The basic meaning of ὡς is 'like', but it has in an early phase developed in different directions: as a dependent conjunction it is in principle comparative, but can also include, for example, a final, modal, consecutive, temporal or causal component.[67] In connection to a participle the causal meaning is evident (BR §274). Then it refers to a cause 'implying the special nature of the circumstances' (Louw and Nida 1988: 89.37).

---

63. To express himself first somewhat obscurely and then more clearly belongs to the style of the author: see Olsson 1982: 198 and Thurén 1990: 21-29.

64. The meaning of the word κατά in this case is discussed more fully in chapter 5.4.f.

65. The κατά expression defines οἱ πάσχοντες: 'you who suffer according to God's will are righteous'. Thus it cannot refer to the main verb.

66. The problems are presented in detail in Thurén 1990, ὡς on pp. 25-26; the participles on pp. 4-20; the solution on pp. 164-76.

67. Bauer–Aland *s.v.*; BDR §453; BR §253,50. When ὡς is connected to a nominal sentence it often signifies an elliptic expression replacing a longer sentence (BR §253,50; Schwyzer 1971: 577, 661-69).

In 1 Peter ὡς occurs 23 times. Half of the cases are likely to have a causal (side-) meaning, and have caused problems for interpretation.[68] Of these 4.15a.b and 5.3 do not motivate an admonition, and in 4.12 ὡς introduces a rejected argument. But in 1.14; 2.5, 11, 14a.b, 16a; 3.6, 7a.b; 4.10 a motivation is possible. In 2.2 (ὡς ἀρτιγέννητα βρέφη) a causal component is found only if the expression is interpreted as a metaphor. This, however, would require a baptismal interpretation of the letter, which in turn is not probable (see Chapter 1 §2.a).

Sometimes the causal meaning is more evident (e.g. in 3.7b: ἀπονέμοντες τιμὴν ὡς καὶ συγκληρονόμοις); in other passages the modal one (e.g. in 3.7a: ὡς ἀσθενεστέρῳ σκεύει), as is the case with the prepositions with a partly causal meaning. There can also be a shift from one meaning to another—in 2.16 only the first ὡς introduces a motivation.[69] In 1.14, 2.11 and 4.10 the expressions are problematic. As signals for a GC relation they are motivations that refer to the good qualities of the addressees—they are obedient children, they are strangers (i.e. they have a Christian identity in the society—for the discussion about ὡς τέκνα see Chapter 5 §3.b n. 70), and they behave well in the congregation. A modal interpretation, however, makes these expressions parts of commands: the addressees ought to be obedient, and so on. I have claimed that this ambiguous use of ὡς is deliberate and serves the rhetorical strategy of the author (Thurén 1990: 164-76); thus both types of interpretation should be taken into account.

καθώς

καθώς refers to an implied comparison 'inasmuch as', or even 'because' (Louw and Nida 1988: 89.34).

In 1 Peter καθώς occurs in 4.10: ἕκαστος καθὼς ἔλαβεν χάρισμα... The meaning is more explanatory than motivating. An appeal can, however, be discerned: the addressees should serve each

68. See Thurén 1990: 26 n. 21. Goppelt counts 1.14, 19; 2.2, 11-12, 13-14, 16; 3.7; 4.10-11, 16 as motivating (Goppelt 1978: 117-18 n. 30) but does not explain which ὡς expressions he means e.g. in 4.10-11. When discussing these sentences in detail, however, he does not see 1.19 (1978: 112) and 2.2 (1978: 134-35) as causal.

69. In 2.16 the addressees are told to do good (a) as (ὡς) free; (b) not as (ὡς) misusing the freedom; (c) but as (ὡς) slaves of God. In (a) the expression is clearly causal, while (b) and (c) are modal examples clarifying (a) which do not motivate the command (against Goppelt 1978: 187 n. 46), since it is unlikely that (b) would be a motivating expression and (c) an antithesis to (b).

other with certain gifts because they possess those gifts.[70] This causal aspect signifies a certain logical GC relation.

καθό

In the New Testament the usage of καθό corresponds to καθώς,[71] but it occurs less often. καθό is found only four times in the New Testament, and is usually translated as a modal: 'in the measure in which', 'to the degree that' (BDR §453.1; Louw and Nida 1988: 78.53). But it also contains a causal component (BDR §456,4 n. 9) and can thereby serve as a signal for a logical relation. Contrary to καθώς, the causal component of καθό is not adjudged strong enough by Louw and Nida.

In 1 Peter καθό occurs in 4.13 καθὸ κοινωνεῖτε τοῖς τοῦ Χριστοῦ παθήμασιν χαίρετε... The causal component is rather weak. However, Goppelt and Brox see the causal meaning as the stronger.[72] Then καθό would signal a GC relation to χαίρετε in the same verse.

f. *Circumstantial Participles*

The circumstantial participles cover a wide range of meanings, but are usually rather easy to assess.[73] However, in the New Testament the usage differs to some extent from the classical language, which causes some problems.[74]

In 1 Peter the interpretation of different participles constitutes one of the most difficult problems. Whereas some independent participles are used instead of imperatives, probably following a Jewish pattern (especially 2.18; 3.1, 7a. b, 9a. b; 4.8, 10),[75] and some are clearly not

---

70. Reicke (1964: 121) offers an interesting modified interpretation, in which a certain amount of causality may be included: 'just as each has received'.

71. BDR §453 n. 1. (Bauer–Aland *s.v.*).

72. Goppelt 1978: 298 n. 8; Brox 1979: 210 'weil'. Cf. also Schelkle 1970: 122. Selwyn (1947: 221) and Kelly (1969: 185) prefer the modal alternative. Cf. Porter (1994: 243) 'as you share'.

73. The circumstantial participle can be translated as an independent clause with a copulative conjunction (BDR §421), but also *inter alia* as a temporal, modal, causal (BDR §418; BR §246; Schwyzer 1971: 387-92: Porter 1994: 191) or relative (BDR §412,1) particle.

74. E.g. the causal participle never has ἅτε as an explanatory addition, which complicates the assessment of the word (BDR §418,1), let alone the use of the so-called imperative participles (see below).

75. See esp. Daube 1947; Thurén 1990: 12-13; Porter 1994: 85-86, 184-86. Martin (1992a: 91-92) challenges Daube's view and, based on examples of the classical language, claims that the 'essential notion of the participle is subordination',

commanding,[76] others can be understood equally well as admonitions or as motivations, but often an objective decision between the alternatives is impossible to make. I hope to have shown in my dissertation that at least the following participles have such an ambiguous character and may serve as signals for motivating expressions: 1.13a.b, 18, 22; 2.1, 4; 5.9. Since, as I believe, the ambiguity of these expressions is deliberate and the correct interpretation depends on the audience, both possibilities must be taken into account in the analysis of argumentation.

In 1.9, 23 the participles serve only as motivations (Thurén 1990: 7). 4.12 μὴ ξενίζεσθε τῇ ἐν...πυρώσει πρὸς πειρασμὸν γινομένῃ is problematic: it is either an explanatory and relative 'which has become...' or a causal 'since it has become'. The expression repeats an idea expressed in 1.6-7, where the word πειρασμός is explained more precisely. It is however difficult to interpret πειρασμός in so positive a way that it alone could serve as a motivation; therefore a relative interpretation is to be preferred.

It is interesting to note that whereas the use of a circumstantial participle as a signal for motivation clearly resembles that of ὡς, the former is concentrated in the first (1.1–2.10) and the latter in the second part of the Letter (2.11–5.14) (Thurén 1990: 2).

A specific case is the Genitive Absolute, which also contains a circumstantial participle and is translated in the corresponding way (Schwyzer 1971: 398-401; Goodwin and Gulick 1981: §1156; Porter 1994: 183-84). The usage in the New Testament corresponds better, however, to the classical one.[77] In 1 Peter there is one motivating GA: 4.1 Χριστοῦ οὖν παθόντος σαρκί. It stands in a GC relation to an exhortation.

g. *Other Expressions with* inter alia *a Causal Meaning: Relative Pronoun,* εἰ, καί

Relative Pronoun
When the predicate in a relative sentence stands in the indicative, but not in the future, it can have *inter alia* a causal meaning.[78] The choice

---

and therefore a participle can never be used instead of an imperative. Daube would certainly agree with that. The problem with 1 Peter is, however, that the participles are *not* used in the ordinary classical manner.

76. E.g. the participles in 1.8 ὃν οὐκ ἰδόντες and 3.6 καλοῦσα, ἀγαθο-ποιοῦσαι καὶ μὴ φοβούμεναι are neither imperatival nor motivating.

77. BDR §423.

78. Goodwin and Gulick 1981: §1461. Other possible meanings are explanatory

between the meanings must be made on the basis of the contents and the context of the sentence (cf. Porter 1994: 266-67). It is often impossible to draw a clear line between the different meanings.

In 1 Peter there are seven relative pronouns that may include a causal component.[79] 1.3 refers to God's activity.[80] The other relative sentences contain motivating expressions, two of which (2.11 ἀπέχεσθαι τῶν σαρκικῶν ἐπιθυμιῶν, αἵτινες στρατεύονται...; 3.4) stand in a direct GC relation to a command. The rest (2.10; 3.6, 21; 4.11) are connected to other motivating sentences with a RR relation. Some of the cases (3.4, 6, 21) also can be interpreted as demonstrative pronouns, but this does not change their meaning in the motivation. A corresponding demonstrative pronoun that also can express a RR relation is found in 1.10.

εἰ *with Indicative*

The conditional conjunction εἰ is one of the most common words in the New Testament (Lüdemann 1980: 931-33). When introducing an indicative sentence, its basic meaning 'if' may acquire a causal significance 'if really' or 'if thus'. Then εἰ can be translated as a causal particle ('since', 'because' [BDR §372,1]) and signify a GC or RR relation. According to Louw and Nida, 'the actual case is regarded formally as a supposition' (Louw and Nida 1988: 89.30).

In 1 Peter there are four instances of εἰ that contain a causal component: 1.17 (εἰ πατέρα ἐπικαλεῖσθε...); 2.3; 4.17b, 18.[81] The first cases are independent motivating clauses indicating a direct GC relation, whereas 4.17b, 18 are connected to one motivation introduce by ὅτι. With the specific semantic meaning of εἰ the author appeals to his addressees by showing how natural it should be to draw the right

(BR §289), qualitative-consecutive, or conditional (indefinite or not fulfilled case) (BR §290).

79. Other relative sentences are clearly not causal: E.g. 1.12 οἷς ἀπεκαλύφθη is not relative but adversative, and 1.6, 8 can be ruled out because of their contents: a GC or a RR relation would not be logical.

80. Thus it marks a RR relation. This technique is typical in hymns (see Deichgräber 1967: 42-43).

81. See Reicke 1964: 13; Goppelt 1978: 119, 137 n. 50; Olsson 1982: 48, 70. See also Kelly 1969: 71. The meaning of 3.17 also comes close to these expressions. In 4.16 ('but if *as* a Christian') there is no GC relation. The shift of the semantic function resembles that in 2.16, where ὡς occurs three times and is similarly modified.

conclusions from their status as Christians, which is for them a known fact.

καί

The coordinate copulative conjunction καί is, after ὁ, the most common word in the New Testament, being far more frequently used than in the classical language (Bauer–Aland *s.v.*; Pridik 1981: 557-60). Having several subsidiary components of meaning (*inter alia* a relative, consecutive, final, explicative and 'weiterführend' meaning [Bauer–Aland *s.v.*; Pridik 1981: 557-60]), it can also indicate a causal relation.[82] In 1 Peter there are three καί sentences, which possibly stand in a GC relation to a command, and thus have a motivating function: 3.13 (καὶ τίς ὁ κακώσων ὑμᾶς ἐὰν τοῦ ἀγαθοῦ ζηλωταὶ γένησθε), 4.6 (εἰς τοῦτο γὰρ καὶ νεκροῖς εὐηγγελίσθη...), and 5.4 (καὶ φανερωθέντος τοῦ ἀρχιποίμενος κομιεῖσθε...). For the nature of 4.18 see above. The first case is a difficult combination of admonition and motivation. The conditional sentence in 3.13b, to which καί partly refers, repeats the exhortation in 3.8-9(10) and can therefore be interpreted as admonishing (you should be zealots for good), which is then motivated with a καί sentence. The whole of 3.13-14 is, however, primarily motivating—the author may use καί only in order to avoid tautology,[83] and to express the 'weiterführend' character of the sentence. In 4.6 we find a clear RR relation. In 5.4 the καί expression motivates the commands in 5.2-3 in a consecutive RR relation. A Means–Purpose interpretation is hardly plausible, since the author uses clearer signals for that purpose (see below).

h. *Additional Motivating Expressions Referring to Grounds*
In 1 Peter there is one motivating sentence, 5.8 (γρηγορήσατε. ὁ ἀντίδικος...περιπατεῖ), which obviously stands in a Grounds–Conclusion relation to the following command with no syntactic signal whatsoever of that relation (also 4.9 may be a similar case). The function

---

82. Especially the consecutive and explicative meanings come close to the causal one (cf. Bauer–Aland *s.v.* I 2f, 3. Louw and Nida surprisingly do not recognize this component in καί.

83. καί may replace a causal particle: every sentence beginning with 3.9b is introduced with a causal conjunction. Goppelt interprets καί here as a consecutive particle (1978: 233. The reference to BDR §448,2 is a misprint—it ought to be §442,2) but also a causal interpretation fits the style of the letter.

of that sentence is so unambiguous that it simply does not need such a signal, which has however been added to the text in some old manuscripts (there is an additional ὅτι in 𝔓⁷² and ℵ²). Instead, 5.10, for example, does not refer to any command, but has a conventional place in the epistolary structure of the Letter.[84]

In 1.13 there is a specific expression ἐλπίσατε ἐπὶ τὴν φερομένην ὑμῖν χάριν, where ἐπί indicates the ground for the hope.[85] There is thus a GC relation between the command and the ἐπί expression. However, the ἐπί expression can also simply describe the hope required.

3. *Motivating Expressions Referring to Purpose*

Introduction

The second type of logical relations that can occur between a command and a motivating expression is the Means–Purpose (MP) relations. According to Beekman and Callow's definition the MP relation answers the question, 'What action was undertaken to achieve the desired result?' (1974: 300). The difference between a MP relation and the similar Means–Result relation is that 'in the Means–Result relation, the result takes place; in Means–Purpose the result is desired, but it is not stated whether it took place or not'.[86] The MP relation can be used in a motivation, since 'there is...an implicit volitional element in this relation, and if this volitional factor is made explicit, then the purpose becomes the motivating cause and the means becomes the result or effect'. In this way the MP relation can be restated as a RR relation. When a MP relation is used in the motivation, the exhortation is called 'Means' and the motivating expression 'purpose': in order to achieve the Purpose one has to use the Means recommended (Beekman and Callow 1974: 303).

When there is a clear marker for the logical relation on the syntactic level, the marker's *final* character constitutes a precondition for a MP relation.[87] Contrary to the GC relation, the position of the motivating

---

84. See Thurén 1990: 86; cf. Goppelt 1978: 343. For the meaning of this sentence for the motivation, see below Chapter 5 §6.

85. Bauer–Aland *s.v.* ἐλπίζω. ἐπί *cum dat.* can refer to a reason (Bauer–Aland *s.v.*, Louw and Nida 1988: 89.27), but here we have an accusative, and in this case the function is weaker.

86. Beekman and Callow 1974: 302-303. According to Cotterell and Turner (1989: 211), the MP relation refers to intention.

87. On the ideological level we can talk about a *teleological* ethic: one ought to do something in order to achieve something good. Cf. above, Chapter 3 §1.

expression does not make any difference: both the primary and the secondary arguments can function as a Purpose in a MP relation.

a. ἵνα

The final meaning 'in order to' of the conjunction ἵνα in the classical language is greatly extended in the New Testament: ἵνα not only functions as a marker of the purpose of events and states like ὅπως (Louw and Nida 1988: 89.59 n. 10), but can also introduce imperatival or consecutive sentences.[88] The consecutive usage can partly be explained with a Semitic influence.[89] Causal, temporal and relative meanings do not occur in the New Testament. Turner claims that ἵνα in 1 Pet. 4.6 is causal (Turner 1976: 130). Such an interpretation is not supported by the modern commentators.[90]

In 1 Peter there are 13 ἵνα expressions. Four of them occur within other motivating statements and explain God's activity (2.21, 24; 3.18; 4.6). Nine ἵνα expressions possibly signify a MP relation to an exhortation: 1.7; 2.2, 12; 3.1-2, 9, 16; 4.11, 13; 5.6. In 1.7 (ἀγαλλιᾶσθε...ἵνα τὸ δοκίμιον...εὑρεθῇ) the contents of the ἵνα sentence may point toward a RR relation, although formally there is a MP relation (thus Selwyn 1947: 129). At least the latter interpretation is the more prominent.

If these sentences are interpreted as including MP relations, they all serve as primary motivations, except for 3.9b, which may also explain God's activity (see further Chapter 5 §4.g).

It is difficult to decide in particular cases between the consecutive and the final meaning,[91] of which only the latter signifies a MP relation.

---

88. For the classical usage, see Schwyzer 1971: 671-74; BR §276,1. Already in the classical language the semantic field of the word was somewhat extended (BDR §388,2; against Zerwick 1963: 352). For the usage in the New Testament, see Bauer–Aland *s.v.*; Lampe 1981: 460-66; Louw and Nida 1988: 89.49; Porter 1994: 210, 235-36, 238-39.

89. Zerwick 1963: 351. According to Lampe (1981: 460-66) the use of ἵνα is a 'Gradmesser für das Sprachniveau eines ntl. Autors', but he does not explain in detail how the measurement is actually done. According to Louw and Nida the alteration between ἵνα and ὅπως as a marker for purpose may be a matter of style (1988: 89.59 n. 10)—possibly they mean that repetition is thereby avoided.

90. See Kelly 1969: 175; Goppelt 1978: 264; Brox 1979: 189.

91. Radermacher (1926: 290) claims that ἵνα occurs in 1 Peter only in a proper final meaning. But since he does not present any arguments for his claim, we must also accept the possibility of consecutive meanings.

Zerwick defines this difference as follows: 'A consecutive clause declares the end which in the nature of things is reached by something, whereas a final clause declares the end which someone intends to reach' (Zerwick 1963: 351). There is also a pragmatic difference between the two types: The semantic difference between the MR and the MP relations can mean, in the motivation, that a consecutive sentence in an MR relation to the exhortation is more cautious and explanatory ('do in this way, and the result will be this'), coming close to a RR relation ('do in this way, since then the result will be this'). A final sentence with an MP relation is more absolute and demanding ('do in this way, in order that the result will be this').

Goppelt interprets ἵνα in 1 Peter always as a final conjunction (so does also BDR §388,3 n. 2) and Brox only once as a consecutive one (3.16). But, Olsson, for example, interprets all the cases that seek to persuade the addressees with a consecutive 'so that'[92] and those referring to God's activity with a final 'in order that'.[93] Clear arguments for the solutions are hard to find. The distinction between the two interpretations obviously has significance for the understanding of the whole type of motivation in the letter: the nature of the motivation is different depending on whether the author appeals to the addressees with teleological ideas. Thus we shall return to this question in the analysis of the structure of the argumentation.

b. εἰς τό *cum inf.*
The preposition εἰς is used in the New Testament almost in the same way as in the classical language (BDR §402). The combination εἰς τό *cum inf.* seldom occurs outside Romans, 1 Thessalonians and Hebrews. This combination is usually seen as equivalent to ἵνα, but according to Louw and Nida εἰς τό marks rather the intent, implying the expected result (Elliger 1980: 965-68; Louw and Nida 1988: 89.57). It refers to the goal or the result of an activity, and can be translated either as a final or a consecutive expression ('in order to' or 'so that': cf. BDR §402; Bauer–Aland *s.v.*).

In 1 Peter εἰς τό *cum inf.* occurs twice: 3.7 and 4.2. Both sentences serve as primary motivating expressions in a Means–Purpose relation to the command, and as parallels to another motivating expression. Goppelt

92. With one exception (2.2). But even this expression is interpreted as explanatory (Olsson 1982: 84)
93. In the problematic case 3.9 ἵνα is translated simply with 'that'.

translates both expressions with a final construction;[94] for example, 3.7c can be seen as standing in a MP relation with a negative 'purpose': 'In order that your prayers are not hindered'. Brox and Olsson interpret them with a consecutive or a temporal sentence (Brox 1979: 141, 189; Olsson 1982: 98, 151); then it serves as an explanatory addition.

1 Pet. 4.2 serves as an provisory example of the use of a rhetorical perspective in semantic assessment. In principle it contains an ambiguity between the consecutive and the final meanings. However, since these parts of the Letter otherwise, due to the unified rhetorical situation, contain no further ambiguities (Thurén 1990: 153-54), the more obvious MP relation is to be preferred.

c. *Infinitive*

In the New Testament the classical usage of the infinitive[95] has been strongly developed, *inter alia* so that the infinitive can be used instead of an final clause (and vice versa) in connection with many verbs (BDR §§388, 390), but also with several nouns (BDR §393). When expressing a purpose the infinitive may signal a MP relation between an exhortation and a motivating expression (see Porter 1994: 199-200).

In 1 Peter there is one such word: 2.5 οἰκοδομεῖσθε οἶκος πνευμα-τικὸς εἰς ἱεράτευμα ἅγιον ἀνενέγκαι πνευματικὰς θυσίας...The final interpretation is supported with 2.9, where a corresponding purpose is expressed with a final conjunction ὅπως. The final expression in 2.9 is not however an independent motivating statement, but explains a nominal clause.

4. *Conclusions*

The text of 1 Peter has been analysed in order to distinguish all the explicit motivating expressions. The meaning of certain expressions remains unclear and must be more precisely determined in the following rhetorical, pragmatic analysis.[96]

---

94. Goppelt (1978: 222, 264), but without presenting any arguments for this solution.

95. Originally the infinitive was used in order to express a purpose (BR §231), and this use was preserved in the classical language, where the infinitive occurs with certain verbs (BR §237).

96. Rhetorical grounds have already been utilized above: see the assessment of 1 Pet. 4.2 in §3.b.

This mostly semantic study shows that in 1 Peter there are several expressions, which primarily signify something else, but which however contain such a strong causal or final component that even they ought to be interpreted as markers for logical relations between exhortations and motivating expressions. Such words are, for example, many comparative conjunctions. The mapping of such expressions is especially important for our goal: if only those expressions signaled with clear and unequivocal markers (such as ὅτι) are taken into account, the picture of the nature of the motivation and the author's ideology behind it remains onesided. The author obviously uses several indirect approaches to the addressees, and such expressions are essential in his persuasion.

The analysis of the logical relations and the classification of certain expressions in the text as motivating yield a point of departure for the forthcoming analysis of the implicit motivating ideas and the function of the different expressions in the argumentation. The difficulties in interpreting certain expressions, which may indicate the author's rhetorical strategy (as seems to be the case with the participles and ὡς expressions), can be better solved or explained in that analysis.

Considering the formal connection between the exhortation and the motivating expressions, some observations can be made.

It has become clear that constant alternation between exhortation and motivating expressions is typical for 1 Peter (so also Neugebauer 1980: 71). With some exceptions it is possible to divide the Letter into exhorting and motivating units. The rhythm is ocasionally broken by long quotations from the Old Testament (e.g. 3.10-12) or by Christological sections (e.g. 2.21-25), which also contain material whose role in the text as a whole is obscure (e.g. 4.6).

An exhorting expression never occurs without a motivation,[97] and often there are several different motivating expressions in the immediate neighborhood. These can be independent or dependent clauses, but it is also typical that short circumstantial expressions in the middle of an exhortation have a distinguishable motivating character. The motivating ideas are often repeated, and the author can introduce an exhortation by referring to an earlier exhortation.

Especially in the case of antithetic expressions it is difficult to distinguish between an exhortation and a motivating expression (e.g. in 3.10).

97. 5.14 is an exception, whereas 2.17 can be seen as being motivated with the preceding sentences, although a clear signal for a logical relation between them cannot be found.

Syntactically we cannot speak of an 'indicative-imperative' model, since the Pauline way of dividing the letter into kerygmatic and paraenetic sections is not found in the text. The motivation and the exhortation are very intimately connected to each other in 1 Peter.

Already this mainly formal analysis has shown that the author uses a rather sophisticated technique when connecting exhorting and motivating expressions to each other. We have also noticed some formal regularities in the use of the markers. Thus the change from ὅτι to γάρ corresponds to the change within the semantic field: γάρ is used for non-theological, ὅτι for theological grounds (2.21 and 3.13 are exceptions in order to avoid tautology). ὡς replaces the participle in the second part of the letter.

The results of this chapter will be used in the next chapter and be displayed in the Greek text.

Chapter 4

THE RHETORICAL SITUATION AND STRATEGY

In order to analyze argumentation it is essential to know the type of situation and audience, or, in other words, the rhetorical situation, which
the author has in mind. We also need to know the plans he follows when
presenting his message.[1] Since these aspects in 1 Peter have already
been studied (Thurén 1990; for approach, see 70-75, for results 93ff.),
only a brief summary is presented here. In the argumentation analysis,
Chapter 5, I shall refer to that study when necessary.

1 Peter is sent to a heterogeneous area, and implies addressees who
have encountered different types of social pressure because of their
Christianity. They are also thought to have reacted in several ways. Two
theoretical types of addressees can be characterized. The 'active' audience wants openly to resist their oppressors by using verbal and even
physical violence. The 'passive' audience does the opposite: they hide
their religious convictions and assimilate to the surrounding culture.[2]

It is important to recognize that these two types of addressees are but
theoretical constructions—the real readers may represent different
combinations of these types.[3]

Since both solutions, and all combinations of them, are unacceptable
from the author's perspective, especially in view of missionary work, he
needs to modify the attitudes and life of both types simultaneously.

The situation becomes more complicated, since both types are suspected of having negative prejudices against the author and his message.
He has to overcome accusations of being too soft and too strict at the

---

1. The difference between logical demonstration and argumentation analysis lies
especially in the role of the audience.
2. Later Martin (1992a: 274) arrived at a similar 'twin purpose' in the rhetorical
strategy of the letter.
3. Thurén 1990: 110. Marshall (1991: 317) misunderstands the study at this
point.

same time. Yet his presentation needs to be rhetorically effective.

The author's strategy is to overcome and reject the negative expectations of both types in the first part of the text (1.1–2.10). He uses ambivalent expressions, which modify the message of the text depending on the addressees.

Toward the end the ambiguities diminish and finally vanish, due to the gradual unification of the rhetorical situation. The author can concentrate on his general message, the positive contact of right suffering and glory, motivated by logical reasoning and Christological examples. The goal is explicated with a revolving theme of unjust suffering, which each time is more explicit. Not until the peroratory sections, where the 'meeting of minds' is sufficient and the rhetorical situation suitable, can the author put forward the message with full force.

Chapter 5

THE STRUCTURE OF ARGUMENTATION

1. *Introduction*

The persuasive argumentation in 1 Peter is many-sided. The grammatic form of the motivations varies from simple causal sentences to ambiguous ὡς expressions and participial forms (see above Chapter 3). The origin and the contents of the persuasive motifs are equally multifarious. There are, for example, expressions that are based on the salvation by God, while other sentences refer to his vengeance; some come from the Old Testament, others are reminiscent of Hellenistic popular philosophy (e.g. 1 Pet. 2.9; 3.12; 2.19-20; 1.16a). The history of research gives us cause to assume that even ideological tensions can be found between these motifs: the scholars have presented different interpretations of the character of the motivation and various views on which factor should ultimately motivate the addressees. The results depend on which motifs the scholars have seen as important or central.[1]

One possible reason for the diversity of the motivation is that the author simply uses different, even opposite motifs from several traditions without attempting to create an ideological unity (thus to some extent Brox 1979: 36-38). Some signs of a corresponding phenomenon occur at the grammatical level in the text.[2]

I have, however, made observations that prompt me to suggest that the variation is premeditated, and that there is some strategic plan and an ideological system that join different motivating themes together. The author thereby uses different techniques methodically and manipulates his material, even Old Testament texts, in order to suit them to his goals.[3] It also seems likely that he utilizes different syntactic and semantic

---

1. See also the history of research, Chapter 1. The various interpretations of 1 Pet. 3.9 provide an illustrative example.

2. E.g. the variation of person and number in a so-called Christological hymn in 2.21-25 could indicate that the author does not mind harmonizing his material.

3. See e.g. a redactional ὅτι in the middle of an Old Testament quotation in 3.12.

features in a specific rhetorical strategy, when appealing to different types of addressee (see Thurén 1990: 175-76). These features could be analogous to the ideological diversity in the motivation.

The explicit elements in the persuasive argumentation were preliminarily identified above. We shall now study how these elements are connected to each other in different units of the text, and what kind of larger structures they may form. Only after such a scrutiny can general comments be made concerning the use of different motifs within the argumentation, and the argumentation as a whole. The analysis will be based on the principles presented in Chapter 2 §4. Here the practical mode of procedure is briefly displayed.[4]

The study of each large unit begins with general remarks and division into subunits. Then the results of the semantic analysis (Chapter 3) will be displayed in the Greek text, and the most important functional elements[5] will be characterized.[6] Within each subunit I shall study the structure of argumentation, and also clarify its rhetorical function in the context. This allows understanding of the motivating factor in the argumentation, viz. in what ways and by what emotions the argumentation is designed to persuade and motivate the addressees. The analysis will thus contain the following steps:

1. Characterization of the context and the rhetorical situation of a large unit; its division into subunits (in a footnote).
2. Display of the text and the explicit expressions used in argumentation within a unit; description of the context and rhetorical situation of a subunit.
3. Characterization of the expressions.
4. Identification of the functional elements and the structure of argumentation (this will be combined with the preceding step when possible).

4. Concerning the rhetorical situation and strategy, and the division of the text into large functional units, I refer to my dissertation (1990); a brief resume is presented above in Chapter 4.

5. By these elements I mean expressions, or combinations of expressions, which play a role in the structure of argumentation, i.e. form a functional unit. For examples of a corresponding approach, see Chapter 2 §2.b.

6. For this kind of identification it serves no purpose to divide the whole text into propositions or 'the minimal semantic units consisting of a concept or a combination of concepts which communicates an Event or Relation' (Beekman and Callow 1974: 273), since a factor in the structure of argumentation may be large, even a long story, which consists of several propositions.

5. Identification of the motivating factor.
6. Concluding remarks about the larger unit and the persuasive argumentation therein.

The tasks of analysing the subunits and the large structures and strategies are related interactively to each other. The last, concluding step leads us already onto an ideological level, since some elements and their functions can be described in a more general terms. By comparing the use of certain motifs and topoi within a larger unit we may find typical ways of using them in the text.

The ideological study in Synthesis (Part III) will be totally built on this analysis. It will present the results in a systematic form and draw the final conclusions. Therefore it is necessary to display the whole analysis here. This even makes it possible to use this study as an independent analysis of the argumentation in 1 Peter, providing material for various purposes insofar as it succeeds in solving puzzling phenomena in the text and in clarifying the role of obscure sections.

For the sake of convenience I shall use subheadings referring to the contents of the section.[7] Further, the basic scrutiny will be displayed only in the beginning (1.1-12) and in some problematic sections. It may still be difficult for a hasty reader to follow up the whole text. In that case it may be a good idea to proceed to some point in the next chapter and return to the analysis when necessary.

2. *Persuasive Description 1.1-12*[8]

The first rhetorical unit is the exordium (1.1-12).[9] It contains no explicit admonition—direct commands are introduced first in the second half of

7. The titles do not always convey the same kind of information; they may refer to the contents of the section, to the type of argumentation used, or to the situation in current research.

8. On the formal, epistolary level the unit can be called a letter-opening; it is divided into a prescript (1.1-2) and an opening thanksgiving (1.3-12) (see Thurén 1990: 84-88; for the distinction between the epistolary and the rhetorical levels, see Thurén 1990: 57-64). The thanksgiving consists of four parts. Verses 3-5 comprise the first part and deal with the addressees' salvation, and the three subsequent parts, all of which begin with a relative pronoun, are combined to this salvation: the addressees' joy (vv. 6-7), their love for Christ (vv. 8-9), and utterances about prophets and angels (vv. 10-12) (cf. the division by Goppelt [1978]: 3-5, 6-7, 8-9, 10-12; Brox [1979: 3-9, 10-12]; Calloud and Genuyt [1982: 3-5, 6-9, 10-12].

9. About the relation between 1.1-2 and 3-12 see Thurén 1990: 89-90.

the chapter. However, the section is important for understanding the motivation due to the form and rhetorical function, which differ from the main bulk of the text. It provides us with an alternative perspective on the author's thinking, since he here expresses similar ideas in a different manner.

According to a solid rhetorical convention a discourse begins by creating a good atmosphere.[10] Another characteristic of an exordium is that main goals of the discourse are introduced, although only briefly, which also indicates that central themes are presented. For these reasons no explicit exhortation can be given. Instead, the addressees and their situation are typically referred to in an over-positive manner, as living in an ideal way. Such a description has two goals, partly depending on the type of the implied addressees: first, to avoid the addressees' possible negative expectations vis-à-vis the author and his message,[11] secondly, to encourage them to live in a particular way by stating that they already do so.[12] Similar themes appear later in the text as exhortations.[13] Here they are connected to different types of reasoning, which seem only to *explain* the addressees' behaviour. However, just as the descriptive expressions can be interpreted as implicit admonitions, the explanation may have a hidden persuasive and motivating task. Because of this persuasive function of the explanation, it is reasonable to analyse this section as well.[14]

The section thus seems to function as a general motivation; the more explicit exhortations appear later in the text. This is further emphasized by opening the next, more exhortatory unit with a signal for a Grounds–Conclusion relation (διό; see above Chapter 3 §2.c) between the units.

---

10. About the functions of an exordium see Thurén 1990: 76-77.

11. This goal is especially important with regard to the 'active' type of implied addressees; see Thurén 1990: 131-32.

12. Thurén 1990: 128-34, 133. The 'persuasive description' is especially suitable for the 'passive' type of implied addressees (see Thurén 1990: 132-34).

13. See 1 Pet. 4.12-13, 16.

14. An explanation of a descriptive statement is actually not a piece of argumentation (Toulmin *et al.* 1984: 6), since formally the goal is not to convince anyone. However, the structure of such an explanation is equivalent to ordinary reasoning and can thus be analysed in a similar way. An example: The sentence 'He was drunk (D), so he did not drive (C), since the law prohibits drunken driving (W)' can be analysed either as an explanation or, if the goal is to convince the audience that he did not drive, as a reasoning.

a. *1.1-2—General Introduction*

1.1   Πέτρος ἀπόστολος Ἰησοῦ Χριστοῦ ἐκλεκτοῖς παρεπιδήμοις
       διασπορᾶς Πόντου, Γαλατίας, Καππαδοκίας, Ἀσίας καὶ Βιθυνίας,
1.2   <u>κατὰ</u> πρόγνωσιν θεοῦ πατρὸς ἐν ἁγιασμῷ πνεύματος
       εἰς ὑπακοὴν καὶ ῥαντισμὸν αἵματος Ἰησοῦ Χριστοῦ,
       χάρις ὑμῖν καὶ εἰρήνη πληθυνθείη.

Formally the section is only a prescript,[15] which names the sender and the addressees, and ends with good wishes. However, it also states something specific: the addressees are strangers (1b), who are chosen to obey (2b): the purpose of the election is that they should be obedient. This is said to have happened as a result of (κατά)[16] God's foreknowledge and the sanctification of the Spirit (2a). God is presented as the Father.[17]

As is typical for opening phrases, the expressions are compact and obscure, and their functions are difficult to explain. 2a can be seen as an indirect ground (D) for the Claim. Furthermore, 2b appears to include an admonition to obey. Thus, the following implicit structure can be discerned in the section:

Fig. 1.1-2

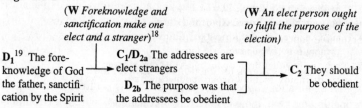

15.   According to Olsson (1982: 19) the expression may have functioned as performative, as a benediction, when the text was read aloud in a service.

16.   Thus Kelly translates (1969: 42). According to Goppelt the κατά expression explains how the election has taken place (1978: 92). For the causal component of κατά see Chapter 3 §2.d.

17.   According to Kelly (1969: 42-43): this emphasizes the love of the Creator, or 'crystallizes the essence of the Gospel' (1969: 47). He does not, however, refer to any ancient source in order to support this thesis.

18.   Purely implicit factors, such as this Warrant (W), are displayed with *italics*; factors consisting of more explicit elements are given in normal text. To every figure (Fig.) is also attached an explanation, which clarifies how the implicit elements are traced from the Greek text. However, since the distinction between explicit and implicit factors is often somewhat blurred, it is often difficult to decide the group to which a factor belongs. In a specific case, the teleological reasoning, I shall use <u>underlined text</u> (see e.g. Fig. 1.6-7b). On the explanation of teleological reasoning, see above n. 41.

19.   When the arguments are chained, Toulmin employs such terms as

Due to the compact nature of the verses it is premature to state anything certain about the Warrants or other implicit factors.[20] The unclear elements and the indistinct structure of argumentation are well suited to the function of the section as a part of an exordium. They give the addressee a hint of the imminent presentation (cf. Goppelt 1978: 79-81), but not yet a clear picture of the author's message. Notwithstanding, central motifs such as election by God, the addressees' status as aliens, sanctification, obedience and Christ are presented.[21]

b. *1.3-5—Grounds for Praise*
The Greek text will henceforth roughly display the results of the preceding semantic analysis.[22] Signals for motivating expressions will be <u>underlined</u>; ambiguous expressions designating either an exhortation or an argument will be printed in **bold**, as in 1.13. Exhortations (or in 1.3-12 statements) beyond doubt will be indented.

1.3   Εὐλογητὸς ὁ θεὸς
         καὶ πατὴρ τοῦ κυρίου ἡμῶν Ἰησοῦ Χριστοῦ,
<u>ὁ κατὰ</u> τὸ πολὺ αὐτοῦ ἔλεος
ἀναγεννήσας ἡμᾶς εἰς ἐλπίδα ζῶσαν,
δι' ἀναστάσεως Ἰησοῦ Χριστοῦ ἐκ νεκρῶν,
1.4   εἰς κληρονομίαν ἄφθαρτον καὶ ἀμίαντον καὶ ἀμάραντον,
τετηρημένην ἐν οὐρανοῖς εἰς ὑμᾶς
1.5   τοὺς <u>ἐν</u> δυνάμει θεοῦ φρουρουμένους διὰ πίστεως
εἰς σωτηρίαν ἑτοίμην ἀποκαλυφθῆναι ἐν καιρῷ ἐσχάτω.

'subground' and 'subwarrant', but in my opinion the use of figures (e.g. D_1) is a more illustrative and precise way of displaying the sequence.

20. The first W is somehow connected with the addressees' nature as elect and strangers. The W between D_2 and C_2 more clearly refers to the fact that as elect they are obliged to fill the purpose of the election or the elector. The emotive content and the motivating factor cannot yet be stated, but since both the words ῥαντισμός and ἐκλεκτοί refer to the Exodus in OT (thus e.g. Selwyn 1947: 117-18), it may be something positive.

21. According to Brox (1979: 59) this kind of presentation is somewhat peculiar. However, it corresponds well to the rhetorical conventions connected with exordium.

22. As we have seen, the semantic analysis is a necessary, but only preliminary, step towards identifying the motivating expressions. Thus the results given here are not final. Further, we have observed many problematic or nuanced cases, which cannot be displayed with a simple typographical system. These will be further discussed in the text.

The first expression 'Praise to God' (3a) is a C, irrespective of the interpretation.[23] It can be modified to a statement: 'God is / should be praised'. It is justified[24] by the D 'He has given us new birth' (3b),[25] which means that 3b contains specific information, on which the Claim is grounded. The reason for God's activity is mercy (ἔλεος).

Now we can ask: how does the fact that God has given the addressees (and the author) a new birth make them praise him? This question consists of two problems: (a) how does new birth provoke praise, and (b) why should they praise just God?

The rest of the text, 3c-5, answers the latter question. Precise information about the new birth is provided: it gives a hope (ἐλπίς), an inheritance (κληρονομία), and salvation (σωτηρία).[26] They can be reduced into a thesis 'A new birth is valuable', which functions as another D beside the expression 'God has given a new birth'.

God has thus done something valuable to the addressees by giving them a new birth. But the first problem remains: how does this indicate that the addressees should praise or thank[27] him? Here we have to construct an implicit Warrant (W): We should/do thank and praise anyone who does us a service. This W does not exist in the text, but it expresses a natural and logical bridge between the two D's and the C. A possible Backing (B) consists of general norms of behaviour.

This analysis leads into the following description, which similarly illustrates one of the merits of the modified version of Toulmin's system: it reveals to us how the argumentation is designed to persuade and be effective.[28]

23. Both 'Praise be to God...' and 'Praise belongs to the God' are possible; see Deichgräber 1967: 30; Kelly 1969: 47, Goppelt 1978: 91 n. 10.

24. For the argumentative character of the expression, signaled with ὁ, see Chapter 3 §2.g. This character is, however, not very strong, since there are no clear semantic signals (such as causal or final conjunctions) of an argumentative logical relation, but only a participle, which has a causal component of meaning.

25. This refers to the addressees' baptism according to Kelly 1969: 48; Brox 1979: 61.

26. Although these ideas are connected with each other, they do not form a clear argumentative structure, but are presented as parallel (all of them are introduced with εἰς). For a detailed presentation, see below.

27. Praise is here equivalent to thanksgiving according to Kelly 1969: 46; Goppelt 1978: 92; Brox 1979: 60-61.

28. Note that due to the open-endedness of argumentation several elements, which as such are important, do not occur in the explicit level. Thus, here the thesis 'Before

Fig. 1.3-5/1[29]

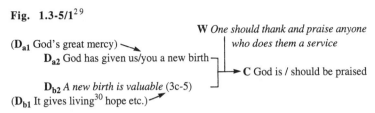

Verses 3c-5 also include expressions that support the D_b above by emphasizing the value and certainty of hope, inheritance and salvation. In principle, the analysis could be pursued by observing that the hope is reliable because of the Resurrection of Jesus Christ (3c). Similarly, the inheritance is valuable, since it is imperishable (ἄφθαρτος, ἀμίαντος, ἀμάραντος); it is imperishable since it is kept in heaven (4b) (cf. Kelly 1969: 51). These thoughts form a chain of arguments, which leads to D_b.

Verse 5 corresponds to 3b: 'God has given us/you salvation'. The emphasis is in the new factor, God's protection (φρουρουμένους): it is certain that they will obtain salvation, since (ἐν—see above Chapter 3 §2.d) God shields them. These ideas can be presented (without Warrants) in the following way:

Fig. 1.3-5/2

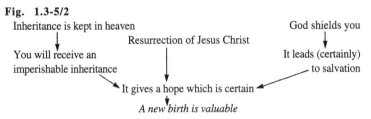

The mention of heaven and the Last Days (ἐν καιρῷ ἐσχάτῳ) may answer a critical question, which might lead to a rebuttal (R): If the salvation is not visible, it is only a dream.[31]

you did not have a valuable inheritance' or 'There is a God' are taken for granted.

29. Explanations:
   /1 = the first phase in the analysis of the unit
   /a = the first alternative explanation for the unit
   1.3a = an explanation of the first part of the verse
30. 'Living' means here 'certain' according to Kelly 1969: 48; Brox 1979: 61.
31. This can be presented in the following way:

D God has given salvation ──────────►	**C** The addressees will be saved
R If it is not visible	**Counter-R** It is in heaven and will be
it does not exist	revealed in the last time

In short, 3-5 claim that the addressees (should) praise God because of his good works toward them. The motivating factor here is thankfulness, but we shall bear in mind that it is not connected with the proper paraenesis.

c. *1.6-7—Emotions Revealed*

1.6   <u>ἐν</u> ᾧ ἀγαλλιᾶσθε
            ὀλίγον ἄρτι εἰ δέον ἐστὶν λυπηθέντες ἐν ποικίλοις πειρασμοῖς,
1.7   <u>ἵνα</u> τὸ δοκίμιον ὑμῶν τῆς πίστεως
            πολυτιμότερον χρυσίου τοῦ ἀπολλυμένου
            διὰ πυρὸς δὲ δοκιμαζομένου
            εὑρεθῇ εἰς ἔπαινον καὶ δόξαν καὶ τιμὴν
            ἐν ἀποκαλύψει Ἰησοῦ Χριστοῦ

This section introduces a new theme, suffering.[32] It begins with a compound Claim about the addressees: They rejoice greatly, even though they have to suffer (6).[33] This C has two types of grounds (D): The first words in 6 (ἐν ᾧ; the expression has a causal meaning: see Chapter 3 §2.d) refer to the preceding unit 3-5, whereas 7 is connected to the claim with an ἵνα expression. This expression consists of four different ideas: (a) Your suffering means that your faith is being tested; (b) the testing of the faith should lead to glory; (c) the faith will prove to be more precious than gold, which is tested with fire; (d) this will happen in connection with the resurrection of Jesus Christ.

The preceding 3-5 refers to the first half of the claim. It gives the reason for the addressees' joy: they will obtain salvation. To receive an imperishable inheritance and salvation causes joy. Thus, an implicit W will be 'If one receives something valuable, one begins to rejoice'.

Fig. 1.3-6a

     W *If one receives something valuable, one begins to rejoice*
                             │
D You will obtain salvation (3-5) ————————————▶ **C** You rejoice (6a)

But the new aspect comes in 6b: The addressees rejoice even in the midst of suffering. It takes into account their situation, which seems to be incompatible with the joy that the author has described. Since the

---

32. Brox rightly notices that there is a rhetorical shift of theme (1979: 63).

33. Actually, the statement has even more elements: The addressees rejoice, they have to suffer (according to Kelly [1969: 53-54] this means real suffering, but not according to Brox [1979: 64]), the sufferings are identified with trials, and the sufferings are said not to affect the addressees' joy.

section deals with a motivating emotion, it is important for the whole motivation (see Chapter 2 §3.b), and thus needs a closer examination.

The argumentation begins with an obscure final conjunction ἵνα. To what does it refer?[34] A natural solution would be λυπηθέντες in 6b, which would mean: 'You suffer in order that your faith would prove to be valuable'.[35] But a comparison with the parallel 4.13 (καθὸ κοινωνεῖτε τοῖς τοῦ Χριστοῦ παθήμασιν χαίρετε, ἵνα καὶ ἐν τῇ ἀποκαλύψει...χαρῆτε ἀγαλλιώμενοι) suggests that ἵνα rather refers to the whole sentence.[36] 'You rejoice even in the midst of suffering, in order that...' This, in turn, leads to an enigmatic idea of a *teleological* joy. How could one rejoice in order that something would happen? The problem can be solved by changing the interpretation of the sentence. There are two possibilities.

(a) The particle ἵνα includes a consecutive, or even a causal, component of meaning (cf. Chapter 3 §3.a), that is, instead of the Meaning–Purpose relation we have a Grounds–Conclusion relation: 'You rejoice even in the midst of suffering, since it results in glory' (thus Selwyn 1947: 129; see Chapter 3 §3.a).

(b) 'You rejoice although you suffer' actually means 'you are ready even to suffer'. The word ἀγαλλιᾶσθε is then interpreted 'you are willing to', 'you are ready to', and the Meaning–Purpose relation would be distinct: the addressees are willing even to suffer, in order that their faith will stand the test and, consequently, result in (εὑρεθῇ) glory in the revelation of Jesus Christ.

I begin by presenting alternative (a).[37]

34. See Chapter 3 §3.a. There are three possible solutions: It explains why the addressees suffer (reference to λυπηθέντες), why it is necessary to suffer (reference to εἰ δέον), or why they rejoice although they suffer (reference to the whole sentence).

35. Thus Brox 1979: 65. He consequently interprets ἔπαινος, δόξα and τιμή as rewards for the addressees.

36. Although not based on such a comparison, also Selwyn (1947: 129) is in favor of this solution.

37. In (a) an implicit W, which should connect D and C, seems to be 'What is glorious causes joy'. The suffering is not, however, presented as a cause for glory. The expression εἰ δέον ἐστίν shows that the word λυπηθέντες should be interpreted as a concession, not as a causal expression. The addressees are said to rejoice although they suffer. Therefore the W_1, the Warrant for the first structure presented above, is misleading: it cannot read 'What is glorious causes joy', but somewhat obscurely 'What is glorious does not prevent joy'.

Fig. 1.6-7/a1[38]

$$W_1 \text{ \textit{What is glorious does not prevent joy}}$$

D_1 Your suffering results in glory ⊥→ C_1 You rejoice even (7ac) when suffering

The argumentation behind D_1 is more crucial than this scheme. The expression in 6-7a functions there as a ground: 'Your suffering means that your faith is being tested'. A generally applicable W, which makes the move from D to C justified, is not explained in the text. However, we do have a typical Backing (B) in 7b, which speaks of gold. It gives a general example of how gold is tested in fire and it leads to a good result.[39] Using this B we can reconstruct a W, which the B supports: severe testing leads to a good result. This analysis is built upon the interpretation (b), according to which the vv. 6 and 7 are in a Reason–Result relation to each other.[40]

Fig. 1.6-7/a2

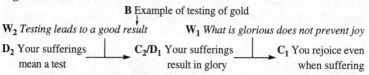

B Example of testing of gold

W_2 *Testing leads to a good result* W_1 *What is glorious does not prevent joy*

D_2 Your sufferings ⊥ C_2/D_1 Your sufferings ⊥ C_1 You rejoice even
   mean a test   result in glory   when suffering

38. More illustratively the structure reads:

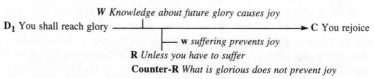

W *Knowledge about future glory causes joy*

D_1 You shall reach glory ————⊥————————→ C You rejoice

             — w *suffering prevents joy*

          R *Unless you have to suffer*

        Counter-R *What is glorious does not prevent joy*

39. This picture is common in Jewish literature (see Brox 1979: 65).

40. Beside this, the example with gold functions also as a *double-hierarchy argument* (Perelman 1969: 337-45), cf. e.g Mt. 6.26-30 and the Jewish *qal wachomer*:

      W The validity of a statement about a subject

     is in a direct relation to the size/value of the subject

D_a Statement about gold ⌐

D_b Your situation is analogous, but ⊢→ C The statement about your

    your faith is more valuable than gold ⌐   faith is more valid

Further argumentation for D_b (as a **C**): **D** Gold is perishable, your faith is imperishable—**W** An imperishable thing is more valuable than a perishable thing. Further, how much better is it for you to endure your testing, since it can be milder (the only quality is ποικίλος) than the testing of gold with fire, especially when the result is more illustrious (δόξα). For problems with analysing the *qal wachomer*, see Wonneberger 1976: 161-62, 174.

(b) The original Means–Purpose relation becomes reasonable in the second alternative (b). The C_1 'You rejoice even when suffering' is formulated 'you are willing even to suffer'. Then we have a *teleological* motivation: You are willing to suffer *in order to produce glory*. This type of motivating expression must be modified in order to be analysed with Toulmin's model, which only applies to causal relations.[41] This gives us the following structure:[42]

Fig. 1.6-7/b

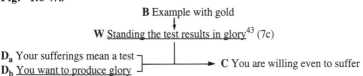

The content of the implicit, but necessary, D_b is interesting. Just as in 7c, it can mean either the addressees' or God's glory.[44] The first interpretation, which can be rephrased 'you want to achieve glory' is almost

41. When seeking volitional elements, motivation presenting the command as a means to an end (do x in order to reach y) is especially important, since it shows us what the persuader sees as the volitional element (Beekman and Callow 1974: 303) in the argumentation.

When there is a Means–Purpose relation between an exhortation and an expression, which is supposed to make the exhortation reasonable and create willingness in the persuadee to obey the exhortation, it is always assumed that the persuadee shares that purpose. The motivation in the discourse 'Dowse the light so that you can sleep' presumes that the listener wants to sleep. Otherwise the motivation would not be effective. Thus, a motivation with a MP relation, or a *teleological* motivation, can be traced back to normal argumentation, where the willingness to reach the Purpose serves as a Ground, i.e., something the listener is assumed to accept.

42. The only possible way in which the motivation can be effective is that the persuader assumes an addressee, who wants to gain the goal of the motivation. Thus the expression 'in order to produce glory' can be modified into a D 'You want to produce glory' and a W 'Doing according to the command results in glory'.

43. Since these modified expressions are not clearly explicit but not totally implicit either, they will be presented as underlined. See above n. 18.

44. The glory comes to the addressees according to Goppelt 1978: 102; Kelly 1969: 55. Selwyn (1947: 130), however, rightly observes that the expression is ambiguous and it also possibly is aimed at God. He refers to 4.2 and 2.9. This ambiguity may be deliberate. Parker (1994: 29) claims that it is God who receives the praise. According to Kelly (1969: 55), the addressees' glory here has '*of course* nothing to do with human commendation or reward' (my italics). However, in 2.11-20 this is exactly the case. See below.

self-evident, while the second 'you want to glorify God' is similar to the
C in the reasoning in 3-5. We thus have three possibilities for interpretation of 6-7, which do not exclude each other:

(a)   You rejoice despite the suffering, since suffering does not
        prevent the joy (on the contrary)
(b₁)   You are willing even to suffer in order to glorify God
(b₂)   You are willing even to suffer in order to obtain glory

The last alternative indicates a new type of motivating factor, willingness
to gain something.

d. *1.8-9—Oxymoron*

1.8   ὃν οὐκ ἰδόντες ἀγαπᾶτε,
            εἰς ὃν ἄρτι μὴ ὁρῶντες πιστεύοντες δὲ
            ἀγαλλιᾶσθε χαρᾷ ἀνεκλαλήτῳ καὶ δεδοξασμένῃ
1.9   κομιζόμενοι τὸ τέλος τῆς πίστεως ὑμῶν σωτηρίαν ψυχῶν.

This unit does not deal with suffering, yet it is parallel to 6-7,[45] since
both deal with obstacles to joy. The importance of faith is emphasized
(πίστις is mentioned in 5, 6, 7, 8 and 9). 8 consists of two parallel
statements about the addressees: they love Christ (ἀγαπᾶτε) and they
rejoice (ἀγαλλιᾶσθε). To these are added three participles, which when
connected to the main verbs express the following idea: they believe in
him, love and rejoice nonwithstanding that they do not see Christ, since
they believe in him. The reason for joy and love is expressed in 9: they
will obtain / are obtaining[46] salvation.

   The C is compound, like the C in 6. It can be separated into two different claims. The first one refers to the preceding text and actually has
two parts: 'You rejoice' and 'You love Christ / believe in him'. The
second, however, which is expressed with participles, contains the
specific message of the section: 'You rejoice/love although you do not
see Christ or the goal of the faith'.

---

45. Against Brox (1979: 65-66), who claims that the author returns to the joyful
tone.
46. The interpretation of κομιζόμενοι is unclear. Have the addressees already (at
least partly) obtained the goal, or will they receive it first in the future? According to
Kelly (1969: 58), the present participle highlights the tension between present and
future. Brox (1979: 66) claims: 'dieses Heil wird jetzt schon erlangt'. In both cases,
however, κομιζόμενοι functions as a reason for joy, that is, it stands in a Reason–
Result relation to ἀγαλλιᾶσθε.

We begin with the first claim, although it has only a secondary position in the text.

Fig. 1.8-9/1[47]

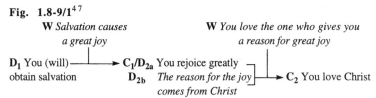

According to the second claim the addressees rejoice over the salvation and love Christ although they do not see it/him. This can be seen as an answer to a possible Rebuttal between D_1 and C_1 in the first structure: if the salvation and Christ are not visible, they lose their meaning.

Fig. 1.8-9/2

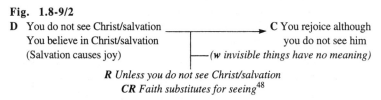

e. *1.10-12—Comparisons*

1.10 περὶ ἧς σωτηρίας ἐξεζήτησαν καὶ ἐξηραύνησαν προφῆται
οἱ περὶ τῆς εἰς ὑμᾶς χάριτος προφητεύσαντες,

1.11 ἐραυνῶντες εἰς τίνα ἢ ποῖον καιρὸν ἐδήλου τὸ ἐν αὐτοῖς πνεῦμα Χριστοῦ
προμαρτυρόμενον τὰ εἰς Χριστὸν παθήματα καὶ τὰς μετὰ ταῦτα δόξας.

1.12 οἷς ἀπεκαλύφθη
ὅτι[49] οὐχ ἑαυτοῖς ὑμῖν δὲ διηκόνουν αὐτά, ἃ νῦν ἀνηγγέλη ὑμῖν
διὰ τῶν εὐαγγελισαμένων ὑμᾶς
ἐν πνεύματι ἁγίῳ ἀποσταλέντι ἀπ' οὐρανοῦ
εἰς ἃ ἐπιθυμοῦσιν ἄγγελοι παρακύψαι.

This unit presents two groups: prophets and angels. Formally they are used to explain the word 'salvation' in 9, but in order to identify the

---

47. An implicit, but evident, factor is that Christ has caused the salvation, which together with joy over the salvation generates love toward Christ. Here an implicit W would read: One loves him who gives reason for great joy.

48. From a rhetorical perspective this idea, although unspoken, plays an important role in the unit.

49. This is not a signal for a logical relation; see Chapter 3 §2.a.

function of the groups and the actual claim of the whole section, they need to be seen as a whole from a rhetorical perspective. A central purpose in the whole larger unit 1.1-12 is to make the addressees appreciate their status as Christians.[50] To this end the author uses *inter alia* the technique of dissociative argumentation by contrasting the addressees' situation with different groups (Thurén 1990: 113-15). In 1.10-12 the prophets and angels function as such groups (cf. also Calloud and Genuyt 1982: 55). The honourable prophets[51] could only search and long for the future salvation, and even the angels are jealous and would like to look upon these mysteries, which have now been given to the addressees.[52] The central purpose of the unit is to point to the merits of the salvation that the addressees have obtained, and thereby emphasize the value of their new situation.

The prophets and angels revere greatly the salvation, which emphasizes its value. How glad should the addressees be when they have obtained this Gospel! The contrast with the prophets and angels is thus neither a Claim nor a D. It is more suitable to see it as a Backing to the W in 8: 'salvation causes great joy' (see above).

Fig. 1.8-12/1

$$\textbf{B} \text{ Comparison with prophets and angels (10-12)}$$

W *Salvation/gospel causes great joy*

D You have obtained salvation (9.10.12b) ⎯⎯⎯⎯→ **C** You rejoice greatly (8)

The unit 10-12 contains also compact motifs, which at least implicitly amplify the proper chain of thought: the Spirit,[53] Christ's suffering and glories.[54] As in 7, it is not explained who receives the glory.[55] The whole

50. Thurén 1990: 113-14, especially for the 'passive', but since it is also against negative expectations, also for 'active' addressees. Cf. Kelly 1969: 58 and Brox 1979: 72.

51. The word refers to OT, not to Christian prophets. See Kelly 1969: 58-59; Goppelt 1978: 105 n. 64 *contra* Selwyn 1947: 134.

52. Thus Kelly 1969: 59; Brox 1979: 72. Against Selwyn 1947: 139; Goppelt 1978: 109-10. For detailed discussion, see Thurén 1990: 114, 70.

53. The prophets have spoken in the Spirit, and the proclamation of the Gospel has taken place through the spirit of Christ. The mention of the Spirit not only serves to increase the reliability of the Gospel, but also shows from whom the salvation comes.

54. Christ's sufferings and glories, which later become a central theme in the Letter, are introduced. However, as is typical for an exordium, this is done only briefly, so that the connection between Christ's sufferings and glories serves here only as a part of a greater issue. It can be seen as a proof of the idea that suffering

of 8-12 serves as an amplification of the argumentation in 3-5.

Fig. **1.8-12/2**

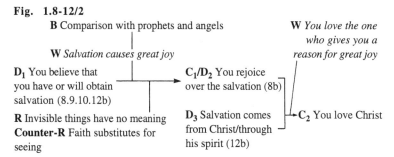

Conclusions

Now the argumentation in the whole 1.1-12 can be summarized and some concluding remarks can be made. This may give us a glimpse of the system of the different motifs behind the text, or, in other words, a structure of motivation on a more ideological level.

The C in the beginning of the section is 'God is / should be praised'. With regard to its function in the motivation, that is, as applied to the addressees and seen from a volitional perspective, it can be restated: 'You want to praise God'.[56]

The primary reason (D) for this praise is explained in 6a, 8: The addressees are rejoicing. This joy is caused by hope of salvation/ inheritance (4, 5, 7, 9, 12), which comes from God (3a) or Christ (3b). Therefore the addressees want to praise just God/Christ. God's grace, providence and protection, along with the suffering and resurrection of Christ, election, and the new birth, serve as grounds for the salvation.

results in glory, functioning thus as a D to the previous C (expressed in 6-7). Another possibility is that the example with Christ corresponds to the example of gold's testing (in 7) and thus is a B. However, a proper B needs to be of a more general nature.

55. Beside thinking of God's or Christ's glory the expression can be interpreted in the light of 12 so that the prophets foresaw the sufferings of Christ, which resulted in the salvation of the addressees, that is, their glory. Due to the ambiguity even this interpretation is possible. It explains how the joy over salvation is combined into love for and faith in Christ: he has produced the salvation.

56. See above. In 1 Peter, the author's way of opening the Letter can with ancient terminology be characterized as an *insinuatio*, which is an alternative to the ordinary exordium (see Thurén 1990: 76). To stress this function means a maximal interpretation of the expression, which also serves e.g. as a benediction, but for the purpose of our analysis such an emphasis is possible.

Thus, we have a simplified structure (the corresponding W's have been presented above) for this type of argumentation in 1.1-12. This *basic chain* of argumentation is then amplified with factors like the certainty and value of salvation.

Fig. 1.1-12/1

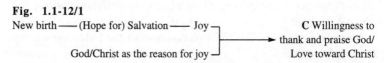

The second issue in the unit 1-12 comprises suffering and not seeing Christ, and their relation to the basic chain. It is not possible to say which issue is the more important, since this greatly depends on the audience (Thurén 1990: 128-34). We shall only focus on the way the arguments are related to each other.

According to 6-7 the addressees' sufferings constitute a test, which will result in glory. This glory seems to come both to (a) God and (b) to themselves. The first alternative fits well into the basic chain.[57] The second alternative leads to a similar structure, but causes changes in D and W. According to a third possibility the addressees rejoice, since suffering does not exclude joy.

Fig. 1.1-12/2

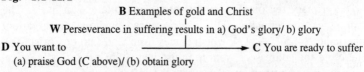

As an answer to a possible Rebuttal in the basic chain comes 8-9: Although not seeing the salvation or Christ, the addressees love him, since their faith compensates for seeing. Seen on the ideological level the willingness to suffer, or perseverance when suffering, seems to be the goal of the argumentation in the unit 1.1-10. This goal is, however, weakly presented in the explicit text and only briefly explained in 6, due to the rhetorical function of the unit.[58]

There are two possible reasons for this willingness: The addressees are

---

57. Since they will praise God (D, v. 3), and perseverance in trial/sufferings result in God's glory (W, 7, alt b), they are ready to suffer (6). The example of gold (7) and Christ (11) function as a B.

58. The rhetorical functions of the unit are typical of exordium (*captatio benevolentiae* and *insinuatio*). The first is especially aimed here at the 'active', the second at the 'passive' type of audience.

rejoicing and therefore want to thank and praise God, or they want to obtain the final salvation. Although the first alternative is emphasized with many expressions about joy and love, the second is also evident. The ambiguous expressions in 7 and 11, from which we cannot decide, whose glories the author is speaking of, may be designed to leave both alternatives open.

It is particularly important for the analysis of the following exhortatory sections that the author here speaks openly about emotions and deals with the readiness or willingness to do something. Such things even function as Claims in the argumentation. As stated above (Chapter 2 §§3, 4), we focus on the emotions when analysing how the exhortations are motivated. Apart from 1.17 (and possibly 3.6) they remain unsaid in the rest of the text until the last, peroratory sections (4.12–5.14), whereas here the exhortations stay implicit. By combining these two it may be possible to construct an 'explicit' picture of the persuasion and motivation in the whole Letter.

3. *General Exhortation 1.13–2.10*[59]

The second rhetorical unit introduces the explicit admonitions in the text—from 1.13 to the end of the Letter the text can in principle be divided into exhortation and motivation. The imperatives and other exhorting expressions are here rather vague compared with the following sections. The tension between the addressees and the non-believers is not even mentioned. Instead, the addressees are simply encouraged to live as good Christians, and the tone of the author is still sympathetic. This indicates that the section is still somewhat preparatory and abstract in nature and thereby closely related to the preceding 1.1-12. The section 1.13–2.10 can be characterized as the first part of the *argumentatio*, or as an extension of the *exordium*, depending on the type of addressees implied.[60]

59. On the formal, epistolary level, the unit begins the letter-body, and 1.13 functions as a letter-opening phrase (Thurén 1990: 84-86). The most natural division line within this long unit goes between 1.25 and 2.1. Thus Spicq 1966: 59, 77; Balch 1981: 124; Olsson 1982: 73; Calloud and Genuyt 1982: 113-14. Goppelt (1978: 128-29) instead sees 1.22–2.3 as a coherent unit. Since the particle οὖν usually serves as a signal for return to the theme or something new (see Chapter 3 §2.c; cf. 1 Pet. 4.1 and 5.1) it is reasonable to see 2.1-3 as an introduction to 2.4-10.

60. Thurén 1990: 145. For the 'active' type of implied audience the commandments serve mainly the *ethos* of the author by portraying him as having the same high

The change of the form from indicative to imperative expressions and from eulogy to paraenesis signify that the reasoning in the text can be analysed as persuasive argumentation. The task is, however, complicated by the use of the *ambiguitas* as a rhetorical device (Thurén 1990: 164-76): the same expressions can be analysed in two ways, both of which are equally legitimate.

The First Half 1.13-25[61]

a. *1.13—introduction*

1.13 διὸ **ἀναζωσάμενοι** τὰς ὀσφύας τῆς διανοίας ὑμῶν
νήφοντες
τελείως ἐλπίσατε
ἐπὶ τὴν φερομένην ὑμῖν χάριν ἐν ἀποκαλύψει Ἰησοῦ Χριστοῦ.

The unit draws a conclusion from the preceding unit (διό; see Chapter 3 §2.c; cf. Brox 1979: 73), which thus serves as a D for 13. It forms a bridge between the eulogy 1.1-12 and the following paraenesis. We find the first explicit, imperatival exhortation in the letter: τελείως ἐλπίσατε. But the actual message and C in 13 is unclear due to the ambiguous nature of the participles ἀναζωσάμενοι and νήφοντες; they can be interpreted either (a) as motivating the imperative (since you are ready) (see also Thurén 1990: 14 n. 35), or (b) as exhortations (be ready).[62] Here a purely semantic reasoning is not enough. The identification of their meaning and the final Claim depends on how the rhetorical situation is assessed, or, in other words, whether the author wants more to admonish or to encourage the addressees.[63] In any case, 13c is a motivation: The grace will be given you (see above Chapter 3 §2.h). The reason for using the topoi 'eschatology' and 'exodus' is

ethical principles as the addressees. It however modestly suggests that the addressees should change their attitudes (see closer Thurén 1990: 145). For the 'passive' addressees the unit already serves as *argumentatio* (see Thurén 1990: 141-42).

61. The first part of the unit consist of four sentences, which may serve as a further division of the text: 1.13, 14-16, 17-21 and 22-25. E.g. Brox (1979: 72-89) discerns the following units: 13-16, 17-21, 22-25.

62. Thus most scholars. However, no solid arguments have been presented. E.g. Goppelt (1978: 114 n. 16) argues for the exhortative nature of the verse, but uses clearly misleading arguments (see Thurén 1990: 13 n. 33).

63. In a sense, the rhetorical function of the participles is exhortatory despite their form: both as imperatives or as 'persuasive description' they encourage the addressees to be ready. But whether such an encouragement is a demand or motivation is difficult to discern.

evident: the addressees are to be ready for the imminent end (cf. Goppelt 1978: 115-16; Brox 1979: 74-75).

(a) We start with an 'indicative' interpretation of the two participles.[64]

Fig. 1.13/a1

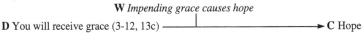

W *Impending grace causes hope*

D You will receive grace (3-12, 13c) ——————————→ **C** Hope

Fig. 1.13/a2

W *Readiness means intensified hope*

D You are sober and ready (13a) ——————————→ **C** Hope fully

(b) With an 'imperative' interpretation the first structure is similar: The addressees are to hope since they will receive grace. But the command 'be ready' as a C leads to a different structure, where hope for the impending salvation implies readiness.[65] A clear motivating factor cannot be discerned.

Fig. 1.13/b

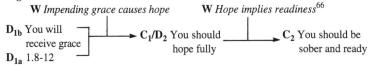

W *Impending grace causes hope*   W *Hope implies readiness*[66]

D₁ᵦ You will ⎤
    receive grace ⎬ ——→ **C₁/D₂** You should ——→ **C₂** You should be
D₁ₐ 1.8-12 ⎦   hope fully   sober and ready

b. *1.14-16—Two Motivating Factors*

1.14   ὡς τέκνα ὑπακοῆς
        μὴ συσχηματιζόμενοι
        ταῖς πρότερον ἐν τῇ ἀγνοίᾳ ὑμῶν ἐπιθυμίαις

---

64. Then the imperative 'hope' or 'hope fully' is the C and there are two D's: 'You are ready' and 'You will receive grace'. This interpretation is natural for the 'active' type of rhetorical situation. Cf. Thurén 1990: 143.

65. The C₂ is motivated with hope (ἐλπίσατε as D). In fact, the exhortatory component of the participles ἀναζωσάμενοι and νήφοντες always makes them stronger than in the actual imperative ἐλπίσατε, which despite the grammatical form does not sound like a requirement (against Goppelt 1978: 110), but rather motivates the participles. As reason for the hope the author refers to the preceding section with διό, but he also explains what is the goal of the hope: 'The grace to be given you in the revelation of Jesus Christ' (13c). Such a chain of reasoning corresponds to 1-12: The author argues for a C which serves as a D for the following C.

66. The meaning of this W remains somewhat obscure. This is only natural, since as a letter-opening phrase the unit is suspected to introduce an idea, which is later explained.

1.15　**ἀλλὰ <u>κατὰ</u> τὸν καλέσαντα ὑμᾶς ἅγιον**
　　　　　καὶ αὐτοὶ ἅγιοι ἐν πάσῃ ἀναστροφῇ γενήθητε,
1.16　<u>διότι</u> γέγραπται[67]
　　　ἅγιοι ἔσεσθε ὅτι ἐγὼ ἅγιος.[68]

The unit consists of two parallel exhortations: μὴ συσχηματιζόμενοι ταῖς...ἐπιθυμίαις[69] and its antithesis ἅγιοι...γενήθητε. They are motivated with a quotation from the OT (16, signaled with διότι).

Here begins the first longer chain of arguments, which makes it possible to commence the actual analysis of persuasion. We start with a simple structure:

Fig. 1.14-16/1

W *OT is authoritative for Christians*

D OT-quotation: 'Be holy' (16) ————⊥——► C Do not assimilate but be holy (14-15)

Each factor, however, contains more material. This makes this obscure argumentation easier to understand and more persuasive. It is evident that the metaphorical language about children and father dominates this unit, but ὡς τέκνα can be understood in two ways.[70]

　(a) We begin with the first, 'indicative' interpretation, which is especially suitable for the 'active' implied audience (Thurén 1990: 144).

Fig. 1.14-15/a

W *An obedient child follows its father's example*

D_1 You are obedient children
D_2 Desires are something negative　　┐
　　　God's example, something positive[71]┘　　C Do not follow desires but
　　　　　　　　　　　　　　　　　　　　　　your father's example

---

67. Thus $\mathfrak{P}^{72}$, ℵ *et al.*; B adds ὅτι.
68. Thus $\mathfrak{P}^{72}$, ℵ adds εἰμί.
69. Due to the structure, the expression is not ambiguous. See Thurén 1990: 14 n. 55.
70. (a) The ambiguous expression 'like (ὡς) obedient children' in 14 can serve as a D 'Since you are obedient children' for the C 'Do not conform to evil desires (but to your father)'. Even κατὰ τὸν καλέσαντα is ambivalent; see Chapter 3 §2.e.
　　(b) An alternative is to see the ὡς-expression as an extension of the exhortation: 'Be obedient children and...' (see Chapter 3 §2.e and Thurén 1990: 26).
Further: the desires belong to a former life, which is characterized by ignorance. As an alternative, positive model for behaviour God's holiness is presented in 15. The author also recalls that God has summoned the addressees, which supports D_2, but also refers to what has already been said and serves as a ground (D_0) to D_1. An implicit W could be: the one who is called by God becomes God's child.
71. The grade of explicitness of this type of expressions is difficult to define.

(b) An 'imperative' interpretation of ὡς τέκνα ὑπακοῆς[72] would serve to render the main command precise. It is motivated with D₂ above, but especially with 16 and with the addressees' status as God's children. The emotive factor in such an argumentation will be studied below.

16 as a whole serves as a D for 14-15: the author's command is supported by reference to the OT and to the will of God.

Fig. 1.14-16/2

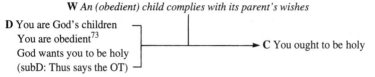

W *An (obedient) child complies with its parent's wishes*

D You are God's children
   You are obedient[73]
   God wants you to be holy   → C You ought to be holy
   (subD: Thus says the OT)

16 has also its C 'Be holy' and a D 'God is holy'. A necessary extra D is here implicit, but found before: 'You are God's children'.[74] The implicit W corresponds to the W above: a child takes after its father.

Fig. 1.16

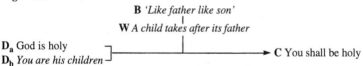

B *'Like father like son'*

W *A child takes after its father*

Dₐ God is holy
D_b *You are his children*   → C You shall be holy

Now the factors can be seen from an *ideological* perspective, as more general motifs. 14c refers to the addressees' former life, whereas 14a speaks of their new status as God's children. The change from old to new is caused by salvation by God, and in 16 the holy life is motivated with God's being. 16 is also an argument from Scripture.

Thus we discern a structure of the whole unit. God's character (16) and the addressees' new status (13) imply that they shall be holy. The former life (14f) adds a negative counterpart to the new status, and argument from Scripture (16) gives authority to the argumentation by

---

Since this idea is rather clearly manifested in the text (μή... ταῖς πρότερον ἐν τῇ ἀγνοίᾳ ὑμῶν ἐπιθυμίαις, ἀλλὰ κατὰ τὸν καλέσαντα ὑμᾶς ἅγιον), I have decided to present it as explicit.

72. This partly fits the 'passive' type of implied addressees (Thurén 1990: 138).

73. According to the 'indicative' interpretation.

74. Thus 1.14. However, if the D_b is not added to the OT quotation, a more obscure W must be implied: 'God's holiness implies that people who are close to him are holy'. As a Backing the quotation lets us assume the Holiness Code in Leviticus, but due to the compact nature of the text, the possibilities remain open.

indicating that the requirement of holiness is not only the author's, but also God's thought.

This analysis of argumentation does not yet explain how the reasoning is designed to persuade and motivate the addressees. In order to study the text from that perspective we have to focus on the volitional aspect and emotions, which the argumentation in the section attempts to provoke.

The question can be formulated: how does the addressees' new status (that they are God's children) motivate them to obey God?[75] On the ideological level there are two possible explanations: (a) since the change to the new status is God's work, the addressees should thank and praise God and therefore obey him. This is explicit in 1.1-12; (b) The addressees want to preserve their new status and thus obey God. Even this idea can be found in 1-12, although due to the rhetorical requirement of a positive tone in the opening section it is not so clearly formulated (see above; it can only be found as underlying in 1.7).

Fig. 1.14-16/3

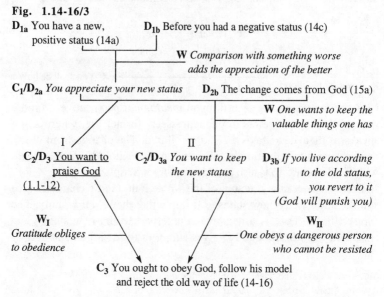

The first D in the chain of argumentation is the addressees' new status (they have been born again, they have hope for salvation, they are

---

75. The commentaries usually do not deal with such issues. Brox (1979: 77) claims that the intimate relationship to God motivates the addressees here just as in 1.17, but does not explain in detail what this means. Cf. also Selwyn 1947: 140-41.

God's children etc.). Compared with the old status (implicit in 1.4—it is not ἄφθαρτος, ἀμίαντος, ἀμάραντος—and explicit in 14.18), it is of inestimable value; thus the addressees rejoice (6.8). Since the change is caused by God (3.15), they praise him (3.7), and therefore obey. But the addressees' dependence on God suggests that he can also take away this status, and in fear of this his will has to be scrupulously obeyed. These alternatives point toward two ideological structures in 1.14-16, seen in the context of 1.1-12 (see Fig. 1.14-16/3, previous page).

According to version I the motivating factor is joy and thankfulness toward God (cf. 1.1-12), whereas in II it is the will to maintain the new status or the fear of losing it.

c. *1.17—Incitatio*

1.17 καὶ εἰ πατέρα ἐπικαλεῖσθε
      τὸν ἀπροσωπολήμπτως κρίνοντα κατὰ τὸ ἑκάστου ἔργον,
      ἐν φόβῳ τὸν τῆς παροικίας ὑμῶν χρόνον ἀναστράφητε

Due to the crucial position and ambiguous nature of 17 it will first be analysed as such, and first thereafter connected with 18-21 in the same unit. 17 consists of the following elements: the addressees' appeal to God as Father, God is an impartial judge, the addressees should live in fear of God, they live now as strangers. It is a parallel to 14-16 (ὡς τέκνα—καὶ εἰ πατέρα). The addressees' status as strangers does not have a distinct function in the structure of argumentation, but only refers to an idea that is expounded later in 2.11 (against Goppelt 1979: 120 and Elliott 1981: 44).

The ground for exhortation to live in fear of God can be interpreted in two alternative ways: (a) 'Since [see Chapter 3 §2.g] you invoke the impartial judge as father', which means 'God is an impartial judge *but* you can appeal to him as father'[76] (= D). This indicates that God cannot punish them (= W);[77] (b) 'Since the father you invoke is an impartial judge', which means 'You call him father *but* he is an impartial judge' (= D). This indicates that God can punish them after all (= W).[78] The

76. About the ambiguity of the word 'father', see Thurén 1990: 24.

77. This alternative is favoured by e.g. Selwyn 1947: 142-43, according to whom the emphatic place of πατέρα in the sentence indicates this 'positive' interpretation. See also Delling 1973: 109.

78. This alternative is advocated by e.g. Kelly 1969: 71; Goppelt 1978: 119; Piper 1980: 228. Brox (1979: 75) claims that since the word 'judge' is here something new, it is dominant.

ambiguity of the expression resembles that of 14.

The command (C) is similarly ambiguous (see Thurén 1990: 24): φόβος can be interpreted either (a) as reverence[79] or (b) as real fear[80] before God. Both interpretations could be justified, if the author had written in slightly different terms. Arguments for the first alternative, especially references to the fourth (fifth) commandment, point toward a hypothetical sentence 'God is your father—live in fear of him', while the second could be well grounded if the author had written 'God is a judge—live in fear of him'. The actual compound sentence makes the interpretation more difficult.

(a) In the first case the emphasis lies on the addressees' new status. God is presented as an impartial and thus terrifying judge. That the addressees now can juridically *appeal*[81] to this judge as father means that their relationship to him has been changed; he will not punish them. This should call them to live in fear of God. In this case φόβος is interpreted as reverent fear. There is thus actually a Rebuttal:

Fig. 1.17/a1

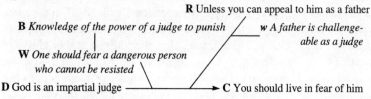

79. Thus e.g. Selwyn 1947: 142. He recalls that reverence for the father (not the judge) is one of the primary principles in *torah*. According to Olsson (1982: 58-59), Ps. 34, which can be seen behind many expressions in 1 Peter, includes an admonition to learn the 'fear of God' as introduction to the verses which are quoted in 1 Peter 3.10-12. Olsson also claims that 'fear' is a typical expression for a right relationship to God in OT, but that in 1 Peter it means also a corresponding humble and holy relationship toward other people (1.15; 2.18; 3.2, 16). He claims furthermore that God as a father strengthens the serious nature of the judgment, but does not explain how. According to Goppelt (1978: 120) φόβος does not mean anxiety, but he also rejects the type of interpretation presented above as 'nachapostolische Vulgär-frommigkeit'—of course without any explanation.

80. Brox (1979: 80) holds this interpretation as possible.

81. Instead of only referring to prayer (thus e.g. Selwyn 1947: 142), ἐπικαλέομαι also has a juridical meaning (Bauer–Aland *s.v.*). The context also supports this interpretation.

In a simplified form this means:

Fig. 1.17/a2

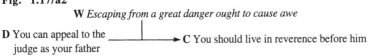

W *Escaping from a great danger ought to cause awe*

D You can appeal to the ──────► **C** You should live in reverence before him
judge as your father

(b) In the second case too the new status has changed the addressees' situation. They now live in such close contact with God that they should be especially careful and afraid of him (thus Brox 1978: 79). An implicit W is that God will detect all their offence. In this case φόβος rather means anxiety in front of God.

Fig. 1.17/b

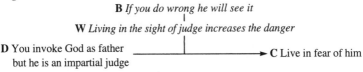

B *If you do wrong he will see it*

W *Living in the sight of judge increases the danger*

D You invoke God as father ──────► **C** Live in fear of him
but he is an impartial judge

Both alternatives are possible, but the first seems more obscure due to the enigmatic nature of the Warrant. The rhetorical situation, that is, the type of the implied addressees, governs the choice between the alternatives (see Thurén 1990: 139, 144). However, in both cases 1.17 serves as the first signal of a threat in the author's message, which has hitherto been mostly positive and encouraging. As such the verse is a climax within the larger unit and for some addressees it should function as an *incitatio* or *deinosis*.[82]

The verse is especially important for the study of persuasion, since here a previously implicit emotion, fear, is expressed. 'Terror' functions as a natural motivating factor in the second alternative, whereas the first motivating function 'positive reverence' is more difficult to explain. In view of the previous argumentation it could possibly refer to the addressees' gratitude to God, because of which they should respect him.

d. *1.18-21—Further Comparisons*

1.18 <u>εἰδότες</u> ὅτι οὐ φθαρτοῖς, ἀργυρίῳ ἢ χρυσίῳ,
ἐλυτρώθητε
ἐκ τῆς ματαίας ὑμῶν ἀναστροφῆς πατροπαραδότου
1.19 ἀλλὰ τιμίῳ αἵματι ὡς ἀμνοῦ ἀμώμου καὶ ἀσπίλου Χριστοῦ,

---

82. Nissilä (1979: 254-55) interprets Heb. 10.26-31 as a *deinosis*. See Lausberg 1960 §257, 3c.

1.20 προεγνωσμένου μὲν πρὸ καταβολῆς κόσμου
 φανερωθέντος δὲ ἐπ' ἐσχάτου τῶν χρόνων δι' ὑμᾶς
1.21 τοὺς δι' αὐτοῦ πιστοὺς εἰς θεὸν
 τὸν ἐγείραντα αὐτὸν ἐκ νεκρῶν καὶ δόξαν αὐτῷ δόντα,
 ὥστε τὴν πίστιν ὑμῶν καὶ ἐλπίδα εἶναι εἰς θεόν.

This lengthy motivation is sometimes seen as diverting from the main theme.[83] It is necessary after the strict exhortation. The command to live in fear of God is motivated with a participial clause in 18-21. Contrary to 17 this half of the unit is mainly positive. It consists of the following elements: the addressees know (or should know)[84] that they have been moved from a vain life to a life characterized by hope of immortality. This is caused by God. He (a) redeemed the addressees with valuable gifts (the blood of Christ is contrasted with perishable gold) and (b) raised Christ from the dead and gave him glory, which also gives the addressees hope.

The section refers to 1.3-5. Beside the main thought it is loaded with various themes.[85] In the analysis, we shall concentrate on the central train of thought. The ultimate C is the command in 17 'Live in (reverent) fear of God'. This is motivated with the addressees' own experience (εἰδότες): they have been redeemed (18b-21a), so that (ὥστε; see Chapter 3 §2.c) they have hope. The hope is based on the analogy[86] of the resurrection and glory of Christ, which suggests that God can raise from the dead also the addressees, who believe in him,[87]

---

83. Thus Kelly 1969: 78. In ancient rhetoric this would mean a technique of *digressio* (see Lausberg 1960 §§340-42, 408).

84. εἰδότες may also be an 'imperative participle': see Thurén 1990: 13-14, 139-40, 144.

85. Such is e.g. the idea of the minor value of gold (earlier in 7), which also refers to its testing. A reference to the imminent end in 20 is another subsidiary theme. Further, it is said that Jesus' sufferings and death led to resurrection and glory, from which an implicit thought can be inferred: since the addressees now have hope of the same glory, they should also be ready to partake in the sufferings of Christ. The author, however, does not go so far—the idea is only suggested here and explained first later (e.g. in 4.13). Such a technique is typical of the author's style.

86. In a section dealing with reasoning from analogy Toulmin characterizes an analogy as a Warrant (since this case is similar to the case x) (Toulmin *et al.* 1984: 216-19). However, since a W typically is a rule, it is more exact to see the analogy as a Backing, which backs up an implied rule (W), which then applies to the case.

87. 'Faith' is here an expression of the addressees' new relationship to God. See Goppelt 1978: 126-27.

(and give them a corresponding glory). This also clarifies the ideological role of the resurrection of Christ in 1.3.[88]

We obtain a preliminary structure:

Fig. 1.17-21/1

However, this figure does not reveal the essential message of the unit, which is not redemption as such. It is emphasized with an antithetic structure,[90] which stresses the quality of the means of redemption (perishable metals versus the blood of Christ), the quality of the result (living hope versus futile life), time (before versus now), and origin (fathers versus God). The contrast is much stronger than in 1.3-5. In order to understand the actual structure of argumentation, we must discern the function of the quality-topos here.

One possibility is that the author wants to undermine the old way of life and show that it is essentially opposite to the new one, so that they cannot be combined. But it is more important that the high value of the alternative is emphasized by the comparison, as in 1.10-12, which the antithesis here resembles. Both stress the extraordinary nature of the addressees' situation. Therefore the comparison between the valuable, but perishable, metals and the blood of Christ is intended to highlight the value of the redemption—the goal is to make the addressees hold the redemption in high esteem. Together with the comparison between old and new status, and fathers versus God, this is aimed at a greater appreciation of the new status.

We can conclude that the actual purpose, and thus also the main C within 18-21, is to increase the addressees' appreciation of their new

88. The ideological role of a theme is not equivalent to its rhetorical function. Since 1.3 formally is a eulogy, and since it is short and logically somewhat obscure, it is not possible to identify exactly what kind of thought the resurrection of Christ is designed to evoke in the addressees. Perhaps it only introduces the theme and hints at its meaning, so that the later explanation becomes more effective. However, the resurrection has a certain place on the ideological level. Thereby the clearer 1.21 also explains 1.3.

89. Joy and gratitude for the hope conferred, or fear of losing it, may give reason for respect or fear.

90. For the use of the quality-topos, see Thurén 1990: 115 n. 71.

relationship to God and their new status as Christians. In 1-12 the merits of the addressees' situation were presented in order to explain (or motivate) their thankfulness toward God. A similar purpose may be suspected here.[91] This, in turn, should motivate the life in (reverent) fear of God.[92]

Fig. 1.17-21/2

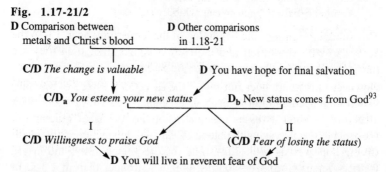

The W in the last move, which would reveal the motivating factor, remains implicit,[94] but as stated above, the positive aspect is much stronger. It even appears that the author is withdrawing the negative aspect in 17 by attaching the positive motivation in 18-21. This, however, does not mean that the negative interpretation of 17 should be disregarded—it is rather a sign of the author's careful strategy.[95] The warning in 17 can well affect the minds of the 'passive' type of audience not despite but because of a 'positive' interpretation of 18-21!

e. *1.22-25—The New Birth*

1.22 τὰς ψυχὰς ὑμῶν <u>ἡγνικότες</u> ἐν τῇ ὑπακοῇ τῆς ἀληθείας εἰς
      φιλαδελφίαν ἀνυπόκριτον,
               ἐκ καθαρᾶς καρδίας
               ἀλλήλους ἀγαπήσατε ἐκτενῶς

---

91. A negative motivating factor is possible, but due to the positive tone of the section it is less evident. The commentators do not take a clear stand on this question.

92. Against Goppelt (1978: 127), who claims that the purpose of 18-21 is simply to give a ground for faith and hope and thereby intensify the imperative in 13-17. Such an interpretation misses the antithetical emphasis on the quality-topos.

93. Although Christ is mentioned he has only a passive role.

94. This is only natural, since the author is not describing his ethics but persuading his addressees. See Chapter 2 §1.

95. Due to the delicate rhetorical situation he has to take care of his *ethos* and not be too severe (otherwise some addressees would close their ears), and yet he has to convey his message.

1.23 ἀναγεγεννημένοι οὐκ ἐκ σπορᾶς φθαρτῆς ἀλλὰ ἀφθάρτου
     διὰ λόγου ζῶντος θεοῦ καὶ μένοντος.
1.24 διότι πᾶσα σὰρξ ὡς χόρτος καὶ πᾶσα δόξα αὐτῆς ὡς ἄνθος χόρτου·
     ἐξηράνθη ὁ χόρτος καὶ τὸ ἄνθος ἐξέπεσεν·
1.25 τὸ δὲ ῥῆμα κυρίου μένει εἰς τὸν αἰῶνα.
     τοῦτο δέ ἐστιν τὸ ῥῆμα τὸ εὐαγγελισθὲν εἰς ὑμᾶς.

This subunit resembles the beginning of the larger unit: as in 13-16 the
author's own exhortation and motivation comes first; then they are
further supported with a proof from the Scripture. 22 includes a command 'love each other',[96] which is more precise than the previous
exhortation. It is motivated with a reference to the addressees' new
birth:[97] they have already cleansed their souls to a brotherly love. A
bridge between this C and D would signify that purification of the soul
(in new birth) will result in pure new way of life. An alternative is to
interpret the whole of 22 as a command.[98]

Fig. 1.22

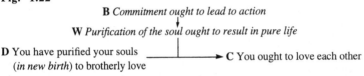

B *Commitment ought to lead to action*

W *Purification of the soul ought to result in pure life*

D You have purified your souls ————————→ **C** You ought to love each other
(*in new birth*) to brotherly love

This reasoning *per se* is not yet persuasive. 22a seems only to suggest
that new birth implies new life[99]—a rule that is essentially similar to the
implicit W above. But why should the addressees take the W into
account? Additional material is needed to show that the argumentation is
also motivating. First the rest of the unit will be treated separately.

96. The command is modified with the words ἐκ καθαρᾶς καρδίας and
ἐκτενῶς. The modifications in 22a also explain the meaning of the command. For
discussion see Evang 1989.

97. Verses 22 and 23 refer to baptism. See Goppelt 1978: 131-32.

98. See Thurén 1990: 19. According to Evang (1989: 113 n. 10), who disregards
Turner (1976: 128), no modern support for this interpretation can be found. He
rejects the imperatival reading on the basis of the 'konzentrische' structure of 22-23,
the meaning and importance of which however remain obscure.

99. This is the message of the whole of 22-25 according to Evang 1989: 117-18.

Fig. 1.23-25

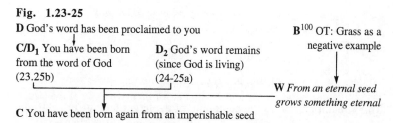

As a whole, 23-25 is connected to the command in 22 with a GC relation. The addressees have been born again of an imperishable seed (D);
thus they should love each other (C). But now we arrive at the crucial
question about the W: how does the birth from an imperishable seed
imply brotherly love—that is, how does it motivate the command in 22?

Evang enumerates different explanations, according to which the
word (Baltz and Schrage 1980: 80), the new birth (Goppelt 1978: 12),
or truth and new life (Brox 1979: 85) is the decisive factor in the unit
(Evang 1989: 111), but not even he explains how they actually are
designed to obligate or motivate the addressees. Kelly claims that the
new existential dimension displayed in 23-25 answers an unspoken
objection: 'How is such love possible in this world?' According to
Evang the purpose of 22a, 23-25 is to function as a ground for 22a by
showing that the origin of the new life is qualified by 'Liebe,
Warhaftigkeit und Dauer' (1989: 118). As such Evang's explanation is
reasonable, and corresponds to the interpretation of 22 presented above.
But is not 22 enough for that purpose? From an argumentative perspective we can ask, how D is designed to function, that is, how the new
birth actually is assumed to motivate the addressees to the required
behaviour?

In my opinion, the scholars have disregarded a factor in 23-25, which
compared with 22 is something new and essential: the quality-topos. The
author describes the new birth from a specific perspective by comparing
it with an ordinary birth and its gloomy result. In this antithetic way he
shows how much more valuable the new birth is since it gives hope of

---

100. For the function of an example as a Backing, see above Fig. 1.17. If necessary, the reasoning can be analysed more precisely. The B above consists of the following factors: Since all flesh is like grass (D), ordinary birth results in death (C),
since grass withers (W). This implies that extraordinary birth, which is not of perishable flesh but of something eternal, does not result in death (the W in Fig. 1.23-25).
The reasoning could be presented even in other ways, but the structure displayed
here sufficiently explains the relations between the arguments.

eternal life. This use of the quality-topos resembles that of 18-21, and their obvious purpose is also similar: the addressees should highly esteem their new birth.

This result supports the motivation in 22. If the addressees' new birth requires a new way of life, and they appreciate the new birth so much, this obligation cannot remain insignificant for them. In view of the structures before, there are two possible alternative Warrants: (a) 'If you highly esteem x, you want to live according to x', or 'If you do not follow the obligation of x, you will lose it'. According to the latter alternative, the antitheses in 23-25 can also serve as warnings not to lose the new status.

Fig. 1.22-25

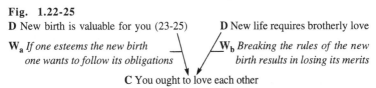

D New birth is valuable for you (23-25)   **D** New life requires brotherly love

W$_a$ *If one esteems the new birth*   **W$_b$** *Breaking the rules of the new*
  one wants to follow its obligations   *birth results in losing its merits*

C You ought to love each other

The C is equal to the W in 22, but it is portrayed from the addressees' perspective. Again, the 'positive' W$_a$ is ideologically more complex. It can be explained with motives like gratitude, but can also be traced back to W$_b$.

With an alternative reading (ἠγνικότες in 22 as an imperative) the structure would be the same but the command more emphatic. As Brox rightly suggests, the meaning (or the rhetorical function) of ἠγνικότες is rather similar irrespective of the interpretation.[101]

In any case, the persuasion here utilizes the change in the addressees' life in both: by referring to the ethical requirements that pertain to the change[102] and by pointing to the hope, which the change has produced. However, the presentation of the salvation and its merits is so long that, although formally connected with an exhortation, it may well serve rather independently as a proclamation of the Gospel.[103]

Conclusions

Now some generalizing conclusions about the first part of the large unit (1.13–2.10) can be made on the ideological level.

---

101. Brox 1979: 86. For a detailed discussion, see Thurén 1990: 140, 144.

102. As Selwyn (1947: 393-400) has shown, the terminology here comes from Early Christian baptismal terminology. See also Nauck 1955: 47-48.

103. Cf. the discussion about the rhetorical situation, genre and purpose of the Letter above in Chapter 4 and Thurén 1990: 124.

The point of departure in the motivation in 13-25 is the addressees' knowledge of what they have experienced: 'as children', 'if you call', 'you know well', 'you have purified yourselves' and 'you have been born again'. The author attempts to show how natural[104] it should be to draw conclusions from this new status and begin to live according to the rules connected with it.

The clearest goal of the motivation is to intensify the addressees' esteem of their new status as Christians.[105] This goal is pursued in different ways.

One means is to refer to the addressees' former life as a dark background to the new one (16, 18, 23-24). The old life was futile, since it contained no hope. The hopelessness is caused by a general perishableness (18, 23-24), but also by God's judgment (17). This judgment can further be seen not only as a theological alternative to the general perishableness, but also as a possible reason for it.

An opposite way of increasing the appreciation of the new status is to refer to its own positive qualities. The new life means hope for imperishableness (13, [17b] 23-25). This hope is reinforced with two types of ground. First, it is supported with grounds that are opposite to the hopelessness of the former life. The addressees are no more under the general principle of perishing (23-25), nor under the judgment of God (17). The first ground is further supported by a new birth through God's eternal word (23) and the resurrection of Christ (24), but also by their status as God's children. Secondly, the author points to the high price that has been paid for the addressees' new life (18-20).

The subsequent goal for the motivation is to show how the appreciation of the new life should lead to willingness to obey God, that is, to lead a holy life in the fear of God. Here two alternatives have been found:

First, the addressees want to thank and praise God and therefore live according to his will. This alternative is supported by 1.3-12, where a

---

104. This is indicated by the way in which these motivating expressions are combined with the exhortations (ὡς, εἰ, participle). For a detailed discussion of the importance of the choice of the way of combining argumentation and exhortation, see Chapter 3 §4.

105. This goal may serve two different purposes, depending on the addressees. It either functions as a real motivation (for the 'passive' implied audience), or it serves the technique of *insinuatio* (for the 'active' audience), restating their own thoughts for a strategic purpose. See Thurén 1990: 134-46.

corresponding ground (new valuable status given by God) is said to lead to joy and praise. The generally positive tone in 13-25 supports this interpretation. The train of thought is as follows: hope for imperishableness causes joy, and since the imperishableness is a gift of God or comes from Christ,[106] the addressees want to praise God and therefore live according to his will, that is, to follow the rules of the new life.

Secondly, the addressees want to preserve their new status and therefore live so that they will not be condemned after all (17). They want to obey the will of the judge and not break the rules of the new life. This idea has been found implicit also in 1.7. The hopelessness of the old life and the judgment of God serve as warning examples. Notwithstanding, the salvation is presented in principle as secure (13b, cf. 5).

A simplified ideological structure of motivation behind 13-25 thus appears as follows:

Fig. 1.13-25

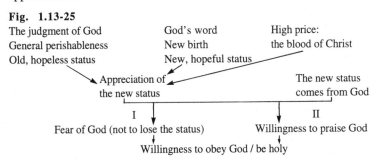

This, in turn, may give motivating power to the reference to God's will, the OT, and the obscure ground 'I am holy' in 1.14-16.

The commands in 13-25 (with the exception of admonition to internal love) speak of general readiness (13) and life according to the will of God or in fear of him. This indicates that, just as in 1-12, the emphasis lies in the motivation for being good and holy. The more concrete way of actualizing the willingness is yet to come. But compared with 1-12 the author adds two aspects: first, the praise of God as the ultimate Claim is replaced by obedience, which lets us assume that there is a connection between the two; secondly, fear of God is introduced as another motivating factor. Seen from the rhetorical perspective these modifications and the development serve as a preparation for the forthcoming concrete message of the author (Thurén 1990: 134-46).

106. *Passivum divinum* in 13, 18; other corresponding expressions are found in 15, 18-19, 23, 25.

The Second Half 2.1-10[107]

The text contains only one indisputable exhortation: 'Crave the pure milk of the word'.[108]

f. 2.1-3—A Catalogue of Vices

2.1   <u>ἀποθέμενοι οὖν</u>
       πᾶσαν κακίαν καὶ πάντα δόλον καὶ ὑποκρίσεις καὶ φθόνους
       καὶ πάσας καταλαλιάς,
2.2   ὡς ἀρτιγέννητα βρέφη τὸ λογικὸν ἄδολον γάλα
       ἐπιποθήσατε,
       <u>ἵνα</u> ἐν αὐτῷ αὐξηθῆτε εἰς σωτηρίαν,
2.3   <u>εἰ</u> ἐγεύσασθε
       ὅτι χρηστὸς ὁ κύριος.

This subunit refers to the preceding subunit (οὖν) and introduces 2.4-10. Contrary to the expressions in 4 and 5, the ambiguous participle ἀποθέμενοι, which is a technical term of baptismal education,[109] has a clear ethical content and an exhortatory rhetorical function regardless of the semantic interpretation—only the grade of explicitness varies (Thurén 1990: 141 n. 14).

(a) If ἀποθέμενοι is interpreted as a motivation, it still has an admonishing tone, because of the catalogue form and the emphasis of the word 'every': 'As you have put away *all kind of* malice...' This corresponds to the exhortation to be holy ἐν πάσῃ ἀναστροφῇ (1.14-16; cf. also Mt. 5.48). It is connected to the imperative in the same way as is 1.23. This interpretation is suited to a 'passive' implied audience (Thurén 1990: 140).

---

107. The latter part of the larger unit 1.13–2.10 consists of three parts, which are determined by their different motifs: 1-3 uses the idea of milk, 4-8 the stone-motif and 9-10 different honorary titles. The text is usually divided into 1-3, 4-5, 6-8 and 9-10 (Goppelt 1978: 110; Brox 1979: 94-95; see also Elliott 1966: 16-49).

108. προσερχόμενοι (2.4) and οἰκοδομεῖσθε (2.5), if interpreted as exhortations, are also rather general. The words clearly have two meanings (indicative and imperative), and this is part of the rhetorical strategy of the author. For discussion see Thurén 1990: 15-19 and *passim*. According to Kelly (1969: 82), 'the detail of [the author's] argumentation seems obscure'—this means a challenge for our analysis.

109. See Selwyn 1947: 19, 393-400; Kelly 1969: 83-84. The catalogue includes also conventional contemporary ethical material (Selwyn 1947: 153; Kamlah 1964: 34, 200).

Fig. 2.1-3/1a

W *Birth should lead to growth*

D You have put away all malice in the new birth (subD: 1.22-25) ——————→ **C** You shall drink milk so that you grow up

(b) ἀποθέμενοι (now C) is motivated with 1.22-25 also as a command. It refers to the addressees' spiritual purification in baptism (1.22. D), but stresses the physical, actual side of the purification: commitment ought to lead to action (W) (cf. 3.21 σαρκὸς ἀπόθεσις ῥύπου). Structurally it is a parallel to ἐπιποθήσατε, which is the main C in the whole unit. This interpretation is more suitable for the 'active' audience (Thurén 1990: 144).

Fig. 2.1-3/1b

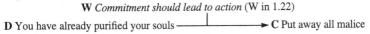

W *Commitment should lead to action* (W in 1.22)

D You have already purified your souls ————→ **C** Put away all malice

The main C ἐπιποθήσατε is further confirmed with two (or three) elements: (a) in order/ so that you may grow up in salvation (2b; for the explanation of a teleological motivation, see Chapter 3 §1); (b) since you have tasted that the Lord is good (3); [(c) since you are newborn babes (2a)].[110] They provide an additional, more precise and better motivated argument for the C than the structure presented above.[111] The picture of a thirsty baby serves also as a general example (= B).[112] The author also refers to the addressees' own experience (εἰ ἐγεύσασθε)—the word itself refers to milk. We find first a general, non-theological example:

Fig. 2.1-3/2

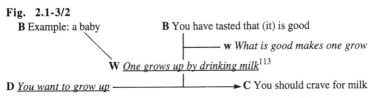

B Example: a baby   **B** You have tasted that (it) is good

— w *What is good makes one grow*

W *One grows up by drinking milk*[113]

D *You want to grow up* ————→ **C** You should crave for milk

110. This ὡς expression may serve either as a metaphor or as an example (see e.g. Kelly 1969: 84). Then it corresponds to τέκνα in 1.14, which also can be either adverbial or a motivating description. See the corresponding analysis above. This interpretation here causes only a slight modification of the structure of argumentation.

111. The author uses a technique similar to 1.22a/b/23-25: cf. 2.1-3/2b/2c-3.

112. The different possible backgrounds (for discussion see e.g. Kelly 1969: 85-86, cf. also Deut. 6.1-3) may further illustrate the use of the example. However, it can be easily understood without any specific previous knowledge.

113. Or, if ὡς τέκνα is interpreted as a D 'since you are children', the example is directly a W.

In the text the words σωτηρία and κύριος give this picture a theological tone:

Fig. 2.1-3/3

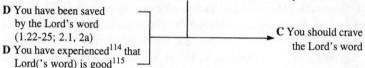

B Example: A growing baby

W *By (continuously) receiving the Lord's word one reaches the final salvation*

D You have been saved
by the Lord's word
(1.22-25; 2.1, 2a)
D You have experienced[114] that
Lord('s word) is good[115]

C You should crave
the Lord's word

The expression λογικὸν γάλα refers to the word of God (cf. McCartney 1991: 132): either to the gospel[116] (corresponding ῥῆμα κυρίου in 1.25) or to the commands of God (so implicitly in 1.16). Again the first alternative is preferable, since a parallel exhortation οἰκοδομεῖσθε[117] more surely has this content. The addressees should listen to the gospel so that they will be saved finally. According to the alternative they should obey the word of God in order to be saved.[118] This again indicates two different motivating factors.

g. 2.4-8—Mixed Metaphors

2.4   πρὸς ὃν προσερχόμενοι λίθον ζῶντα
       ὑπὸ ἀνθρώπων μὲν ἀποδεδοκιμασμένον παρὰ δὲ θεῷ
       ἐκλεκτὸν ἔντιμον,
2.5   καὶ αὐτοὶ ὡς λίθοι ζῶντες
       οἰκοδομεῖσθε οἶκος πνευματικὸς εἰς ἱεράτευμα ἅγιον
       ἀνενέγκαι πνευματικὰς θυσίας εὐπροσδέκτους τῷ[119] θεῷ διὰ Ἰησοῦ
       Χριστοῦ.

114. So e.g. Goppelt (1978: 137) interprets ἐγεύομαι.

115. The Greek text plays with the words χριστός and χρηστός, which were pronounced similarly. See Thurén 1990: 165 n. 7.

116. So Selwyn 1947: 154; Kelly 1969: 85. The adjective ἄδολον adds an aspect, which is not otherwise explained in the argumentation—it may refer to theological tensions.

117. The content (grow up / let oneself be built), the form (imperative), and the function (exhortation) of the two words correspond to each other, depending of course on the interpretation of οἰκοδομεῖσθε.

118. Cf. 4.17 ἀπειθούντων τῷ τοῦ θεοῦ εὐαγγελίῳ, which may also have two different meanings. According to Selwyn (1947: 164), 4.17 does not refer to refusal of intellectual assent.

119. Thus 𝔓[72], ℵ[21] *et al.*, omitted in ℵ*, A, B, C. The longer form is to be preferred, since alliteration is typical of 1 Peter.

2.6   <u>διότι</u> περιέχει ἐν γραφῇ·
       ἰδοὺ τίθημι ἐν Σιὼν λίθον ἀκρογωνιαῖον ἐκλεκτὸν ἔντιμον
       καὶ ὁ πιστεύων ἐπ' αὐτῷ οὐ μὴ καταισχυνθῇ.
2.7   ὑμῖν <u>οὖν</u> ἡ τιμὴ τοῖς πιστεύουσιν,
       ἀπιστοῦσιν δὲ λίθος ὃν ἀπεδοκίμασαν οἱ οἰκοδομοῦντες,
       οὗτος ἐγενήθη εἰς κεφαλὴν γωνίας
2.8   καὶ λίθος προσκόμματος καὶ πέτρα σκανδάλου·
       οἳ προσκόπτουσιν τῷ λόγῳ ἀπειθοῦντες
       εἰς ὃ καὶ ἐτέθησαν.

4-5

The participle προσερχόμενοι in 4 is either (a) a ground for the imperative command,[120] or (b) a further parallel command. We shall start with
alternative (a).[121]

The C stands between two motivating sections 4 and 6-8. The section
consists of many different pictures, which are combined in one,
confused, train of thought.[122] Every thought incorporates a picture of
a stone, which signifies Christ. This motif does not occur as an
independent ground.

The first D is in 4: The addressees are coming to the Living Stone.
Thus they themselves become similar stones (C_1, 5a). An implicit W
must read: he who comes to the Living Stone also becomes such a stone
himself.[123] As a motivational addition we have 4b, which stresses that
the Stone is valuable in God's eyes—thus it is good to be such a
stone.[124] As living stones (D_2) the addressees are to be built up as a

120. The unit includes only one possible imperative, οἰκοδομεῖσθε (5), which in
that case is parallel to ἐπιποθήσατε. But even as an indicative it serves as the C of
the unit.
121. If the words are interpreted as indicatives, the rest of the unit *explains* them in
the same way as the indicatives do in 1.3-12. This does not affect the structure of the
reasoning. We take as a basis for our analysis an interpretation, according to which
οἰκοδομεῖσθε is an imperative and προσερχόμενοι an indicative ground for it,
since other alternatives are only simpler versions of such a structure. The rhetorical
difference between the alternatives is slight (see Thurén 1990: 140-41, 144).
122. First the addressees ought to be built up as a temple, then the temple is
identified with its priests. The priests, which are identical to living stones (note the
technique of *oxymoron*) should then offer spiritual sacrifices. Here the traditional
background can make the picture easier to understand.
123. According to Brox (1979: 97) the expression (as an imperative) means 'Sie
sollen sein was er ist'.
124. So also Kelly 1969: 89. The comparison 'rejected by people' refers to the
forthcoming theme of Christ, who was similarly rejected and elected, as a model for

temple (C₂)—a W might be that a stone is to be built into a temple.[125]

Fig. 2.4-5/a1

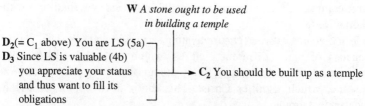

W When one comes to LS one becomes a similar living stone

D_1 You are coming to the Living Stone (4a) — → C_1 You are/become living stones (5a)

The argumentation continues with an emphasis on the value of the Stone (4bc), which is aimed at increasing its appreciation (cf. the corresponding use of the quality-topos in 1.17-21). Since the addressees are presented as similar stones, they should also appreciate their own status.

Fig. 2.4-5/a2

W *A stone ought to be used in building a temple*

D_2 (= C_1 above) You are LS (5a)
D_3 Since LS is valuable (4b)
    you appreciate your status
    and thus want to fill its → C_2 You should be built up as a temple
    obligations

The exhortation is further supported with a *teleological* motivation (5b): 'In order to offer spiritual sacrifices, which are acceptable to God'. In order to be relevant for the addressees, this motivation requires that they already want to do something that is acceptable to God, viz. to offer something to God (the same phenomenon occurs in 2.2b, where a desire to grow up is implied), which can possibly be identified with the praise of God.[126]

---

the addressees. This idea is not yet fully explained.

125. According to Selwyn (1947: 158) λίθος means a worked stone, which is used in a building, in contrast to a πέτρος.

126. According to Kelly (1969: 91) the sacrifice here means thanksgiving, as in Heb. 13.15; Selwyn (1947: 161-62) claims that such a thanksgiving also leads to good conduct and ἀγαθοποιΐα (he connects the sacrifice with eucharistia, which idea is rejected by Best [1971: 104]). Brox (1979: 99) claims that the sacrifice here means directly a good way of life, and Goppelt (1978: 146) combines all these aspects by referring to a 'Hingabe des ganzen Menschen', which means praise, proclamation, mission, martyrdom etc. Goppelt's interpretation may be the most adequate here, since it is typical for the author of 1 Peter to express himself first with obscure, loaded words, which are later explained. A development of the suggested human response from praise to sacrifice, good works, mission, and finally martyrdom can be later discerned. See below.

(b) When the C reads: 'You should become a temple/priests', the factors can be identified as follows:

Fig. 2.4-5/b

W *Priests and temple are required for offering*

D₁ <u>*You want to do something*</u>
    <u>*pleasing to God (praise him)*</u>   C You should become
D₂ Spiritual sacrifices are pleasing to God   a temple/priests

6-8

These verses give an OT ground (connected with διότι) to the preceding reasoning, especially 4b, which was supposed above to explain why the stone-motif is so important, valuable, and thus motivating for the addressees. It explains the preceding short expression,[127] as is typical for the author. Again an antithetic technique is used.

Fig. 2.6-8/1

W *Whoever despises the Stone/disobeys/does not believe etc. will fall*
Dₐ They despise/disobey/disbelieve ——————|——————➤ **Cₐ** They will fall

As an antithesis (D_b), the addressees believe (7a) and thus appreciate the Stone (7b; it is implied that they also obey).

Fig. 2.6-8/2

B God's attitude (according to the Scripture)
|
W *The one who trusts in him will not be put to shame (6c)*
D_b You appreciate/believe/*obey* ——|——➤ **C_b** *You will not be put to shame* (9-10)

Now, to what result do the two C's lead when put together? Especially in view of 9-10, where the other C is amplified, and which is certainly intended to emphasize the value of the addressees' new status (see below), it seems plausible that the other people's destiny functions as a dark background to this new status. Thus, an implied W would read: a negative example adds the appreciation of the positive. Just as presumed in the preceding 4, the C would be that the addressees appreciate their new status as Living Stones/Christians. The whole structure then serves as a subD for D₃ in F 2.4-5/a2 or D₁ in F 2.4-5/b.

Two underlying ideas can be found: First, we find an implicit

---

127. Cf. Brox (1979: 99-100), according to whom 6-8 do not give a ground for 4b but enlarge the idea. However, at least the reference to the OT is motivating by giving authority to the Claim.

warning.[128] The author does not explicitly talk about the Gentiles, but about 'those who do not believe' and 'disobey'. Although not expounded, obedience seems to be a characteristic of the addressees, who believe. If the addressees do not believe and appreciate the Living Stone, and if they *disobey*, they too will fall.[129] Faith and obedience are thus implicitly identical.

Secondly, the Christological picture contains the same idea as 4b. The stone was rejected, but yet, or because of that, it is honoured by God. More clearly than before (1.11; 2.19-21) this anticipates the idea, which is unfolded later: it is only natural, if the addressees, like living stones, meet corresponding trouble, which will however analogously result in glory. This can also be reversed: in order to achieve the same glory they should be ready to resist the same oppression.

h. *2.9-10—Honorary Titles*

2.9 ὑμεῖς δὲ γένος ἐκλεκτόν, βασίλειον ἱεράτευμα, ἔθνος ἅγιον, λαὸς εἰς περιποίησιν
ὅπως τὰς ἀρετὰς ἐξαγγείλητε
τοῦ ἐκ σκότους ὑμᾶς καλέσαντος εἰς τὸ θαυμαστὸν αὐτοῦ φῶς·
2.10 οἵ ποτε οὐ λαός, νῦν δὲ λαὸς θεοῦ,
οἱ οὐκ ἠλεημένοι, νῦν δὲ ἐλεηθέντες.

The first part of the letter closes with praise of the addressees' status as Christians.[130] The comparison with the addressees' old status (9c, 10ac) and the positive description of the new seek to enhance the addressees' appreciation of their new status (9a).[131]

Although the basic function of 9-10 is already clear, we shall take a closer look at the argumentation.

Fig. 2.9-10

D₁ Comparison with old (9c,10ac) ⌐	C *Appreciation of*
D₂ Positive description of the new (9a) ⌐ ⟶	*the new status*

---

128. According to Kamlah (1964: 200) 4-10 is a clear warning for the addressees, but Brox (1979: 102) rightly rejects this interpretation.

129. However, the non-believers are said to be predestined to fall (2.8c), whereas the addressees are predestined to obedience (1.2).

130. Because of the contents 9-10 correspond to the eulogy in 1.3-12 and thus form a rhetorical *inclusio*.

131. For a detailed analysis of the honorary titles, see Elliott 1966; Kelly 1969: 95-99. The idea of the addressees as priests has caused much discussion, which however has nothing to do with the function of the expression in the text.

The short final expression in 2.9 introduces a new motif in the argumentation:[132] a teleological motivation 'that you may declare his ἀρετάς', his great deeds.[133] The goal of the exhortation is not only that the addressees should be holy and steadfast in their faith, but that they should proclaim God's works. Moreover, this explains the corresponding teleological expression in 2.5. Although no explicit and clear explanation is offered in the text, the expression can be analysed in order to see how it is designed to function in the argumentation and persuasion.

In order to be reasonable and effective, the teleological structure requires willingness to reach the goal mentioned; thus willingness to declare the great works of God is presupposed here. The proclamation is however presented as the purpose of God's activity or God's plan, which the addressees are expected to fulfil: the addressees have been called by God to be royal priests (etc.) in order to proclaim.

These ideas correspond to the more clearly indicated willingness to offer to God in 2.5. The development from the liturgical to the missionary/educational function of the priests can be explained with the following implicit structure behind the 2.9-10:

Fig. 2.9-10/2

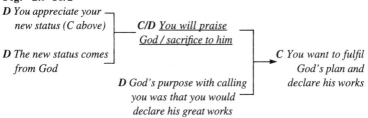

D You appreciate your new status (C above)
D The new status comes from God
C/D You will praise God / sacrifice to him
D God's purpose with calling you was that you would declare his great works
C You want to fulfil God's plan and declare his works

Conclusions

Now a common ideological structure can be sought behind 2.1-10. The section as a whole corresponds to 1.13-25. This unit, too, has a preparatory and motivating role.[134] The addressees are admonished to be ready

---

132. Since this structure is not clearly explained in the text, the new motif cannot be the most visible message of the verses; it is only briefly introduced here. This is typical for the author, especially since 2.9-10 closes a long rhetorical unit and leads to a new one.

133. ἀρετάς used of a god does not signify virtue but manifestations of power (Bauernfeind 1933).

134. For the 'passive' type of addressees it serves a general *argumentatio*, while for the 'active' ones during the first reading it is only a surprisingly long exordium. See Thurén 1990: 145-46.

and willing to live according to the will of God. What this means in practice will be revealed in the next section.[135]

The point of departure is again the addressees' new status, which they (ought to) appreciate because of God's saving activity.[136] This idea is now more clearly expressed. The deliberate use of ambiguous expressions utilizes the status for both motivating and exhorting purposes (see Thurén 1990: 145-46). As a counterpart to the new status there is a negative example, which this time is not so much the addressees' own former life (only in 2.10) as the destiny of the people who continue to live in the old way. Such a life is no longer merely vain, μάταιος (1.18), but bad, κακός (2.1), and the result is characterized as disastrous (2.8; the words πρόσκομμα and σκάνδαλον are used).

The word 'hope' does not recur as an explicit ground in the argumentation, but the idea remains: the addressees, contrary to the non-believers, shall not be put to shame. Together with the honorary titles of Israel this hope is designed to intensify the appreciation of the new life.

How does the appreciation produce willingness to obey the exhortations? The same alternatives for motivating factors as in 1.13-25 are found: [137]

(a) Since God has given the addressees their new status, they want to make spiritual offerings to him. This idea corresponds to the praises in 1.3-12. A new explanation of what form these praises should take is given in 2.9: the addressees shall proclaim the deeds of God.

(b) They want to preserve their new status in order avoid the destiny of the non-believers.

The exhortations to be built into a temple and to grow up into salvation are thus in principle motivated in two ways: either with thankfulness, which can be realized by fulfilling God's plan, according to which his great works should be proclaimed, or with willingness to obtain the final salvation and to avoid the negative destiny. Again the

---

135. Goppelt's statement is correct in principle, but hopelessly static and does not take into account the persuasive and interactive aspect of the text: 'Aus der so im ersten Hauptteil umschriebenen Basis christlicher Existenz werden nun im zweiten Hauptteil Folgerungen für das Verhalten der Christen in den Strukturen der Gesellschaft gezogen' (1978: 154).

136. According to Kelly (1969: 82) the 'broad message' of the unit is to stress the 'surpassingly glorious vocation', which should motivate the addressees 'not to be shattered by their present afflictions'.

137. Even the reference to OT serves a goal similar to 1.16 and 24-25: it should confirm the author's claims.

first alternative is more clearly expressed, especially in 2.9-10.

Fig. 2.1-10/a

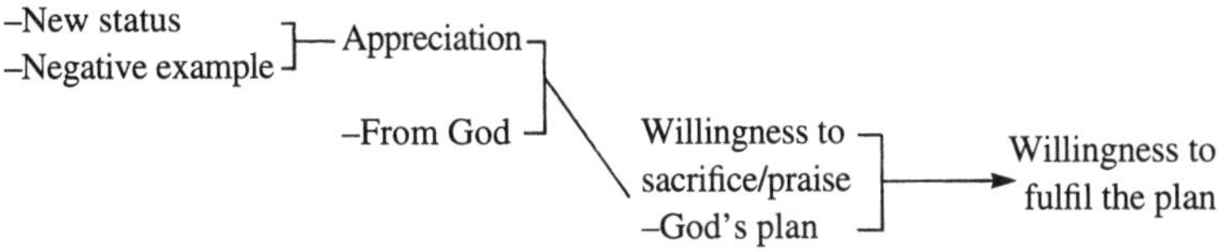

An extra purpose with 2.1-10, which also has occurred before, is to show how important Christ is to the addressees: Through him they have obtained their new status. Christ was rejected by people, but rewarded by God. Since the addressees believe in him, they also are / should be corresponding 'living stones', and similarity to Christ implies a share in his fate. Due to the connection between sufferings and glory the addressees shall not be afraid of them. This chain of thought is implicit in 2.4-8, without being presented clearly yet.

4. *Specific Exhortation 2.11–3.12*[138]

This unit introduces a new tone in the letter. While even the preceding unit was preparatory,[139] 2.11–3.12 is more specific. Instead of admonishing the addressees with polite and ambiguous formulations to grow as Christians and be holy, the author tells them how to do so in practice, thus giving orders which are implied to be more difficult to accept.[140] The unit belongs to the central *argumentatio* of the letter,[141] which also plays a decisive role in the author's rhetorical strategy.[142]

---

138. To call this section a 'household code' is problematic. After two introductory verses (11-12), the author first gives general instruction (13-17), then an exhortation to the slaves (18-20) with a long Christological motivation (21-25), women (3.1-6), men (7) and again to everybody (8-12). Thus e.g. Goppelt (1978: 156-231) and Brox (1979: 111-55). Although a simple exhortation to these groups may not be the only or even main rhetorical function of the unit (see Thurén 1990: 146 n. 55; even Brox 1979: 139-40), this natural division can well serve as a point of departure for our analysis. A stronger dividing line may be set before 3.1.

139. The whole of 1.1–2.10 has been characterized above as a kind of extended exordium.

140. Thurén 1990: 146-47. According to Kelly (1969: 102-103) the unit draws the practical implications of the addressees' changed status.

141. According to Olsson (1982: 120) it is the 'key text of 1 Peter'.

142. The unit is especially important for the 'active' type of implied audience. Their superchristian behaviour is here characterized as 'desires of the flesh', and the

This change in the exhortation lets us assume that the motivation is developing in a corresponding way.

The epistolary level does not yield a more precise division of the unit; it is simply a part of the body middle. The word παρακαλῶ in 2.11 serves, however, as a conventional signal, introducing a central message of the author.[143] Rhetorically the unit seeks not only to persuade, but also to convince the addressees concerning a controversial issue (see Thurén 1990: 104-105, 120).

The First Half 2.11-25
a. *2.11-12—A Loaded Introduction*

2.11   ἀγαπητοί, παρακαλῶ
ὡς παροίκους καὶ παρεπιδήμους
        ἀπέχεσθαι τῶν σαρκικῶν ἐπιθυμιῶν
        αἵτινες στρατεύονται κατὰ τῆς ψυχῆς·
2.12   τὴν ἀναστροφὴν ὑμῶν ἐν τοῖς ἔθνεσιν ἔχοντες καλήν,
        ἵνα ἐν ᾧ καταλαλοῦσιν ὑμῶν ὡς κακοποιῶν
        ἐκ[144] τῶν καλῶν ἔργων ἐποπτεύοντες
        δοξάσωσιν τὸν θεὸν ἐν ἡμέρᾳ ἐπισκοπῆς.

This subunit serves as a transition and introduction to the new unit. There are two exhortations, παρακαλῶ ἀπέχεσθαι... ἐπιθυμιῶν and τὴν ἀναστροφὴν ἐν τοῖς ἔθνεσιν ἔχοντες καλήν. The first, referring to the previous section, still has a general ethical content, but the second is determined more precisely by the words 'among the Gentiles', thus serving as a title to the whole unit.[145] The exhortations are explained by expressions that to some extent have a motivating function:[146] 'you are strangers (ὡς)' and 'desires fight against the soul' (relative, partly causal clause).

---

author attempts to show that only submissive behaviour is a Christian solution even in different situations. See Thurén 1990: 148-50.

143. Bjerkelund 1967: 189. Rhetorically the expression serves as a *propositio* for the 'active' type of audience (Thurén 1990: 148-49).

144. According to Louw and Nida (1988: 89.25) ἐκ marks a reason with focus upon source.

145. According to Goppelt (1978: 159), 'Diese Weisung zieht sich wie ein roter Faden durch die folgende Paränese...'

146. Simultaneously the expressions can be interpreted as exhortation; thus the motivating function is not clear.

2.11

In 11, the exhortation is a C, while the other expressions serve as D's, telling us on which ground the C is based. It is difficult to see any logical contact between the two D's; they express two different entities. Thus we have two different argumentative structures for the Claim.[147] The second D, 'The desires of flesh fight against the soul', is easy to explain.[148]

Fig. 2.11b

B *General religious and philosophical ideas*

W *One should abstain from things which fight against the soul*

D Desires of the flesh fight against the soul   **C** You should abstain from desires of the flesh

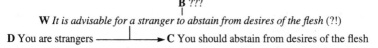

The first D, 'since you are strangers' (for discussion of the interpretation, see Chapter 3 §2.e), is more difficult to connect to the C.[149] This, however, may well be a tactical device: the lack of explanation wakes the interest of the audience and attunes it for the following message.

Fig. 2.11a

B ???

W *It is advisable for a stranger to abstain from desires of the flesh* (?!)

D You are strangers ——————▶ **C** You should abstain from desires of the flesh

2.12

In the following 12 the exhortation 'behave well among the Gentiles' serves as the C. This new motif in the exhortation is motivated with a teleological ἵνα expression: 'so that / in order that they may glorify God

---

147. This phenomenon is not exceptional within argumentation. See e.g. Huth 1975: 99.

148. An implicit W reads 'One should abstain from things which fight against the soul'. Both D and W may refer to a B implied from general religious and philosophical opinions and ideas. Such ideas were common as well in popular philosophy as in Jewish and Christian religion. This interpretation challenges Goppelt (1978: 158 n. 13) and Brox (1979: 112), who claim that the 'fight' here has clear Jewish character. See the Excursus in Chapter 6.

149. A simple W could read, 'It is advisable for a stranger to abstain from desires of the flesh', but before this W can function in the argumentation, a B is needed, which explains how it is relevant. Although some suggestions have been made by the scholars, such a B is not even implied in 11. Even the W sounds strange. Thus the structure of argumentation presented in 2.11 is hardly acceptable.

(on the day he comes)'.[150] As is typical of a teleological motivation, the ground, in order to be persuasive, implies a will to reach the goal (see Chapter 5 §3.h). Thus the D, viz. the statement with which the audience is assumed to agree, is here 'You want the Gentiles to glorify God' and the W which combines the D and C 'If you behave well among the Gentiles, they will glorify God'.

This reasoning is further supported with an explanation, which can be rephrased: 'They accuse you of doing wrong, but when they see your good works, they will praise God'. The theological element may be a deliberate addition,[151] and if it is reduced the expression suggests a common rule: 'People praise or blame others on the basis of their observations', or 'When you do good so that others see it, they will praise you'. This rule not only clarifies the logically implied Warrant presented above, but can replace it as a more accurate W.[152]

Fig. 2.12

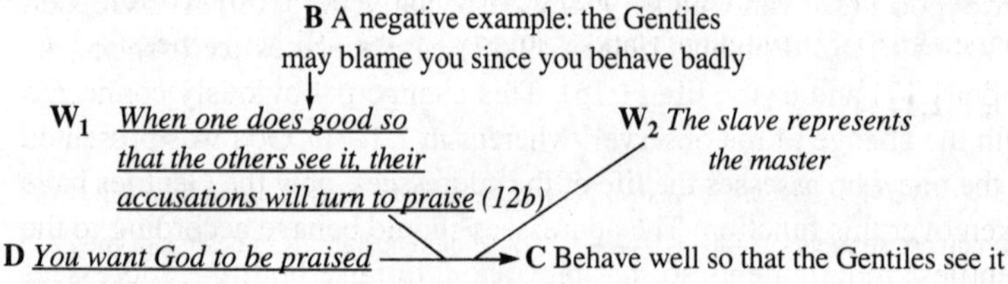

B A negative example: the Gentiles
may blame you since you behave badly

W₁ *When one does good so*
that the others see it, their
accusations will turn to praise (12b)

W₂ *The slave represents*
the master

D *You want God to be praised* ⟶ **C** Behave well so that the Gentiles see it

---

150. This is a close parallel to Mt. 5.16 (there the relation is marked with ὅπως). In 1 Peter the idea is 'awkwardly expressed' (Kelly 1969: 106)—maybe the author puts the clarity of the logical relations before style. About ἵνα see Chapter 3 §3.a.

151. It would be more coherent to say, 'The result of your good behavior is that you will be praised'. Then a theological aspect could be added (thus *T. Naph.* 8.4 according to Selwyn 1947: 171). Kelly even claims that 1 Peter cannot represent a 'bourgeois second generation Christianity', since the theological part appears somewhat abrupt both in 1 Peter and in Mt. 5.16 (Kelly 1947: 107).

152. Again, the grade of explicitness is difficult to assess. Here the use of italics is too rough a means of displaying that grade. The W is backed up (B) with reference to a negative example: The addressees are rebuked for their bad behavior. Thus, analogously, they would be praised for their good behaviour. That the praise surprisingly comes to God can be explained by a further rule (W): 'a slave represents his master' (on the basis of 2.16), or 'a child represents its father' (on the basis of 1.14-17). This is a logical explanation of why the praise is not only aimed at the addressees, as is the blame in 12b, but at God. A W like 'a slave represents his master' implies the following reasoning: The praise or blame is aimed at God (C_1), since you represent him (D_1/C_2). This is true, since you are his slaves (D_2), and a slave represents his master (W between D_2 and C_2).

The compressed nature of the introductory verse 12 is typical in 1 Peter (cf. 1.1–2.13 etc.), thus making the analysis complicated. The ideas can, however, be further clarified.

For our analysis, the clearly implied D[153] is especially important, since it reveals a volitional aspect, which is needed in order to study the persuasive dimension of the argumentation (see e.g. Fig. 2.11a). As stated above, the implicit willingness to ensure that God is praised resembles the explicit praise of God in 1.3-5, and we have seen that the same volitional factor can be assumed as implied in the motivation also in 1.13–2.10, which thus displays or creates motivation for this praise.

An obscure W between willingness to praise and holy life was the missing link in the preceding sections. Now the author explains it. He shows that good life results in more praise for God by affecting the Gentiles.

It is interesting to note that the clearly Hellenistic expression καλὴ ἀναστροφή (see van Unnik 1954/55, especially 107, 109; even Goppelt 1978: 159, 162; Pohlenz 1948: 119-23) here replaces ἀναστροφή ἐν φόβῳ 1.17) and ἅγιος life (1.16). This change is obviously connected with the change of the observer: whereas in 1.14-17 God was presented as the one who assesses the life of the addressees, now the Gentiles have taken over this function. The addressees should behave according to the Gentiles' requirements so that *they* should praise both the addressees and their Lord when he comes. The Gentiles are thus no longer depicted as a dark background to the addressees' positive status,[154] but as judges of the addressees' behaviour (and even as target of some kind of 'missionary'[155] activity).[156]

---

153. In the sentence: 'Behave well in front of the Gentiles in order that they will praise God' (12b) the only logically possible D is, as claimed above, 'You want the Gentiles to praise God' or more simply 'You want God to be praised'.

154. Against Brown, who claims that the Gentiles have only a negative role in 1 Peter (1985: 83).

155. Here the author only speaks of the day of Visitation, but the same idea is later modified and explained e.g. in 3.1, where the women shall change the minds of their husbands by proper behaviour. Brox (1979: 113 n. 373) calls this a missionary tendency. According to Kelly (1969: 106) the Gentiles are supposed to be converted to the same faith, whereas Goppelt (1978: 161) assesses the expression as ambivalent.

156. Brox (1979: 113-14) sees here 'eigentümliche Dialektik' in the argumentation of 1 Peter.

11-12

The fact that verses 11 and 12 are grammatically connected may signify also a deeper contact between them. At least one such aspect is the philosophical background of both the ethical ideas, the fight between the soul and 'the desires of the flesh', and καλὴ ἀναστροφή (see the Excursus). A life dominated by the desires of the flesh violates the high ethical norms of the Gentiles. There may also be a contact between the picture of the addressees as strangers and the presentation of the Gentiles as observing their behaviour: according to a natural W the neighbourhood watches strangers especially carefully.[157] This enhances the validity of the whole argumentation in 11-12 (serving thus as the missing B in 11a), since it shows how the addressees' behaviour can affect the Gentiles.

Fig. 2.11-12

W *People watch strangers carefully*

D You are (like) strangers ——⊥——▶ **C** (= **B** in Fig. 2.11a) Gentiles observe your
behaviour and praise or blame depending on it

b. *2.13-17—Basic Obedience*

2.13 ὑποτάγητε πάσῃ ἀνθρωπίνῃ κτίσει
  διὰ τὸν κύριον,
2.14 εἴτε βασιλεῖ ὡς ὑπερέχοντι,
  εἴτε ἡγεμόσιν ὡς δι' αὐτοῦ πεμπομένοις
  εἰς ἐκδίκησιν κακοποιῶν ἔπαινον δὲ ἀγαθοποιῶν·
2.15 ὅτι οὕτως ἐστὶν τὸ θέλημα τοῦ θεοῦ
  ἀγαθοποιοῦντας φιμοῦν τὴν τῶν ἀφρόνων ἀνθρώπων ἀγνωσίαν,
2.16 ὡς ἐλεύθεροι
  καὶ μὴ ὡς ἐπικάλυμμα ἔχοντες τῆς κακίας τὴν ἐλευθερίαν
  ἀλλ' ὡς θεοῦ δοῦλοι.
2.17 πάντας τιμήσατε, τὴν ἀδελφότητα ἀγαπᾶτε, τὸν θεὸν
  φοβεῖσθε, τὸν βασιλέα τιμᾶτε.

The unit is aimed both at specific groups and at every addressee by using them as examples of the Christians' situation in the society.[158] It

157. Cf. Neighborhood Watch Areas, which are common in some cities in the USA and the UK. This W builds neither on a spiritualized interpretation nor on a historical reconstruction of the addressees' social status (Elliott 1981), but focuses on the character of a stranger as such. See Thurén 1990: 147-48.

158. See Thurén 1990: 120. It hardly formulates any theory about the relation between Christianity and state (against Goppelt 1978: 179-89), but is intended to admonish and persuade. Cf. also Olsson 1982: 118.

consists of five imperatival commands: 'Submit yourselves to every human authority' (13a), and four more precise exhortations: 'Give due honour to everyone: love to the brethren, fear to God, honour to the king' (17). These commands do not include anything particularly Christian,[159] and thus may well reflect the contemporary ethics in the society[160] (maybe one exception is the Christian ἀγάπη in 17).[161] The exhortation in 17 goes well with the command in 13 and can be seen as motivated with the same expressions as ὑποτάγητε in 13. If the addressees live according to these rules, they will not cause any offence to those around them.[162]

The admonition is motivated in three ways. (1) punctual reasoning after each application, which is connected only to that specific command.[163] (2) The will of God (13.15), which in 15 is combined with a unequivocal GC relation to the admonition in 13-14 and thus functions as a D for it. (3) The addressees' status in 16, which explains 15.

(1) The punctual structures are both theological and non-theological:[164]

---

159. E.g. 'fear of God' can in this context be a normal Hellenistic idea. Cf. Strobel 1956: 83-84; Goppelt 1978: 180, 188. Here φοβέομαι means reverence, being parallel to τιμάω (cf. 1.17).

160. Although a 'household code' as a form cannot be found in ancient literature. Dijkman (1986: 264-66) argues that 2.15 has a clear Jewish origin. See also van Unnik (1954/55: 108-109) and the Excursus in Chapter 6.

161. Pohlenz 1948: 406. See also Goppelt (1978: 188), who states that the paraenetic tradition here comes from both Christian and Hellenistic sources. He also refers to Mk 12.13-17; Rom. 13.7 (1978: 181).

162. Thus Balch 1986: 81. For discussion, see Thurén 1990: 36-38. Thereby 2.13-17 shows how the principle in 2.12 can be executed. See Snyder 1991: 213-14.

163. E.g. 'Give honour to the king, since he has the supreme authority'. From the persuasive perspective these grounds are weak, since the motivating factor of the implied W (in this case: He who has the supreme authority shall be honored) remains unclear.

164. 13a is a title for the unit, which the other commands explain. The motivation is double-sided. On the one hand κύριος simply means the king or emperor (cf. Deissmann 1923: 299-304)—according to 2.14a submissiveness to authorities like governors actually means submission to the king, since they represent him. Thus 2.14a serves as a Backing to 2.13a. However, κύριος can also mean Christ (Goppelt 1978: 183 n. 19) or God (Kelly 1969: 109).

Fig. 2.13a

                    B The governors are to be obeyed
                       since they are sent by the king
                    |
                W *Submissiveness to all human authority*
                    means submissiveness to the κύριος
                             |
D The will of the κύριος ————————▶ **C** Be submissive to all human authority

Fig. 2.13b

                W *One who has supreme authority is to be honoured*
D The king has the supreme authority ————————▶ **C** Submit yourselves to him

Fig. 2.14

            W *One should be submissive to the representative of the king*
D The governors are sent by the king ————————▶ **C** Submit yourselves to them

(2) The weightiest motivation is in 15.

Fig. 2.15

                    W *Submissive behaviour silences insults*
D God insists that the ignorant |
    individuals' insults are inhibited ————————▶ **C** You shall submit yourselves

The addressees ought to submit themselves to every human authority
(13a = C), since God wants the ignorant Gentiles' ἀγνωσία[165] to be
silenced (15) (D). What is this ἀγνωσία of the Gentiles and how can
submissive behaviour silence it? Obviously the word refers to talk, since
it can be silenced. Only three verses earlier the addressees were told to
silence the καταλαλία of the Gentiles. The two words probably have
the same meaning. In order to stop καταλαλία the addressees should
live well. We may thus assume that submissive behaviour, which is the
means of silencing ἀγνωσία, shows what the good life in the introduction (12) means in practice. Moreover the implied W between D and G
is similar to the earlier W (Fig. 2.12), but due to a different D is
expressed in negative terms: if one is submissive, the others' insults will
be silenced.

   In 14 the governors' principle to punish the bad and reward the good
serves as a B to the W above. From this general policy we can deduce a
more precise rule: people speak good of one who does good and they

---

165. The choice of word is here prompted by a stylistic reason, *alliteration* (see
Bühlmann and Scherer 1973: 16-17): ἀγαθοποιοῦντας...ἀφρόνων ἀνθρώπων
ἀγνωσίαν. Cf. the D in Fig. 2.15.

speak ill of one who does ill. This replaces the W above, whereas the governors' principle serves as a B.

When asking for the motivating aspect in this argumentation, the main question is: how is the reference to the will of God expected to oblige the addressees? In order to be relevant, the use of God's will implies that the addressees already want to obey God. In 16 the addressees' status as slaves of God serves as a D for such a will (C), and we can assume a W: A slave obeys his or her master. But why do the addressees want to be God's slaves? An answer may be found in 16a: as God's slaves the addressees are free. This positive status refers to the first part of the letter. Thus an ideological structure in the text can be described as follows:

Fig. 2.13-16/a

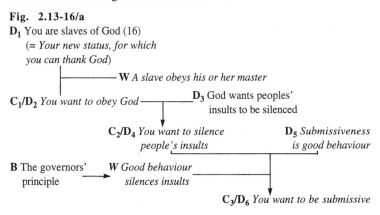

D_1 You are slaves of God (16)
(= *Your new status, for which you can thank God*)

W *A slave obeys his or her master*

C_1/D_2 *You want to obey God* — D_3 God wants peoples' insults to be silenced

C_2/D_4 *You want to silence people's insults* D_5 *Submissiveness is good behaviour*

B The governors' principle → **W** *Good behaviour silences insults*

C_3/D_6 *You want to be submissive*

The train of thought resembles 12: silencing the ignorant people's insults is the negative side of evoking the praise in 12. When these two goals are put together, they form a cohesive train of thought: God wants the Gentiles not to insult but to praise. Due to the ambiguity of the text, both the present addressees and God on the day he comes can be the aim of the praise, since according to 4.4 both are insulted by the Gentiles.

The motivation in 13-16 can however be interpreted in a totally opposite way.[166] The heart of this type of persuasion can be described as follows:

166. The motivation starts from the 'negative' interpretation of the motivating factor in 1.13–2.10, according to which the willingness to obey God comes from fear of losing the new status, or even a wish finally to be rewarded and avoid sanctions. Since the governors punish the bad and reward the good, and since God as an impartial judge is similar, the addressees should behave well in the eyes of both authorities.

F 2.13-16/b

B Statements of governors (and God)

W Good works will be rewarded, bad works punished (14)[167]

D_1 *You want to avoid punishment and be rewarded*

D_2 God wants you to do good and be submissive (12, 13, 15)

C You shall do good and be submissive

This alternative is modified by the fact that the addressees are not coerced as being submissive, but described to be free (16, cf. the function of the children in 1.17). However, 16b stresses that the freedom cannot or shall not be misused.

c. 2.18-20—Petitio Principii

2.18   οἱ οἰκέται, ὑποτασσόμενοι ἐν παντὶ φόβῳ τοῖς δεσπόταις,
        οὐ μόνον τοῖς ἀγαθοῖς καὶ ἐπιεικέσιν ἀλλὰ καὶ
        τοῖς σκολιοῖς.

2.19   τοῦτο γὰρ χάρις
        εἰ διὰ συνείδησιν θεοῦ ὑποφέρει τις λύπας πάσχων ἀδίκως.

2.20   ποῖον γὰρ κλέος
        εἰ ἁμαρτάνοντες καὶ κολαφιζόμενοι ὑπομενεῖτε;
        ἀλλ' εἰ ἀγαθοποιοῦντες καὶ πάσχοντες ὑπομενεῖτε,
        τοῦτο χάρις παρὰ θεῷ.

According to Olsson, 2.18-25 is the heaviest part of the whole letter, revealing its 'theological logic'.[168] Formally the unit is aimed at slaves, but the slaves simultaneously function rhetorically as an example of every addressee's situation in the society or most of the addressees' position in the congregation.[169] The command is motivated with four γάρ expressions[170] and with one ὅτι clause. The train of thought can be divided into two parts: 18-20 and its Christological argumentation in 21-25.

---

167. Thus Brox (1979: 120).

168. Olsson 1982: 120. Brox (1979: 129) calls it a theological 'Schlüsselstext'. A similar motivation is repeated in a slightly modified form in 3.13-14, 17 and 4.14-16.

169. Olsson 1982: 20; Brox 1979: 128; Thurén 1990: 120. Against Elliott, according to whom '... the reference to slaves but omission of a reciprocal exhortation to owners in 2:18-20 seems to point to a generally inferior economic position of the addressees...' (1981: 79). Thus also Kelly 1969: 114.

170. An argumentation introduced with γάρ occurs here for the first time in 1 Peter.

In the exhortation of 1 Peter a clear development can be found. Now it again moves one step in a more specific and controversial direction. The addressees shall not only do good or be submissive, but be submissive even to unjust masters (18a). Despite this command, the author does not speak of submissiveness but unjust suffering (19c, 20) in the following argumentation.

The only way to see any contact between the explicit D (unjust suffering) and C (submission) is to assume that the author here identifies these two concepts:

Fig. 2.18-19

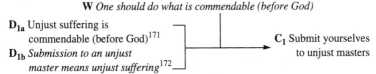

W *One should do what is commendable (before God)*

D_{1a} Unjust suffering is
   commendable (before God)[171]
D_{1b} *Submission to an unjust
   master means unjust suffering*[172]

C_1 Submit yourselves
   to unjust masters

In the chain of reasoning 20 functions as a D for 19 (connected again with γάρ). If the technique of a *rhetorical question* is resolved, it yields the following D:

Fig. 2.19-20

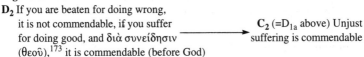

D_2 If you are beaten for doing wrong,
   it is not commendable, if you suffer
   for doing good, and διὰ συνείδησιν
   (θεοῦ),[173] it is commendable (before God)

C_2 (=D_{1a} above) Unjust
   suffering is commendable

Here the D partly refers to an example and to common sense, but also uses the questionable but effective persuasive technique of repetition, since a W is not needed. Actually, 20 resembles a rule, and should therefore be a W, not a D. Thus the D is missing. In formal logic this case means a fallacy, a *petitio principii*.[174] As such the expression can be

171. This is 19 in short form. χάρις may mean a (Pauline) grace (thus Brox 1979: 133-34), but as a parallel to κλέος it rather signifies something commendable; thus Kelly (1969: 116) translates it 'fine thing'.

172. An alternative would be that the author changes the topic without any explanation, and the argumentation remains meaningless.

173. The expression is ambiguous. According to a simple interpretation it means 'for conscience sake (before God)'. More precise and theological interpretations (e.g. those rejected by Kelly 1969: 117) have no actual support in the text. See Selwyn 1947: 176-77; Goppelt 1978: 195-96.

174. Toulmin *et al.* (1984: 135-37) assesses this technique as not fatal by itself, but says that the actual Grounds [= Data] are missing. Perelman (1969: 112-13) is

traced back to a general Hellenistic idea 'Better to suffer as not guilty than as guilty'.[175] It is striking to notice how the argumentation appeals to reason. The theological elements (διὰ συνείδησιν) θεοῦ (19)...παρὰ θεῷ (20) could well be deduced.[176] Yet the word θεός first gives the expression new content thus making it a proper D.

On the ideological level the train of thought can be described in the following way: Obedience to the command 'submit yourself even to unjust masters' means that the addressees have to suffer, although without cause. In order to motivate this, the author refers both to a philosophical maxim and to the will of God. The elements support each other.

d. 2.21-25—The Intention of Christ

2.21 εἰς τοῦτο γὰρ ἐκλήθητε,
      ὅτι καὶ Χριστὸς ἔπαθεν ὑπὲρ ὑμῶν ὑμῖν ὑπολιμπάνων ὑπογραμμὸν
      ἵνα ἐπακολουθήσητε τοῖς ἴχνεσιν αὐτοῦ,

2.22 ὃς ἁμαρτίαν οὐκ ἐποίησεν οὐδὲ εὑρέθη δόλος ἐν τῳ στόματι αὐτοῦ,

2.23 ὃς λοιδορούμενος οὐκ ἀντελοιδόρει, πάσχων οὐκ ἠπείλει,
      παρεδίδου δὲ τῷ κρίνοντι δικαίως·

2.24 ὃς τὰς ἁμαρτίας ἡμῶν αὐτὸς ἀνήνεγκεν ἐν τῷ σώματι αὐτοῦ ἐπι' τὸ
      ξύλον,
      ἵνα ταῖς ἁμαρτίαις ἀπογενόμενοι τῇ δικαιοσύνη ζήσωμεν,
      οὗ τῷ μώλωπι ἰάθητε.

2.25 ἦτε γὰρ ὡς πρόβατα πλανώμενοι,
      ἀλλά ἐπεστράφητε νῦν ἐπὶ τὸν ποιμένα καὶ ἐπίσκοπον τῶν ψυχῶν
      ὑμῶν.

The preceding step in the development of the exhortation, a call for submissiveness, presupposed among other things a will to avoid suffering (cf. the use of the governors' principle to punish and reward as motivation). Since, however, the author now admonishes his readers to submit themselves even if this involves unjust suffering, a reference to a general maxim or to the will of God is not enough in order to persuade them, but a stronger and more thorough motivation is required. This is done with a long Christological section 2.21-25, which functions at least

misleading when calling this technique an error of rhetoric. Although poor reasoning, as rhetoric it is good and persuasive (cf. Alexandrova 1987: 270-71).

175. Cf. Goppelt 1978: 196-97. An implicit exhortation can also be discerned: You should not suffer as guilty of any offence. This is explicitly stated in 2.18.

176. According to Brox, the author here uses an idea of popular philosophy, to which he then adds some words in order to suite it to his own purposes (1979: 134).

as a general motivation to the author's message.[177]

Formally the unit explains the C in 20c '[unjust suffering] is commendable before God'.[178] The D refers to God's intention, as in 12 and 15. For the first time the purpose of the salvation is revealed. We start with this connection:

20-21a

Fig. 2.20-21a/a

      W *What serves a person's purpose is seen as commendable by them*

D It was for this that you were called (by God) ⌐►C It is commendable before God

If, however, the unit is seen as a direct D for the command to be ready for unjust suffering, the W could be 'One should fulfil God's intention'. 21a also serves as a basic C inside the unit.

Fig. 2.18-21a/b

         W *One should fulfil God's intention*

D God's intention ──────────────► C Be ready for unjust suffering

18-25

In 21bc the idea 'Christ suffered for you (and saved you) in order that you may follow in his footsteps' is a D for the C in 21a 'You were called for that reason', viz. for readiness for submissiveness and unjust suffering (τοῦτο refers to 18 and partly to 19-20). 22-24a explains what these footsteps are. Thus we have a continuous chain of thought: [179]

---

177. It is difficult to decide the role of 19-21a (signaled with γάρ) and 21b-25 (ὅτι). Are they parallel motivating expressions (both in a GC relation to the command), or does the latter support the former (a GC + an RR relation)? In both cases they serve the motivation even independently.

178. Kelly (1969: 118) argues that the purpose of baptism is also meant.

179. 21b-25 consists of the following four elements:

    21b   Christ also suffered, and he suffered for you. Repeated in 24c, with addition 'by doing so he healed you', whereas 21b continues 'by doing so he gave you an example'.

    21c   His purpose thereby was that you should follow in his footsteps. Repeated in 24b, where Christ's footsteps are identified with ceasing from sin and living for righteousness.

    22-24a Description of Christ's footsteps, which corresponds to the exhortation in 18 (and 19-20).

    25   Reference to the addressees' old and new status as a ground for the first element.

Ia Christ suffered for you and saved you   Ib Christ's example means
    in order that you may follow   submissiveness and
    his example (21b, 24cb)   unjust suffering (22-24a)

II You were called in order that you may be submissive and ready for unjust
    suffering (21a)

III Submissiveness / Unjust suffering is commendable before God (19-20)

IV You should be submissive even to unjust masters (which indicates readiness
    for unjust suffering) (18, the main C in 18-25)

The behaviour of Christ serves as an example (for the function of an
example, see the analysis of 1.7):

Fig. 2.18-25/1

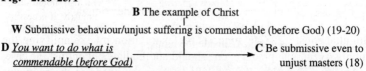

B The example of Christ

W Submissive behaviour/unjust suffering is commendable (before God) (19-20)

D *You want to do what is*   **C** Be submissive even to
    commendable (before God)   unjust masters (18)

Next we shall search for the ideological structure in order to find the
motivating factor(s). To use the intention of God and the purpose of
Christ's saving act in persuasion indicates that the author attributes to
them an obligating power of them over the addressees; otherwise their
use would remain irrelevant. The grounds for such a power are briefly
mentioned in 21b (ὑπὲρ ὑμῶν and in 24c-25, which emphasize the
saving function of Christ's suffering. They correspond to 2.10 and 1.18
by referring to the old and new status, and show why the D above
ought to be important to the addressees: since the act of Christ changed
their status from negative to positive, they want to fulfil his intention
and be ready to follow his example. Thus 24c-25 repeat the basic
structure of creating motivation, which we have met earlier. We obtain
the following ideological structure:

Fig. 2.18-25/2

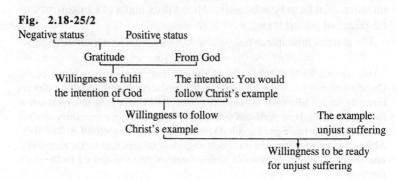

Negative status   Positive status

         Gratitude   From God

Willingness to fulfil   The intention: You would
the intention of God   follow Christ's example

         Willingness to follow   The example:
         Christ's example   unjust suffering

                              Willingness to be ready
                              for unjust suffering

Here the 'positive' motivating factor is superior. The good works of Christ toward the addressees are supposed to create in them willingness to obey him. What will happen if they do not follow God's plan or Christ is not discussed.

The example of Christ can also have other independent functions, such as emphasizing solidarity. Further, the addressees are shown that it was the very submissiveness and unjust suffering of Christ that yielded their salvation. By this is implied that unjust suffering will produce a good result also in the case of the addressees.[180]

Fig. 2.18-25/3

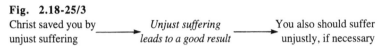

| Christ saved you by unjust suffering | → | *Unjust suffering leads to a good result* | → | You also should suffer unjustly, if necessary |

Simultaneously 22-24b supports the exhortation by exemplifying the submissiveness in practice: one should not retaliate but entrust the case, and vindication (thus Kelly 1969: 121), to the hands of the righteous judge. This briefly mentioned theme will be explained later, in 3.9-12.

Conclusions
The exhortation in this unit becomes more precise and harder for the addressees to accept. They are no more told only to be ready, holy or submissive, but even submissive to unjust masters and ready for unjust suffering. A similar development from general to deeper and more specific can be distinguished in the argumentation and motivation.

The argumentation in the unit builds on the preceding basic structure, by which the author attempted to intensify the addressees' appreciation of their new status and modify that appreciation to willingness to obey God/Christ by emphasizing their role in the salvation. Now he tries to show that the salvation by God obligates the addressees to fulfil God's intention, that is, to be submissive. Here the example of Christ serves as the principal ground.

The general principle is also specified by a distinctive train of thought.

180. Against Kelly (1969: 199), who argues that 'the vicarious nature of the Christ's suffering is... strictly irrelevant to the conduct of slaves', and that it appears here only since it belongs to the sentence quoted. As we have seen, no expression in the text has so far been irrelevant to the topic. Incidentally, the imaginary original form of the unit has caused much discussion (see e.g. Goppelt 1978: 204-207). Although knowledge about the traditional origin may be important for the addressees' assessment of the unit, the possible hymnic form has little significance for the unit's function.

In 1.1-12 the addressees were presented as (and, rhetorically, persuaded to be—see above Chapter 5 §1) rejoicing and praising God because of the salvation. Now the author shows how God can receive more praise in practice: if the addressees live in a way that is respected by the Gentiles, these will stop insulting and instead praise God one day. Thereby the addressees' right behaviour leads to the result that they themselves desire: God will be praised. This is presented as the intention and purpose of God and Christ.

Another specific feature is that the author motivates his commands not only on theological grounds, but also by appealing to common sense and to ideas familiar in the popular philosophy.

The Second Half 3.1-12
e. 3.1-6—Feminist Theology

3.1   ὁμοίως αἱ γυναῖκες, ὑποτασσόμεναι τοῖς ἰδίοις ἀνδράσιν,
         ἵνα καὶ εἴ τινες ἀπειθοῦσιν τῷ λόγῳ,
         διὰ τῆς τῶν γυναικῶν ἀναστροφῆς ἄνευ λόγου
         κερδηθήσονται,
3.2   ἐποπτεύσαντες τὴν ἐν φόβῳ ἀναστροφὴν ὑμῶν.
3.3   ὧν ἔστω οὐχ ὁ ἔξωθεν
         ἐμπλοκῆς τριχῶν καὶ περιθέσεως χρυσίων ἢ ἐνδύσεως
         ἱματίων κόσμος
3.4   ἀλλ' ὁ κρυπτὸς τῆς καρδίας ἄνθρωπος
         ἐν τῷ ἀφθάρτῳ τοῦ πραέως καὶ ἡσυχίου πνεύματος,
         ὅ ἐστιν ἐνώπιον τοῦ θεοῦ πολυτελές.
3.5   οὕτως γάρ ποτε καὶ αἱ ἅγιαι γυναῖκες αἱ ἐλπίζουσαι εἰς θεὸν
         ἐκόσμουν ἑαυτὰς ὑποτασσόμεναι τοῖς ἰδίοις ἀνδράσιν,
3.6   ὡς Σάρρα ὑπήκουσεν τῷ Ἀβραὰμ κύριον αὐτὸν καλοῦσα
         ἧς ἐγενήθητε τέκνα
         ἀγαθοποιοῦσαι
         καὶ μὴ φοβούμεναι μηδεμίαν πτόησιν.

Formally the unit exhorts only women, but it also illuminates the situation of all the addressees in the society.[181] The word ὁμοίως in the beginning signifies that the unit is a parallel to the preceding unit; thus we can expect corresponding commands and motivation (cf. Selwyn 1947: 182).

The unit consists of two commands ὑποτασσόμεναι τοῖς ἰδίοις

---

181. Cf. Thurén 1990: 120. According to Brox (1979: 142) the author here utilizes ethical tradition for his own purposes (cf. the use of 'imperative participles', Thurén 1990: 176).

ἀνδράσιν (1) and ὧν ἔστω οὐχ ὁ ἔξωθεν...ἀλλ᾽ ὁ κρυπτός (3-4). They are motivated with a teleological motivation in 1b-2, and with a short expression in 4c. A longer example of the holy women, especially Sarah (5-6), is presented as an additional ground.

1-2

The use of a teleological argument in persuasion (3.1b-2) presupposes assent to the goal presented. Thus, the verses can be traced back to the following, possibly non-theological,[182] structure:

Fig. 3.1-2[183]

> W *A person can be won with submissive behaviour*
> *even when they do not listen to anything you say*

D <u>You want that your husband will be won</u> ——————▶ **C** You ought to be submissive

A new factor here is the contrast between words, which have proven to be an ineffective means of persuasion (ἀπειθοῦσιν), and behaviour.

3-4

The command in 3.3 explicates the preceding one:

Fig. 3.3-4

> W *One should do what is good (before God)*

D Inner beauty is valuable before God ⌐
                                    ├———▶ **C** Your beauty should be inner...
D *The inner is better than the outer*[184] ⌐

182. The meaning of τῷ λόγῳ is ambiguous. As such it indicates the gospel or God's will, but the counterpart ἄνευ λόγου refers to normal speech, so that the structure of thought functions also as a general example. In that sense it resembles 2.20, which also indicates that the argument is not only religious but contains a more general core. Women can win their husbands by submissive behaviour when the latter do not listen to them (W).

183. The structure of the unit resembles the argumentation in 2.11-25: The command (Claim) to be submissive is connected to a teleological argument, which also enlarges on the contents of the command. This time submissiveness is not identified with suffering but with life in purity and reverence (2) and ἀγαθοποιΐα (6) (cf. Goppelt 1978: 220), which are further exemplified in 3-4. To obey the rule is similarly said to be commendable (this time not χάρις but πολυτελές) before God. The W resembles the implied W in 2.12 'When you do good and the others see it, they begin to praise (you/God)'.

184. We have seen that the author is wont to use theological grounds only as parallels to reasons which have a more general nature. This is the case here too: the idea, according to which the inner is more valuable than the outer, is a familiar Hellenistic

5-6

The main D, according to which submissiveness is of great value before God, is also supported with an example (5-6), the content of which is strikingly feminist.[185] This simply indicates how carefully the author aims his message at different addressees (cf. Thurén 1990: 167-70).

Fig. 3.5-6/1

D_1 The example[186] of Sarah
|
C_2/D_2 Holy women made themselves beautiful by being submissive
|——— **W** *God appreciates the behaviour of holy people*
C_2 To make oneself beautiful by being submissive is valuable before God

The example of Sarah can also be seen as an independent persuading unit.[187]

Fig. 3.5-6/2

D_1 You have become children of Sarah
|——— **W** *Daughters want to be like their mother*
C_1/D_{2a} *You want to follow her example* D_{2b} Sarah was submissive to her husband
                        |
           C_3 You should be submissive to your husband

---

maxim. See the Excursus in Chapter 6; Pohlenz 1948: 421; and Selwyn 1947: 434. For the custom of criticizing women's ornament, see Kelly 1969: 129.

185. Instead of Christ and his behaviour, the model for women is Sarah, and the salvation is similarly modified: the women have become children of Sarah. When to this is added that the unit advises the women how to change their husbands' mind, we can state that 1 Peter here shows feminist theology. However, to search for support for or against a patriarchal view of the society behind this unit is off the mark. As Brox (almost) rightly notes, the women's example, Sarah in v. 9 (sic!), is not presented as changing something (Brox 1979: 144 and Olsson 1982: 120; against Goppelt 1976: 503, who claims that women are here urged to change their status). Applegate's (1992: 603-604) interpretation of 3.1-6 is, in turn, unnecessarily antifeminist. The reason for the change of argument is primarily rhetorical, not ideological. However, for the tension between the two, see below, the final conclusions.

186. This time the example does not function as a Backing, since C_2 is not a Warrant, but a D.

187. For the addressees it is suggested to become obligating because of the change in their status: they have become (a reference to baptism according to Kelly 1969: 131) her children (or daughters). The basic structure of argumentation resembles that of 1.14 (children of obedience). Kelly assesses the sentence in a misleading way: 'The writer...collects his thoughts together'. The sentence is by no means a conclusion of the unit but a subD which exemplifies the D about holy women.

The implicit W is important for describing the motivating force. How does the status as Sarah's children imply willingness to live as she did? There are two possibilities: (a) the positive effect of the status and its merits—to which 6d refers: 'you do not fear anything';[188] (b) strive after maintaining[189] the status—thus 6c ἀγαθοποιοῦσαι can be interpreted as a condition.[190]

f. 3.7—Reasonable Men

3.7   οἱ ἄνδρες ὁμοίως, συνοικοῦντες
<u>κατὰ</u> γνῶσιν
<u>ὡς</u> ἀσθενεστέρῳ σκεύει
τῷ γυναικείῳ ἀπονέμοντες τιμὴν
<u>ὡς</u> καὶ συγκληρονόμοις χάριτος ζωῆς
<u>εἰς τὸ</u> μὴ ἐγκόπτεσθαι τὰς προσευχὰς ὑμῶν.

The unit consists of a Claim,[191] according to which the husbands ought to be considerate to their wives.[192] Beside exhorting actual husbands, the command may illustrate the other aspect of the main exhortation:[193] the addressees should not act aggressively even if this is possible; they shall not seek vengeance.

Three types of ground are presented: (a) common sense (κατὰ γνῶσιν, the female weakness),[194] (b) theological expressions (as heirs

188. The expression can of course be interpreted the other way round: 'As her children, you must not fear anything'.

189. Goppelt (1978: 219 n. 49) notices that ἀγαθοποιοῦσαι (present tense) does not indicate that the aorist ἐγενήθητε should also be interpreted as a present form.

190. Thus Kelly 1969: 131. The word φόβος clearly has here two meanings: The wives ought to live in φόβος (2) by not being φοβούμεναι (6). It hardly presents here a clear motivating factor (cf. 1.17).

191. συνοικοῦντες is here a typical 'imperative participle', see Thurén 1990: 12.

192. Or: in the similar way, viz. like every Christian in the society, the husbands should be considerate (so Goppelt 1978: 221). According to Selwyn (1947: 186), the expression possibly has two meanings.

193. It is indicative that Brox (1947: 147) does not recognize the admonition to men as an example, but assesses it as a deviation from the theme 'submissiveness'. This is due to negligence of the bipolar rhetorical situation in the letter with 'active' and 'passive' types of implied addressees. It is not possible to reconstruct here the author's attitude to sexuality, as Kelly (1969: 133-34) does.

194. According to Brox γνῶσις means 'ganz simpel die Einsicht in das Richtige und Gute' (1979: 147). The expression can be interpreted in two ways. As a non-religious expression κατὰ γνῶσιν refers to a general custom: 'Since you are reasonable'. The husbands should take account of the natural weakness of women.

with you of the grace of life, γνῶσις as a Christian concept),[195] and (c) a teleological motivation: 'in order that your prayers may not be hindered'. Ground (a) is simple:

Fig. 3.7a

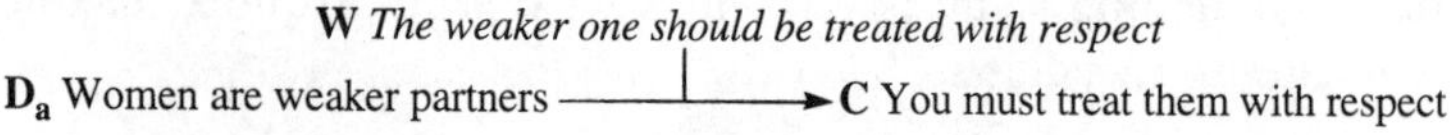

W *The weaker one should be treated with respect*

D_a Women are weaker partners ──────┴──────► C You must treat them with respect

Grounds (b) and (c) form together a teleological motivation:[196]

Fig. 3.7b

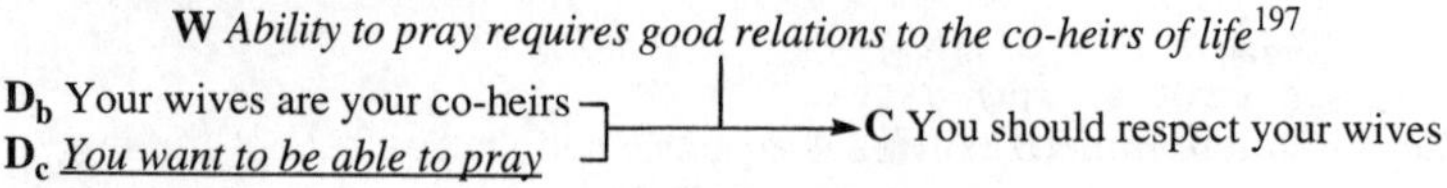

W *Ability to pray requires good relations to the co-heirs of life*[197]

D_b Your wives are your co-heirs ┐───────┴──────►C You should respect your wives
D_c *You want to be able to pray* ┘

A motivating factor, willingness to pray, is here taken for granted,[198] but can be aroused in the two ways that have been discussed earlier (see Chapter 5 §3, the first half, conclusions). The 'negative' interpretation again becomes possible. It is also imaginable that the MP relation is so weak here that the εἰς τό expression is to be seen as a consecutive clause and the analysis is an overinterpretation.[199]

g. *3.8-12 Crux Interpretum*

3.8   τὸ δὲ τέλος πάντες
            ὁμόφρονες, συμπαθεῖς, φιλάδελφοι, εὔσπλαγχνοι,
            ταπεινόφρονες,

---

195. If γνῶσις is here a Christian concept, it refers to the addressees' faith and love (so Goppelt 1978: 221).

196. If interpreted as being in a MP relation to the command, 7c implies a wish to be able to pray (D_a) (see Chapter 3 §3.b.). Another ground (D_b, 7b) is that the wives are co-heirs of the grace (Brox 1979: 148 sees this as a specifically Christian expression). Then a logical Warrant would be: Ability to pray requires good behaviour toward a co-heir of the grace.

197. According to Brox (1979: 149), behaviour which violates the presented obligations is a sin and therefore makes the prayers ineffective. Thus the expression becomes a warning.

198. The short text gives only a clue to the idea behind it. One possibility is that the husbands also are heirs—to this refers also the Christian interpretation of κατὰ γνῶσιν—and a heir will have good relations to the one from whom the inheritance is to come. Attached to a reference to God this indicates a custom to pray.

199. Chapter 3 §3.b. The interpretation depends on the rhetorical situation, i.e. what type of audience is implied (see Thurén 1990: 124-25).

3.9   μὴ ἀποδιδόντες κακὸν ἀντὶ κακοῦ ἢ λοιδορίαν ἀντὶ
        λοιδορίας,
        τοὐναντίον δὲ εὐλογοῦντες
        ὅτι εἰς τοῦτο ἐκλήθητε
        ἵνα εὐλογίαν κληρονομήσητε.

3.10   ὁ γὰρ θέλων ζωὴν ἀγαπᾶν καὶ ἰδεῖν ἡμέρας ἀγαθὰς
        παυσάτω τὴν γλῶσσαν ἀπὸ κακοῦ καὶ χείλη τοῦ μὴ λαλῆσαι
        δόλον,

3.11   ἐκκλινάτω δὲ ἀπὸ κακοῦ καὶ ποιησάτω ἀγαθόν
        ζητησάτω εἰρήνην καὶ διωξάτω αὐτήν·

3.12   ὅτι ὀφθαλμοὶ κυρίου ἐπὶ δικαίους καὶ ὦτα αὐτοῦ εἰς δέησιν αὐτῶν,
        πρόσωπον δὲ κυρίου ἐπὶ ποιοῦντας κακά.

This subunit summarizes (this is signaled with τὸ δὲ τέλος) the larger unit by again addressing everybody.[200] The exhortation is now even sharper and more explicit than before. The addressees are not only told to be humble and sympathetic (8), or ready for unjust suffering. They are forbidden to avenge insults and enjoined to bless their enemies (9). This main C of the unit goes even further than the high ethical standards of the Hellenistic popular philosophy (Piper 1979: 63-65); therefore also a specific Christian motivation is needed. The fleeting reference to his example in 9a (cf. 2.23a) indicates that this is the right way of following the example of Christ, but the explicit argumentation in 9b-12 carries more weight. It consists of the author's own reasoning (9b), which is justified with a quotation from the OT (10-12).

As the concluding subunit in the larger 2.11–3.12, its central exhortation and motivation have formally an important position in the letter (Thurén 1990: 150). The author uses a rhetorical technique of *entrapment* by which he attempts to unify the complex rhetorical situation (see further Thurén 1990: 151). Thus, the central verse 3.9 can be characterized as a climax in the rhetorical strategy of the letter. These notions indicate that the verse is also crucial for understanding the nature of motivation in the text.

In 9b we have a ὅτι expression which is clarified with a ἵνα expression. Two opposite interpretations are possible.[201]

200. Thus, we have an *inclusio*. According to Brox (1979: 152) the unit draws a general conclusion of what has been exemplified by the household code.

201. The interpretation depends on the word to which τοῦτο refers: (a) 'For you have been called to inherit the blessing' (e.g. Selwyn 1947: 190; Schelkle 1970: 94-95; Delling 1973: 105; Goppelt 1978: 228); (b) 'For you have been called to bless (in order to inherit the blessing)', thus e.g. Piper 1980; Olsson 1982: 103, 132; see

(a) 'For you have been called to inherit the blessing.' This version resembles the basic motivation in 1.1–2.10: The addressees ought to be willing to obey God, even if this means blessing their enemies, since God has given / will give them an inheritance. A logical W is: 'If you are blessed, you shall also bless'.[202]

In order to identify the motivating factor a specific B must be reconstructed, since a general B gives us nothing new. According to the 'positive' alternative the blessing is something valuable (implied D) and thus the addressees are thankful to God. This attitude in turn obliges them to be obedient. The 'negative' alternative reads 'Blessing others is a condition for maintaining the blessing',[203] which indicates that the volitional factor is fear of losing it.

Fig. 3.9/a

B *Thankfulness for a valuable present involves obedience*	(B *Blessing others is a condition for maintaining the blessing*)

W *If you are blessed, you shall also bless*

D_1 You have been called
    to inherit the blessing
(D_2 To inherit a blessing is valuable)

C You shall bless your
enemies (and not seek revenge)

(b) 'For you have been called to bless (in order to inherit the blessing).' This version resembles the motivation in the 'household code', where the basic motivation is completed with reference to the intention of God/Christ (Christ died for you in order that you may follow in his footsteps). Then the ἵνα expression formally only explains[204] God's activity,

Thurén 1990: 24 n. 17. The scholars have not reached any final solution. According to my suggestion, the obscurity has a purpose (Thurén 1990: 150-51). Thus we shall take both possibilities into account in our analysis.

202. A more general alternative 'You should do to the others what has been done to you' is not suitable, since the addressees are forbidden to repay evil with evil. Goppelt's explanation (1978: 229), according to which the addressees have become capable of blessing those who curse them, is not particularly good either, since the author is not explaining here why the addressees bless but urging them so to do.

203. This idea is expressed e.g. in Jesus' parable of the Unmerciful Servant (Mt. 18.21-35). See also Thurén 1990: 151 n. 72.

204. According to Kelly the ἵνα expression is aimed at motivating the addressees whereas the ὅτι expression is in this alternative an awkward parenthesis (Kelly 1969: 137). This is not correct, since the ὅτι expression is unequivocally connected to μὴ ἀποδιδόντες... εὐλογοῦντες with a Grounds–Conclusion relation (see above Chapter 3 §2.a).

but is obviously also aimed at motivating the addressees. A formal structure of reasoning, which is enlarged with a teleological explanation, appears as follows:

Fig. 3.9/b1

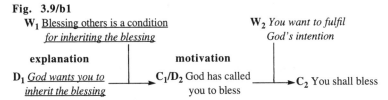

Since the W_2 seems rather surprising and unnatural in this context, we may assume that behind the structure lies another, purely motivating scheme, where not only God, but also the addressees, want the addressees to inherit the blessing. Thus we arrive at the following simple but implicit structure:

Fig. 3.9/b2

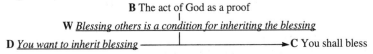

Although the structure can be presented in slightly different ways,[205] it is important to note that irrespective of the interpretation, the volitional factor, which is crucial for persuasion, can rise either from a 'positive' thankfulness to, praise of and reverence for God, or from a 'negative' fear of God, fear of losing the blessing or anxiety in earning it.

There is hardly any 'correct' interpretation; instead the expression seems to be made open and ambiguous on purpose.[206] Thus the whole of 3.1-12 culminates in an encouraging but simultaneously warning statement.

Verse 9 is explained with a long quotation from the OT. As such it gives authority to the author's statement. The redactional ὅτι in 12 indicates that the whole quotation is designed to function in the

205. E.g. in the first case a W: The inheritor wants to please him from whom he will inherit (B refers either to gratitude or a wish to ensure the inheritance).

206. Against Piper (1980: 212), according to whom only one interpretation can be right. He admits that the problem can be solved only from a general view of the author's thinking (see Thurén 1990: 25), but since the author appears to use ambiguous expressions frequently, and since there are signs of corresponding ambivalence even on other levels in his thought (Thurén 1990: 26-28) it is more plausible that even here the ambiguity is deliberate.

argumentation. 10-11 can be paraphrased: 'Whoever wants to prosper in life must turn from evil and do good' (speech in particular is mentioned here, as in 9).

(a) Formally it is a general rule, which according to Toulmin's definition lets us assume that it functions as a W.[207]

Fig. 3.9-12/a

> **B** OT quotation: God is for the righteous and against the evil
>
> **W** Whoever wants to prosper in life must turn from evil and do good

D_a *You want to inherit the blessing*
D_b God wants you to inherit the blessing, → **C** You shall bless, not avenge
   therefore he has called you to bless

(b) It is not, however, necessary to base the interpretation on the *form* of 10-12 and see it as a W or B. It can also be seen as an OT parallel to the author's own ὅτι expression in 9b (Brox [1979: 154] calls it a 'Wiederholung' of 9) and as a direct motivation for the command to bless in 9a: 'God has called you to inherit the blessing' (9) is equivalent to 'The eyes of the Lord are on the righteous...' (12a).[208]

Fig. 3.9-12/b1

> **B** The example of Christ (2.23)
>
> **W** *Avoid unnecessary work / A human being must not do what belongs to God*[209]

D_a The Lord punishes the bad
   (and rewards the good)   **C** You shall not seek revenge
   (12 is a specific version of 10-11)   → (= *you do not need to seek*
D_b *You are righteous, those who insult are not*   *revenge* but only bless)

The logically necessary, and thus implied D_b results also in the following implicit structure behind 10-12, which formally is not a motivation but an explanation:

207. Goppelt (1978: 224) calls 10-12 a 'Weiterführung' of 9. Indeed, as a W for 9 it corresponds to the more specific W above in Fig. 3.9/b1-2: 'Blessing others is a condition for inheriting the blessing'. 10-11 can be seen as a warning: 'If you do not cease from evil you will not prosper' or in the context of 9, 'you will not inherit blessing'. Verse 12 is connected to 10-11 with a redactional ὅτι, which signifies a GC relation and thus serves as a ground for 10-11. It is a B: 'God is for the righteous and against the evil'. Similarly it serves as a theological support for the general rule.

208. This suits 2.23b well: Christ, who is portrayed as an example for the addressees, left his case to God, who judges righteously. A similar thought can be found e.g. in Rom. 12.19 and Rev. 14.11-12.

209. Osborne (1983: 397-98) favours this interpretation.

Fig. 3.9-12/b2

D_1 God is for the righteous and against the evil (12)

C_1/D_2 *The righteous will prosper* (10-11)

|————Q *So, presumably* ——R *Unless you are evil (do not bless)*

C_2 *You will prosper*

Summing up, the argumentation in 8-12 has a new specific tone compared with the earlier thoughts. The content in the motif 'God's intention' is extended. A teleological argument, which builds on this intention, is used not only when speaking of the Gentiles' destiny on the last day, but also about the destiny of the addressees. Fulfilment of the intention leads to glory in two ways. Whereas the Gentiles' destiny was connected with the glory of God (2.12), the addressees' salvation, also intended by God, can be identified with their own glory. This double goal corresponds well to the two ways of interpreting 1.7b: εὑρεθῇ εἰς ἔπαινον καὶ δόξαν κὰι τιμὴν ἐν ἀποκαλύψει... Another specific feature in 3.9 is that the 'negative' aspect in the motivation is clearer than before. As in 1.17 God is presented as a righteous judge; in ch. 1 the addressees were called and thus urged to be obedient children, here they are also meant and thus admonished to be righteous.

Conclusions

The large unit 2.11–3.12 can be said to be the central *argumentatio* of the letter. The exhortation becomes more precise. The addressees ought to be submissive even to non-Christian masters and ready to suffer for their faith. They shall not seek revenge or blame their oppressors, but bless them. Thus also a clearer, more specific motivation is presented.

The motivation builds upon the preceding basic structure, but now the author first attempts to show how the salvation, joy and praise oblige to submissive behaviour. The example of Christ serves as an important ground, but a distinct structure can also be discerned: the best way of praising God is submissive behaviour and a life according to high ethical standards. Such a life causes admiration among the Gentiles and thereby prevents them for insulting the addressees and their God. Instead, they will praise him one day. This is the purpose of God and Christ. Here the author uses not only theological grounds, but also ideas of Hellenistic origin.

The unit culminates in 3.9-12 where the addressees are forbidden seek revenge from those who insult them. A 'positive' motivation is possible even here: the addressees are formally presented as righteous—thus they shall leave their case in the hands of God, just as Christ did. However, the 'negative' or warning argument is clearer than before: if the addressees do not bless their enemies, they will not inherit the blessing. Both interpretations include a new version of God's intention, which seeks not only the Gentiles' praise, but also the addressees' salvation.

5. *Modifications and Clarifications 3.13–4.11*[210]

The text is more forthright and implies a fairly unified rhetorical situation.[211] As a part of the *expolitio* (Lausberg 1960: §842), the ideas of the preceding unit appear, albeit more lucidly expressed.[212] The analysis will be displayed in a reduced form.

a. *3.13-17—Non-Theological Factors*[213]

The motivation extends that of 2.19-20. But the exhortation is different. The author also urges the addressees to play an active missionary role. In this way the subunit combines 2.1-25 and 3.1-12.

3.13 καὶ[214] τίς ὁ κακώσων ὑμᾶς ἐὰν τοῦ ἀγαθοῦ ζηλωταὶ γένησθε;
3.14 ἀλλ' εἰ καὶ πάσχοιτε διὰ δικαιοσύνην, μακάριοι.
        τὸν δὲ φόβον αὐτῶν μὴ φοβηθῆτε μηδὲ ταραχθῆτε,
3.15   κύριον δὲ τὸν Χριστὸν ἁγιάσατε ἐν ταῖς καρδίαις ὑμῶν,
        ἕτοιμοι ἀεὶ πρὸς ἀπολογίαν παντὶ τῷ αἰτοῦντι ὑμᾶς λόγον
        περὶ τῆς ἐν ὑμῖν ἐλπίδος,

210. The structure corresponds to the previous unit: 3.13-17 is comparable to 2.19-20, the following Christological section 3.18-22 corresponds to 2.21-25, and 4.1-6 draws the conclusions as does 3.1-12. The unit ends with a peculiar, peroratory section 4.7-11, which formally corresponds to Dibelius's original definition of the paraenesis including different exhortations which are loosely connected to each other.

211. Thurén 1990: 153. All addressees are now supposed to be persuaded to lead a holy life, which means that it is not only approved by God but also respected by the Gentiles. They shall be submissive, ready for unjust suffering and, especially, they will not repay evil with evil.

212. Kelly (1969: 139) goes too far when saying that from 3.13 to the farewell greetings we have the 'main section' of the Letter. Against Kelly also Goppelt (1978: 201).

213. The unit consists of four motivating expressions 13, 14a, 16b and 17. ἐλπίς in 15c can be also interpreted as motivating. There are two exhortations, too: 14b, and 15a with its further addition in 16b.

214. For the discussion about the role of the word see Chapter 3 §2.g.

3.16   ἀλλὰ μετὰ πραΰτητος καὶ φόβου,
         συνείδησιν ἔχοντες ἀγαθήν
         ἵνα ἐν ᾧ καταλαλεῖσθε καταισχυνθῶσιν οἱ ἐπηρεάζοντες ὑμῶν
         τὴν ἀγαθὴν ἐν Χριστῷ ἀναστροφήν.
3.17   κρεῖττον γὰρ ἀγαθοποιοῦντας,
         εἰ θέλοι τὸ θέλημα τοῦ θεοῦ,
         πάσχειν ἢ κακοποιοῦντας.

Apart from some inserts, the argumentation is not theological. The main
C is in 14b:

Fig. 3.13-17/1[215]

D_1 Suffering when doing good is commendable (17)

└──────────w Doing good makes one happy (cf. 3.10-12)

C_1/D_2 Even if you suffer for doing good you are happy (14a)

└──────────r As far as you are zealots for good (13b)

C_2/D_3 Nobody can harm you if you are a zealot
    for good[216] (13) (even if that means suffering 17b)

└──────────W *If nobody can harm you, you shall not be afraid*

C_3 You shall not be afraid of them/ anybody (14b)[217]

The counterpart to C_3, viz. the second exhortation to be ready to sanctify[218] Christ, is as such not motivated in any way, if unless with the reference to the addressees' hope in 15c. Instead, the larger form of the
exhortation, to sanctify Christ by 'answering' respectfully 'to everyone
asking about their hope', is given teleological support in 16b:

215. The main D in 13a is further grounded with a general and/or theological
statement in 14: 'If you suffer for doing good you are happy (μακάριοι)', which in
turn is based on a general and theological rule in 17 (D_1): 'Suffering when doing
good is good, suffering when doing bad is bad'. The rhetorical figure can be
resolved in this way (see Thurén 1990: 154 n. 79). For the Hellenistic background
see the Excursus in Chapter 6.

216. The expression 'zealots for good' has a double meaning, depending on the
addressees (see Thurén 1990: 154; cf. Kelly 1969: 141). The 'active' addressees are
enthusiasts (Selwyn 1947: 191; Kelly's 'devoted to' is too mild a translation), who
are enjoined to avoid false eagerness, the 'passive' addressees are told to have more
enthusiasm when doing good. For the Hellenistic and Jewish background of the
verse, see Kelly 1969: 140; Goppelt 1978: 233 n. 5.

217. For the interpretation, see Goppelt 1978: 235-36.

218. According to Kelly (1969: 142) ἁγιάζειν means 'to acknowledge as holy',
according to Goppelt (1978: 236) it means proclamation of the gospel.

Fig. 3.13-17/2[219]

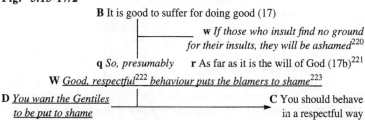

For the motivation, the crucial question is again: why are the addressees supposed to want those who blame their behaviour to be put to shame? As before, there is a double solution.

Not only the addressees, but also Christ's reputation is meant, since the addressees' life *in Christ* is blamed. Cf. the counterpart in 15a (Χριστὸν ἁγιάσατε). The motivating factor is similar: willingness to prevent blame of Christ is comparable to the willingness to praise him in 2.12 and 3.1.[224] This will is identical with the intention of God in 2.5, 9. As stated above, the motivation for this will is presented here only with a reference to the addressees' hope, which in turn recalls the basic structure of motivation in 1.1–2.10.

b. *3.18-22—Baptism Interpreted*
As in 2.21b-25 now follows a Christological ground for what the author has said. The author mentions stories unknown to us and therefore obscure (cf. Brox 1979: 169). This deficiency, however, has little effect on the assessment of their function in the argumentation. As such the subunit forms a closed entity.[225] Thus its contents will be treated not

219. The teleological motivation as such implies that the addressees are assumed to want those who speak maliciously against them to be ashamed of their slander (= D), similarly as in 2.12b (and 3.1b).

220. This is an implied side-W between B and the main W. A W can be displayed between almost every one of the elements in the structure of argumentation.

221. 13-14 repeat a possible rebuttal 'Unless you have to be afraid of them'.

222. Here, according to Goppelt (1978: 237), φόβος means reverence.

223. εἰ θέλοι τὸ θέλημα τοῦ θεοῦ corresponds to εἰ δέον ἐστίν (1.6) which is only implicitly theological. Now the theological component is distinctly expressed, since the previous Christological explanation (2.21-25) has made it clear that unjust suffering can be the will of God.

224. See above. The new aspect here is that the others' destiny is here described only as negative.

225. The unit has a chiastic construction: (A) the death of Christ—(B) the spirits in

only in relation to the preceding and following subunits, but also separately.[226]

3.18 ὅτι καὶ Χριστὸς ἅπαξ περὶ ἁμαρτιῶν ἔπαθεν,[227] δίκαιος ὑπὲρ ἀδίκων,
ἵνα ὑμᾶς προσαγάγῃ τῷ θεῷ
θανατωθεὶς μὲν σαρκὶ ζῳοποιηθεὶς δὲ πνεύματι·

3.19 ἐν ᾧ καὶ τοῖς ἐν φυλακῇ πνεύμασιν πορευθεὶς ἐκήρυξεν,

3.20 ἀπειθήσασιν ποτε ὅτε ἀπεξεδέχετο ἡ τοῦ θεοῦ μακροθυμία
ἐν ἡμέραις Νῶε κατασκευαζομένης κιβωτοῦ
εἰς ἣν ὀλίγοι, τοῦτ᾽ ἔστιν ὀκτὼ ψυχαί, διεσώθησαν δι᾽ ὕδατος.

3.21 ὃ καὶ ὑμᾶς ἀντίτυπον νῦν σῴζει βάπτισμα,
οὐ σαρκὸς ἀπόθεσις ῥύπου ἀλλὰ συνειδήσεως ἀγαθῆς ἐπερώτημα
εἰς θεόν,
δι᾽ ἀναστάσεως Ἰησοῦ Χριστοῦ,

3.22 ὅς ἐστιν ἐν δεξιᾷ τοῦ[228] θεοῦ πορευθεὶς εἰς οὐρανὸν
ὑποταγέντων αὐτῷ ἀγγέλων καὶ ἐξουσιῶν καὶ δυνάμεων.

1. *The Christ Story*
The basic story about the suffering of Christ, its purpose and results is *per se* coherent.[229] Therefore it can be analysed first, and the baptismal

the prison—(B) the salvation of Noah and the addressees—(A) the resurrection of Christ.

226. See below. According to Kelly (1969: 147) there are ideas which 'go beyond the strict requirements of the argument'. This is correct, but the example he gives, the atoning effect of the death of Christ, is required for the motivation (see below).

227. Thus most modern commentators, based on B, P, M. An alternative ἀπέθανεν is found in 𝔓⁷², ℵ*, A, and preferred by Kelly 1979: 147-48; Windisch and Preisker 1951: 70; Olsson 1982: 134. Even the alternative should be seen as a synonym to 'suffer', since 18 formally is a ground for 17. It is imaginable that the example of Christ is assumed to mean for the addresses even a possibility of dying for their faith (Reichert 1989: 310-35). The following 4.1 indicates, however, that the primary connotation here is the ἔννοια of Christ.

228. Thus 𝔓⁷², ℵ²; omitted in ℵ* *et al.*

229. The following elements can be discerned:

- Christ suffered as righteous and once for all (18a), he died in the flesh (18c)
- The purpose of his death was to bring the addressees to God (περὶ ἁμαρτιῶν, ὑπὲρ ἀδίκων 18a; ἵνα -expression 18b)
- he was made alive in spirit (18d)
- he preached to the spirits in prison (19)
- his resurrection saves the addressees (21ad)
- the result of his death and resurrection was that he went to Heaven and reigns there over angels / different powers (22)

section in 20-21abc is assessed as a *digressio*.[230]

(1a) Formally the unit is connected to the W and B in 17b with ὅτι, and to the D in 4.1 (Christ suffered in the flesh) with οὖν. The GC relation between 17b (It is good to suffer unjustly) and the unit indicates that the unit should provide support for the idea of the positive value of unjust suffering.[231] Moreover, the author does not speak of the *exemplum* of Christ as such,[232] but rather about the *consequences* of Christ's sufferings for himself, for the addressees, and for those who do not obey (so also in 2.21-24). Thus the story as such is a B_1 for the rule in 17 by giving an example of how unjust suffering leads to a good result (see Fig. 3.13-17/2).

Fig. 3.13-22/a

B_1 The example of Christ (3.13-22)

B_2 It is good to suffer for doing good (3.17)

W Respectful and good behaviour puts the blamers to shame (3.16)

The basic story tells us that the effect of Christ's righteous suffering σαρκί was that he himself received great glory, and salvation for the addressees (it is also implied that the addressees will obtain such glory). The angels or powers appear here in order to enhance the glory of Christ in a similar way as in 1.12. The spirits in prison perform a similar function, insofar as the expression is interpreted so that Christ only proclaimed his victory.[233] Another reason why Christ's sermon is used here

230. See Lausberg 1960 §§340-42, 408. This rhetorical technique is commonly misunderstood as a later interpolation (for discussion see Brox 1979: 168 n. 538). My claim is based on the rhetorical function of the section, and does not require that an earlier form of the baptismal section be historically reconstructed. Even in that case the author has heavily manipulated his material, since everything has now its place in the motivation. For discussion see Goppelt 1978: 240-41. Kelly (1969: 147) rejects any attempt at reconstruction as 'sheer guesswork'.

231. Against Kelly (1969: 147), according to whom it only refers to the whole of 13-17. Kelly stresses that Christ is not portrayed here as an example, since his suffering was unique (*hapax*). However, as 4.1 clearly shows, the author even here presents Christ's behaviour as a model for the addressees.

232. Cf. Selwyn 1947: 195: 'We pass from the *Christus patiens* to *Christus victor*'.

233. See Selwyn 1947: 200; Kelly 1969: 156. Then Christ is presented as superior to the powers in Hades, just as he is said to rule over different powers in 22. It is not essential for understanding the argumentation to decide whether the spirits mean people (Goppelt 1978: 247-50), supernatural spirits (Kelly 1969: 154) or sons of God (Brox 1979: 172). An interpretation according to which a positive contact

may be that it conveniently leads to Noah and the baptism.

(1b) The unit can also be seen as a parallel motivation to the main thesis in 13-17.

Fig. 3.13-22/b

D The example of Christ: modest behaviour (3.18-22)[234] **D** *You shall follow the example of Christ*	**C** You shall be modest etc., (3.15-17), and ready to suffer unjustly (4.1)

What makes the example of Christ obligating to the addressees, and why are they expected to follow him? The emphasis on Christ as Saviour (18, 21) and the addressees' salvation can be seen as intended to answer this question. Like the basic motivation in 1.3–2.10 they are designed to enhance the addressees' willingness to obey Christ. They are also connected to the baptismal section in the unit, which we shall analyse in greater detail in what follows.

2. *The Baptismal* Digressio—*A Key Factor in the Motivation*

In the problematic subunit 19-21abc,[235] which can be characterized as a partial *digressio*, we can discern the following elements:

1. The spirits who now are in prison were disobedient in the days of Noah, when God waited patiently.
2. The (obedient) Noah with few other people was saved in the Ark through the water.
3. The baptism saves you in a similar way (the water separates you from the evil people and their destiny).[236]

between Jesus and the worst sinners is aimed at enhancing the addressees' adherence to him would be reasonable, but is poorly supported in the text. My solution, which is based on the function of the sermon in the argumentation, is the most natural as far as the existing form of 1 Peter is concerned. It however does not deny that the story may originally have had different connotations.

234. This function is clearly indicated by 1 Pet. 4.1; see below, against Kelly (1969: 147) and Goppelt (1978: 209), according to whom the example is 'parenthetic'.

235. According to Luther (WA XII: 367) and Kelly (1969: 152) this is the most difficult and controversial section in the New Testament.

236. I presented this interpretation in Thurén 1990: 116 n. 75. Cf. also Brox 1979: 177: 'Es vernichtete...das Sündhafte und reinigte somit'. According to the common explanation the water saved by buoying the Ark (e.g. Kelly 1969: 159), which however leaves unsolved from what the baptism saved Noah and consequently the addressees. A local interpretation of διά, i.e. Noah running into the Ark through

4. an obscure statement: 'not putting away the dirt of flesh but an ἐπερώτημα of good conscience εἰς θεόν through the resurrection of Jesus Christ'.

Before going further we shall clarify the last antithetical element. The majority of modern commentators interpret ἀπόθεσις σαρκὸς ῥύπου as physical washing (Holmer and de Boor 1976: 133; Goppelt 1978: 257-58; Brox 1979: 177), but as Hill rightly observes, such an insert would be 'a rather inconsequential point to be making',[237] that is, it would be rhetorically odd. Moreover, the word ἀπόθεσις is hardly suited to washing. Instead, it resembles ἀποθέμενοι in 2.1 where the object is a list of sins. According to Selwyn, ἀποτίθημι and such a catalogue is typical of Early Christian baptismal education (Selwyn 1947: 393-400). Thus, ἀπόθεσις σαρκὸς ῥύπου connected with baptism rather means the designed effect of the baptismal ethical education.

The crucial question here is, why would the author suddenly insert a dogmatic and static definition of the essence of baptism[238] in the middle of the paraenesis. Since he says in 21a that baptism saves, it is more plausible that in 21b he simply explains how it saves, instead of discussing its essence. The baptism saves, but not as an ἀπόθεσις, that is, because of the putting away of malice, enlisted in 2.1. In other words, it is not the ethical consequences of baptism, to which he referred above,

---

water (see e.g. Cook 1980: 76) requires too much imagination.

237. Hill 1976: 186. He is right to interpret the expression as 'abandonment of the moral weakness of the pre-Christian life' (1976: 189). Kelly (1969: 161) also assesses it 'hard to believe that such a view of baptism needed refuting'. According to him (161-62) the expression opposes circumcision (so also Dalton 1965: 215-24, Best 1969/70: 147, Manke 1976: 182). According to Selwyn (1947: 204-205) the expression utilizes the distinction between inner and outer (thus also Goppelt 1978: 257; Brox 1979: 179; cf. 3.4): the baptism is presented as a deeper purification as opposed to circumcision. Against this view I claim (1) that the circumcision is a Pauline question—there is no evidence of such a problem in 1 Peter; (2) The expression does not refer to the distinction between inner and outer—the possible counterpart to σάρξ is rather ψυχή. Suffering in σάρξ means e.g. in the following 4.1 the *inner attitude, which is commendable* for the addressees. For a correct understanding of the expression, we need to focus on its counterpart in the text. Hill's interpretation becomes problematic because of his understanding of ἐπερώτημα, as Brox (1979: 179 n. 579) has shown.

238. E.g. according to Brox (1979: 177) the expression explains 'was die Taufe nun ist'; on p. 178 he calls the expression a 'definition'. See also Reichert 1989: 261.

that saves in baptism, but the ἐπερώτημα of a good conscience.[239]

The author thereby rejects a false interpretation of the motivating character of baptism, which might be used here as a Rebuttal against the saving effect of baptism. The ethical aspect is important for him, but he wants to ensure that the addressees do not misunderstand him.[240] Instead, baptism saves the addressees as an ἐπερώτημα. This is a controversial term, which in the light of ancient sources is best understood as a technical term for a contract, *stipulatio*.[241] Here it is an agreement of good conscience between God, the stronger partner, and human beings, who agree to have a good conscience (not 'good works').

Fig. 3.19-21

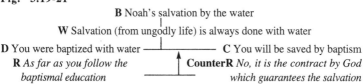

B Noah's salvation by the water

W Salvation (from ungodly life) is always done with water

D You were baptized with water ——————— **C** You will be saved by baptism
   R *As far as you follow the*   **CounterR** *No, it is the contract by God*
     baptismal education   *which guarantees the salvation*

Returning to section 19-21 as a whole we can say that like the resurrection of Christ, the use of baptism emphasizes the certainty of the salvation (which is also argued for with the *exemplum* of Noah) and that the addressees will obtain the glory (Thurén 1990: 155). This in turn adds to the value of the addressees' new status and shows from whom it comes. In so doing the section corresponds to the basic motivation and is aimed at intensifying the addressees' appreciation of Christ's suffering and death and their willingness to obey him. The motivating force of the baptism is mainly positive, since the addressees, who are also in the

239. Reichert (1989: 277-78) rejects Hill's interpretation of ἀπόθεσις as an abandonment of moral failures, because Hill gives too modest a translation, 'not so much...as', of the antithesis οὐ...ἀλλά. Although the comment is right, Reichert fails to see that if the expression is not a static definition, Hill's translation of the antithesis is not necessary for the whole interpretation.

240. At least modern readers have done so. E.g. Kosala (1984: 31-32) understands baptism in 1 Peter in exactly the way which the author here presumably rejects. (I presented this interpretation in an unpublished licentiate thesis [1988a], and in Thurén 1988b, which resulted in a corresponding translation in the new Finnish Bible [Pyhä Raamattu 1992]).

241. According to Reicke (1946: 182-85; see also Aalen 1972: 161-75; Goppelt 1978: 259 n. 3) at least shortly after the writing of 1 Peter ἐπερώτημα was used in a similar sense to the Latin *stipulatio*. The stronger and active partner presents a formal question. Thus Brox's translation 'promise' (1979: 178) and even Hill's 'response' (1976: 188) give too narrow a picture of the agreement.

minority, are identified with those who will be saved. However, the reason for the gloomy destiny of the spirits is disobedience, and they may serve as a warning, as a counterpart to Noah.

The author stresses the implication of baptism for the addressees' life. It should make a division between the addressees and the Gentiles just as in the days of Noah, and as a contract it also obligates the addressees. On the ideological level, however, the most important feature in the baptismal *digressio* is that the author rejects a possible misunderstanding of the ethical nature of the baptismal theme. Salvation is not achieved by living according to the education; but it is based on the contract with and by God. The idea deals with the tension between the 'positive' and 'negative' argumentation, and this time the positive line is given clear preference.

Conclusions

Summarizing, we can say that the Christological and baptismal section 3.18-22 (a) backs up the idea of unjust suffering as commendable, and (b), rather similarly to 1.3-12, seeks to intensify the addressees' willingness to live according to their status as Christians by assuring them of the merits of that status and contrasting it to the other possibility. This is supposed to enhance their appreciation of their own position. The role of Christ in the salvation is stressed in order to direct that appreciation into adherence to his example and the will of God. The unit thus takes up the basic motivation of the first unit in the letter.

Here in particular we meet the problem of identifying the genre and status of the text. Although the unit formally functions as a factor in the ethical motivation, it can also simply be a matter of preaching the gospel, that is, it can be seen as aimed at intensifying the addressees' adherence to the Christian faith as such. It is difficult and even unnecessary to distinguish in 1 Peter between the Christian faith or the gospel *sensu stricto* and the ethics, since they belong together. The behaviour is not seen as an absolute value, but as indicative of faith.

Together with the preceding subunit (3.13-17), 18-22 repeats and modifies the themes in the earlier unit. The addressees are admonished both to passive suffering and to active good life, and the relation to the counterpart, 'the others', is double-sided: they serve as the goal for missionary activity, but also as a warning example. In order to avoid contradictions the negative counterpart to the addressees is taken from the OT, but the positive from their own surroundings.

c. *4.1-6—Enough!*[242]

The unit involves a step forward in the rhetorical strategy of the text, but nothing new appears as far as the contents are concerned. The author makes an even more explicit demand for good moral behaviour by all types of addressee. No more *pia desideria*, tactical courtesy or theoretical considerations are seen; instead the author requires the addressees to cease from their current behaviour. This is made possible by unification of the rhetorical situation (Thurén 1990: 155-56) and by repetition of the basic motivation in the preceding unit. We can also discern a shift of focus in the relation toward the Gentiles: they are now presented exclusively as bad and to be avoided. The exhortation is also changed. The addressees are no more directly admonished to submissive behaviour vis-à-vis the Gentiles, but as in 1.13–2.10 to a more general life according to the will of God. However, this holy life is now identified with unjust suffering.

4.1   <u>Χριστοῦ οὖν παθόντος</u> σαρκὶ
        καὶ ὑμεῖς τὴν αὐτὴν ἔννοιαν ὁπλίσασθε,
    <u>ὅτι</u> ὁ παθὼν σαρκὶ πέπαυται ἁμαρτίας

4.2   <u>εἰς τὸ</u> μηκέτι ἀνθρώπων ἐπιθυμίαις ἀλλὰ θελήματι θεοῦ
    τὸν ἐπίλοιπον ἐν σαρκὶ βιῶσαι χρόνον.

4.3   ἀρκετὸς <u>γὰρ</u> ὁ παρεληλυθὼς χρόνος τὸ βούλημα τῶν ἐθνῶν
    κατειργάσθαι
    πεπορευμένους ἐν ἀσελγείαις, ἐπιθυμίαις, οἰνοφλυγίαις,
    κώμοις, πότοις καὶ ἀθεμίτοις εἰδωλολατρίαις.

4.4   ἐν ᾧ ξενίζονται
    μὴ συντρεχόντων ὑμῶν εἰς τὴν αὐτὴν τῆς ἀσωτίας ἀνάχυσιν
    βλασφημοῦντες,

4.5   οἳ ἀποδώσουσιν λόγον τῷ ἑτοίμως ἔχοντι κρῖναι ζῶντας καὶ νεκρούς.

4.6   εἰς τὸ <u>καὶ</u> νεκροῖς εὐηγγελίσθη,
    ἵνα κριθῶσι μὲν κατὰ ἀνθρώπους σαρκὶ ζῶσι δὲ κατὰ θεὸν
    πνεύματι.

The first verse has caused much trouble for the interpreters. It has been unclear what is meant by the attitude of Christ and whether the ὅτι expression gives a reason (because...) or an explanation (namely that...); thus what is the meaning and purpose of that expression (cf. Chapter 3 §2.a)? When starting from the most probable, clear GC and MP relations

---

242. The unit consists of a command 'arm yourselves with the attitude of Christ' (1b). It is surrounded with different grounds: a cryptic maxim in 1c, reference to the preceding unit (4.1a), a teleological motivation in 2 and a longer section about the Gentiles (3-5), to which is added an explanation about the dead (6).

(see Chapter 3 §§2.a and 3.b), Toulmin's model provides us with a simple explanation. The ὅτι sentence resembles a typical Warrant. First we have a rough structure:

Fig. 4.1-2

$\mathbf{W}$ One who suffers in the flesh has ceased from sins (1c)[243]

$\mathbf{D_a}$ Christ suffered in the flesh (1a)[244]
$\mathbf{D_b}$ *You want to cease from sins* (2)[245]
$\longrightarrow$ $\mathbf{C}$ You should adopt the attitude of Christ (1b)

A detailed analysis leads into a more precise structure:[246]

Fig. 4.1-2

$\mathbf{B_{1a}}$ Christ has suffered $\mathbf{B_{1b}}$ Suffering in the flesh means
    in the flesh (1a)   ceasing from sins (1c)

$\mathbf{B_2}$ *Christ's example: he has ceased from sins by suffering in the flesh*

$\mathbf{W}$ *In order to cease from sins one should do as Christ did*

$\mathbf{D}$ *You want to cease from sins (2)* $\rightarrow$ $\mathbf{C}$ You should adopt the attitude of Christ (1b)

From this argumentation we cannot, however, deduce whether the author assumes that the addressees are suffering in the flesh and need only a better attitude, or whether he encourages them to be ready to do so, since their suggested model, the ἔννοια of Christ, is equivocal. This corresponds well to the different types of audience which the text implies (Thurén 1990: 156).

The rest of the unit, 3-6, is connected to the teleological motivation in 2 with a clear GC relation. When the rhetorical technique of *irony* is

243. As a rule this is probably a W—and this does not depend on how its grammatical connection to the imperative is assessed. For discussion about the meaning of ὅτι here see Chapter 3 §2.a above.

244. Cf. 2.4, which is also backed up with the preceding section.

245. The teleological ground can be resolved 'You do not want to live according the desires of the Gentiles, but according to the will of God', or as paraphrased 'You want to cease from sins'.

246. From the scheme above we can conclude that the attitude of Christ is readiness to suffer in the flesh, which also means ceasing from sins. This is identical with the unjust suffering in the preceding sections, and summarizes the main exhortation in the letter: Christ lead a righteous and holy life, and was ready for unjust suffering. As such the teleological ground (2) involves not only the willingness to live according to the will of God and cease from sin, but since it gives a reason for the command to adopt the attitude of Christ, it also implies a W: In order to cease from sins one should adopt the attitude of Christ. The general rule in 1_c together with 1_a backs up the Warrant. In order to clarify the presentation an auxiliary conclusion from these elements is offered as the B.

resolved into normal text, we obtain the following structure:[247]

Fig. 4.3-6

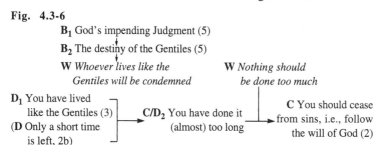

The meaning of 6 has been widely discussed. It can imply two questions which the addressees have raised. Against the majority of the scholars I claim, in the light of the general rhetorical situation, that the author here seems to be playing with words when discussing the problem of the dead Christians' fate.[248]

---

247. We can identify the C as the thesis which is deduced from v. 2: You want to live according to the will of God, not according to the desires of the Gentiles. At least 3 serves as a D for this C, whereas 4 is a short *narratio*. The author uses the rhetorical technique of *irony*. For this technique, see Perelman 1969: 207-209. If the statement is taken as such, it involves a rule: 'He who has done something long enough does not have to do it anymore'. However, like a rhetorical question, also an irony can be translated into a normal statement: 'You have lived (almost) too long like the Gentiles'. Such way of life is exemplified with a conventional catalogue of vices in 3b and characterized pejoratively with αὐτὴν ἀσωτίας ἀνάχυσιν (again the alliteration). Finally the author states that the Gentiles will answer for their sins before the Judge, i.e. they will be condemned.

248. (a) The addressees wonder, how everybody can be judged, although the dead have no opportunity even to hear the gospel (thus more or less Reicke 1946: 204-206; Dalton 1965: 51-56 (on pp. 257-77 he however rejects the idea); Kelly 1969: 174-76; Brox 1979: 161; Olsson 1982: 196). Then νεκροί refers to everybody who has died before Christ. (b) The addressees ask, what use is it to be a Christian, if one will die anyhow (thus Selwyn 1947: 337-39). According to this interpretation, dead Christians are discussed.

Which problem is more urgent and plausible in the addressees' situation? (a) suggests that the author begins to discuss an interesting, but too modern, question. The contact between this question and the addressees' acute situation is less clear than the contact in (b). Just like the question about a possible evangelization of the spirits in prison (3.19-21) which this solution also implies, the fate of people who have died before Christ is an issue of great interest for many Christians, but in either case there are no other signs in 1 Peter that such a problem would clearly belong to its rhetorical situation. The alternative (b) has a parallel in 1 Thess. 4.13-18, and fits well into one

The verse seems to be added to 3-5 because of the *Stichwort* νεκρός in 5b: 6 also speaks of the dead (cf. 7-8), but this time he is referring to those to whom the gospel has been proclaimed. Instead of basing the interpretation on extratextual evidence or theological assumptions, it seems most reasonable to interpret 6 by searching for its function in the argumentation.

The people to whom the gospel has been preached and who thus live κατὰ θεόν (cf. 1.15) can be certainly identified with Christians. The verse becomes reasonable if it is seen as a counterargument to a possible rebuttal: 'What benefit does the righteous suffering and even death for the faith do for some Christians, if they are now dead?', or, 'for us, if we die suffering righteously?'[249] The author claims that even those people live κατὰ θεόν, from God's perspective, although condemned and dead κατὰ ἀνθρώπους, that is, they are reckoned to be dead.[250] The author plays with words: such Christians have according to 1.14-15 and 4.2 lived κατὰ τὸν καλέσαντα ὑμᾶς ἅγιον, and θελήματι θεοῦ, not ἐπιθυμίαις. If one lives now κατὰ θεόν (according to God's will/ example), one will live κατὰ θεόν (from God's perspective) even when dead.

The dead and yet living Christians' example is a counterpart to the example of the Gentiles. It exemplifies the positive side of the W above ('he who lives like Gentiles will be condemned') by stressing that those living according to the will of God will be saved. As such the verse is not a loose addition to the argumentation, but serves as an additional B to the W by rejecting a possible Rebuttal (see Fig. 4.3-6).

The motivating factor thus has a double character, positive and negative. The choice depends on which B the motivation is based on. Only the example of the dead Christians refers to God's intention: the purpose of the proclamation of the Gospel was that they should live even though dead.

---

type of the general rhetorical situation of the Letter, viz. the question about social pressure and the merits of the Christian faith. Thus (b) is to be preferred. For interpretation of the κατά expressions, see above Chapter 3 §2.d.

249. Selwyn 1947: 214, 337-39; 1 Thess. 4.13-18.

250. According to Selwyn the first κατά expression means 'in men's estimation' (1947: 215), while the second one is 'as God lives', since the parallelism is not exact (1947: 216). Selwyn gives no motivation for this statement. Brox (1979: 199) also claims that the two κατά expressions must be translated in different ways. The explanation is almost as short as in Selwyn: 'Natürlich'.

d. *4.7-11*—'*Paraenesis*'

This formally genuine paraenesis[251] consists of short conventional rules of behaviour and their motivations. The unit has several parallels in the NT (e.g. Rom. 12.6, 13; 13.12). It deals with the addressees' internal relations and has already a peroratory style with elements of a higher pathos.[252] The rhetorical situation is homogeneous (Thurén 1990: 156-57).

4.7   πάντων δὲ τὸ τέλος ἤγγικεν.
      σωφρονήσατε <u>οὖν</u> καὶ νήψατε εἰς προσευχάς
4.8   πρὸ πάντων τὴν εἰς ἑαυτοὺς ἀγάπην ἐκτενῆ ἔχοντες,
      <u>ὅτι</u> ἀγάπη καλύπτει πλῆθος ἁμαρτιῶν.
4.9   **φιλόξενοι εἰς ἀλλήλους ἄνευ γογγυσμοῦ,**
4.10 **ἕκαστος <u>καθὼς</u> ἔλαβεν χάρισμα**
      εἰς ἑαυτοὺς αὐτὸ διακονοῦντες
      ὡς καλοὶ οἰκονόμοι ποικίλης χάριτος θεοῦ
4.11   εἴ τις λαλεῖ, ὡς λόγια θεοῦ ·
      εἴ τις διακονεῖ, ὡς ἐξ ἰσχύος ἧς χορηγεῖ ὁ θεός,
      <u>ἵνα</u> ἐν πᾶσιν δοξάζηται ὁ θεὸς διὰ Ἰησοῦ Χριστοῦ,
      ᾧ ἐστιν ἡ δόξα καὶ τὸ κράτος εἰς τοὺς αἰῶνας τῶν αἰώνων,
      ἀμήν.

The first verses are formally easy to interpret, but the ambiguous verse 8 as a W causes familiar ideological problems.

(a) If the addressees' own love and own sins are meant in W, they should love each other, because they will thus be helped to survive the Last Judgment.[253] (b) As a theological statement it refers to the love of God and its saving effect:[254] since the love of God saves them from the imminent judgment, they should feel obligated to show similar love to each other. Contrary to a common opinion among the interpreters of Peter, the imminent End is here designed to function as an effective

251. Cf. Chapter 1 §2.a. E.g. the commands in 7 and 8 are connected to each other with the *Stichwort* πάντων, according to the paraenetical convention.

252. The change of the rhythm from long sentences to a short, intensive style, the use of the imminent End, the mention of several emotional factors such as ἀγάπη, χάρις, φιλοξενία, δόξα, and the praise formula serve this purpose.

253. So Windisch and Preisker 1951: 75; Brox 1979: 205. According to Kelly forgiveness is God's free mercy, yet love or lack of love is decisive at the final assize (1969: 178).

254. So Goppelt 1978: 284-85; according to Selwyn (1947: 217-18) the statement is ambivalent.

D.[255] The sentence is so short that a detailed analysis and the identification of the motivating factor would be too arbitrary.

Fig. 4.7-8

W Love covers over the multitude of sins (8)[256]

D The End (last judgment
  in 3.5) is at hand
  [Thus sins have to be covered]

C You should love each
  other and be ready
  (cf. 1.14, 22)

Verses 9-10 yield the following structure:[257]

Fig. 4.9-10

B *General idea of the* οἰκονόμος

W *An* οἰκονόμος *serves others*

D You are good οἰκονόμοι
  of the grace of God (10c)[258]

C You shall serve each other (10b)

The teleological motivation in 4.10-11 resembles the general reasoning in 2.11-12.[259]

255. Brox, who has a tendency to emphasize the pseudepigraphical nature of 1 Peter, claims that the Letter does not indicate any acute 'Näherwartung' (1979: 203), since (a) eschatology is used as a ground for ethics (Brox's D requires a W: 'what is used as an ethical motivation is not acute or real'); (b) the expression in 4.7 is an Early Christian phrase (W: 'If a text contains Early Christian material it cannot be from an Early Christian period'); (c) On the whole the ethic of 1 Peter is 'Leidensethik' (W: 'Suffering was unknown to the first generation'). For a different assessment of the nature of 1 Peter see e.g. Olsson 1982: 162-63.

256. As a general rule, this is a typical W.

257. Verse 9 is a motivation or a command. The first alternative means that it builds on 7-8: 'Since you (thus) love each other, this means that (10-11) you shall serve each other' (the problem is assumed to be common to all types of addressee: Thurén 1990: 156-57). If 9 is a command, 10-11 explain it: 'Be thus φιλόξενοι, which means that...'

258. ὡς gives the subjective ground (see Chapter 3 §2.e). According to an alternative, adverbial interpretation, the addressees are urged to follow the example of οἰκονόμοι. Cf. ὡς τέκνα in 1.14 and ὡς παροίκους in 2.11.

259. In 2.11-12 the praise of God is presented as the ultimate goal for the addressees' activity. But instead of affecting the Gentiles the addressees are here told to serve people inside the congregation. 11a exemplifies the word ποικίλος in 10b, but the ὡς expressions in 11 have no motivating component. This structure (one partly motivating ὡς expression combined with two only adverbial ὡς expressions) corresponds to 2.16.

Fig. 4.10-11[260]

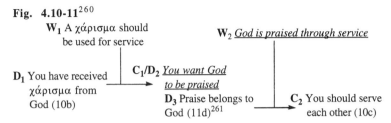

We have seen that despite the traditional form the unit is skilfully constructed and closes the larger rhetorical unit 3.13–4.11 or even the whole of 2.11–4.11. Verses 1-6 summarize the central motifs in the exhortation and motivation, and 7-11 direct these ideas into personal relations and into the internal relations in the congregation. The climax of the pathos at the end demonstrates the good rhetorical sense of the author.

Conclusions

On the whole the unit 3.13–4.11 repeats the preceding section with some variations. The addressees are admonished to both active and passive obedience. Contrary to 2.11–3.12 the Gentiles are now also described in a pejorative light. The addressees' status is again important. Only here is baptism mentioned explicitly—before the author has only used baptismal material and allusions. A misinterpretation of baptism is rejected, but its motivating aspects are emphasized. The baptismal section also serves as a *digressio* and reiterates the basic structure of motivation.

---

260. The primary motivation for the exhortation in 9-11 is the expression connected to the admonition with ἵνα in 11c: 'In order that God may be praised in all things'. This is not only a solemn phrase, although Kelly (1969: 181) calls it an 'insert' after the climax or (182) 'outburst underlining the majesty of God or Christ'. As typical for such teleological argument, the expression is reasonable as a motivation only if we assume the D_2 and W_2 in the scheme. The only reason for the willingness to praise are the χάρισμα which the addressees are said to have received, but maybe the whole act of salvation is meant, as above.

261. So Goppelt 1978: 291 and Kelly 1969: 181-82 and (according to Selwyn 1947: 219-20) Jesus.

6. The Final Phase 4.12–5.7[262]

Although not yet the last unit of the letter, 4.12–5.7 includes an increasing number of features that are typical of a *peroratio* (Thurén 1990: 157-58): the theses of 1.3-12 are repeated (*recapitulatio*, see Thurén 1990: 77). Instead of the indicative the author now uses imperative forms (1.6//4.13; 1.8//4.16) which serve as an *inclusio* of the letter.[263] What the addressees are described to be in 1.3-12 has now become an exhortation. The *ethos* and *pathos* aspects are now also clear (*affectus*, see Thurén 1990: 77). The contact between the author and the addressees is emphasized (the addressees are called ἀγαπητοί, first person singular in 5.1) and dramatic motifs are used (the addressees' situation is dramatized [4.12] and the final Judgment is stressed ([4.17-18]). Both the exhortation and the motivation are presented in a clear form without any sign of *insinuatio*. This is especially obvious, if the section 4.14-15, 16 is compared with the parallel 2.19-21 and 3.14-17. The tone is consolatory and warning (Thurén 1990: 158).

a. *4.12-13—Joy with a Purpose*
The verses consist of two parallel antithetical commands: μὴ ξενίζεσθε...ἀλλὰ...χαίρετε. Together they form the C in the unit. The clearest ground, which is aimed at both of them, is the teleological motivation in 13c, but both commands are also supported punctually with less clearly motivating expressions πρὸς πειρασμόν...(12b) and καθὸ κοινωνεῖτε...(13a). Since this analysis concentrates on the motivation, we shall treat these expressions primarily as persuasive.

4.12   ἀγαπητοί, μὴ ξενίζεσθε τῇ ἐν ὑμῖν πυρώσει
          πρὸς πειρασμὸν ὑμῖν <u>γινομένη</u>
          ὡς ξένου ὑμῖν συμβαίνοντος,
4.13   ἀλλὰ <u>καθὸ</u> κοινωνεῖτε τοῖς τοῦ Χριστοῦ παθήμασιν
          χαίρετε,
   <u>ἵνα</u> καὶ ἐν τῇ ἀποκαλύψει τῆς δόξης αὐτοῦ χαρῆτε ἀγαλλιώμενοι.

---

262. The unit consists of two parts, which are introduced with signals on the pragmatic level: ἀγαπητοί in 4.12 and πρεσβυτέρους οὖν παρακαλῶ in 5.1. The first half consists of two antithetical commands and their motivations in 4.12-13, and 14-16 which explains these ideas in detail.

263. Thurén 1990: 157. Since the rhetorical function of the unit is so clear, there is no need for the earlier thesis, according to which the section begins a new letter. The thesis is commonly rejected by modern scholars for other reasons (see Kelly 1969: 183-84).

Fig. 4.12-13/1[264]

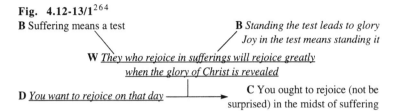

B Suffering means a test

B *Standing the test leads to glory*
Joy in the test means standing it

W <u>They who rejoice in sufferings will rejoice greatly</u>
<u>when the glory of Christ is revealed</u>

D <u>You want to rejoice on that day</u>

C You ought to rejoice (not be surprised) in the midst of suffering

This structure, although clear in itself, includes an undeniable difficulty. If the author would admonish the addressees to be steadfast in or prepared for suffering, the reasoning would serve as a good motivation. But to command the addressees to *rejoice* in order to gain something sounds unnatural.[265] An alternative solution could be that the imperative 'rejoice' is interpreted as consolation and ἵνα consequently as signifying a consecutive or causal connection: 'You can rejoice even now, since you are going to rejoice when Christ is revealed'. Then the word καθό

264. This is a combined structure of 12 and 13. In the peroratory 12 the C is 'Do not be surprised at suffering...' 12b is interpreted as a D 'Since the suffering means a trial', if the *causal* component of γινομένη (see above Chapter 3 §2.f) is emphasized (thus Brox 1979: 213; Kelly [1969: 185] calls it explicative). This further implies an additional D from 1.6-7 and 4.13 'Perseverance in trial leads to glory' (and a W 'What leads to glory shall not cause surprise'). The *relative* interpretation is however to be preferred, see above Chapter 3 §2.f. Although only underlying, the dramatic redefinition (Thurén 1990: 73) of the sufferings here may well be designed to recall the reasoning in the corresponding 1.6-7 and thereby to prepare the addressees for 13c.

In 13 the C 'rejoice' is a counterpart to the C in 12 'do not be surprised' (the possibly consolatory expressions are here overinterpreted in order to make the argumentation more lucid). It repeats the motif of joy from 1.3-12. The difference is the change from indicative to imperative. The shift of form is not to be seen as occasional, although the function of the indicative there is 'persuasive' and the imperative here may be consolatory.

The C is motivated with a ἵνα expression in 13c, which indicates a teleological motivation, if ἵνα is interpreted as a signal for a Means–Purpose relation. In that case it contains the D and W of Fig. 4.12-13/1. The statement in 12b, according to which the addressees sufferings mean a trial, gives material for a B as a reference to 1.6-9. There the addressees are presented as joyful in the midst of sufferings, in order that (ἵνα) they may stand the test and reach the glory, or since they will reach the glory (κομιζόμενοι). There the joy is clearly combined with readiness to suffer.

265. Cf. Brox, according to whom the unit reflects an original Christian 'logic' (1979: 214). The commentators usually just seek the origins of the combination between joy and sufferings (e.g. Goppelt 1978: 299-304), which however is of little use when attempting to understand what the author means.

in 13a is a signal for a Qualifier and a Rebuttal (the expression is not causal: see above Chapter 3 §2.e).

Fig. 4.12-13/2

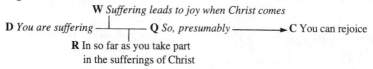

Or, in a more straightforward form, if καθό is simplified to a marker for a GC relation:

Fig. 4.12-13/3

> **W** *Taking part in the sufferings of Christ*
> *will result in joy when he comes*
>
> **D** You take part in the sufferings of Christ ────────┴──────► **C** You can rejoice

But even this solution has a weakness: to translate ἵνα καί only with 'since' and the imperative with 'can' or 'may' results in a rather narrow interpretation, especially since the imperative form is used here instead of the indicative in the corresponding 1.6, 8.

The two interpretations, the exhorting and warning 'be ready to suffer in order to gain salvation' and the consoling and encouraging 'rejoice when suffering, since you will attain salvation' are both possible ways of understanding the expression, but neither gives its full significance. It is obvious that both solutions must be taken into account. The problematic relation between the two could be paraphrased: 'You will reach salvation; therefore you rejoice, in order to reach salvation'. The tension may serve a rhetorical purpose: Between the lines of the consolation the addressees are allowed to surmise a command or a warning.[266]

b. *4.14-19—Joy and Fear*[267]

14-16 repeats the reasoning in 2.19-20 and 3.13-14, 17. This time the general motif ('common sense') is even weaker than in the second

266. It is noteworthy that the author never admonishes the addressees to suffering, not even here; it is only implied that visible Christian faith resulted in some type of suffering in the addressees' situation. Nor is it said explicitly that suffering results in, or is a reason or requirement for, joy when Christ comes. The author rather admonishes to a right attitude or says that the addressees should rejoice in spite of suffering.

267. 14-16 is explained and supported with 17-18, while 19 draws a conclusion (ὥστε), presenting thus the final C of the unit: Those who suffer according to the will of God should/may entrust themselves to God and do good.

version, and the theological one is correspondingly stronger.

4.14 εἰ ὀνειδίζεσθε ἐν ὀνόματι Χριστοῦ μακάριοι,
<u>ὅτι</u> τὸ τῆς δόξης καὶ τὸ τοῦ θεοῦ πνεῦμα ἐφ᾽ ὑμᾶς ἀναπαύεται.

4.15 μὴ <u>γάρ</u> τις ὑμῶν πασχέτω
ὡς φονεὺς ἢ κλέπτης ἢ κακοποιὸς ἢ ὡς ἀλλοτριεπίσκοπος·

4.16 εἰ δε ὡς Χριστιανός,
μὴ αἰσχυνέσθω, δοξαζέτω δὲ τὸν θεὸν
<u>ἐν</u>᾽[268] **τῷ ὀνόματι τούτῳ.**

4.17 <u>ὅτι</u> καιρὸς τοῦ ἄρξασθαι τὸ κρίμα ἀπὸ τοῦ οἴκου τοῦ θεοῦ·
<u>εἰ</u> δὲ πρῶτον ἀφ᾽ ἡμῶν,
τί τὸ τέλος τῶν ἀπειθούντων τῷ τοῦ θεοῦ εὐαγγελίῳ;

4.18 καὶ <u>εἰ</u> ὁ δίκαιος μόλις σῴζεται, ὁ ἀσεβὴς καὶ ἁμαρτωλὸς ποῦ
φανεῖται;

4.19 <u>ὥστε</u> καὶ οἱ πάσχοντες κατὰ τὸ θέλημα τοῦ θεοῦ
πιστῷ κτίστῃ παρατιθέσθωσαν τὰς ψυχὰς αὐτῶν
ἐν ἀγαθοποιΐᾳ.

Fig. 4.14/1[269]

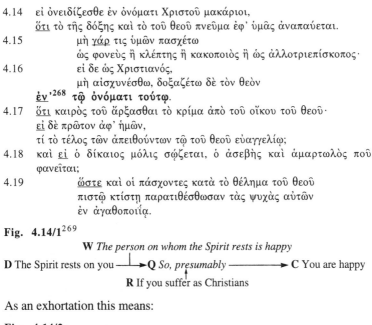

W *The person on whom the Spirit rests is happy*

D The Spirit rests on you ——┴—▶**Q** *So, presumably* ————————▶ **C** You are happy

R If you suffer as Christians

As an exhortation this means:

Fig. 4.14/2a

W *The person on whom the Spirit rests is happy*

D *You want to be happy* ⎤
D *The Spirit rests on everyone* ⎬————————▶ **C** You should be ready
  who suffers as a Christian ⎦   to suffer as Christians

As consolation the structure is slightly different:

Fig. 4.14/2b

W The spirit rests on the person who suffers as a Christian

D You suffer as Christians ————————┴————————▶ **C** You are happy

In 15-16 the structure is seemingly simple, if the C is found in 16:

268. The word is a signal for GC relation; see above Chapter 3 §2.d.
269. **D** The Spirit of God ————————————▶ **C** You are happy if you
  rests on you   suffer as Christians

The argumentation in the text is simple. The D is in accordance with most modern
commentators; Selwyn (1947: 222) however translates: 'The Presence of Glory, yea
the Spirit of God'.

Fig. 4.15-16

      B The known result of the opposite type of suffering (15)

        W *Suffering as a Christian leads to glory* (14b)

D You suffer as Christians[270]

D *Reaching the glory causes praise of God*   → **C** You should praise God

However, the actual text is less straightforward. Instead, we have an antithetic structure with a striking asymmetry:[271]

Fig. 4.15-16	**Fig. 4.16**
D *Suffering as a criminal leads to shame*	**D** *As a Christian it leads to glory* (14b)
C Do not suffer as a criminal	**C** Praise God if you suffer as a Christian

Here one could expect a different C in 16: '(Be ready to) suffer as a Christian' and a W 'One should do such things as cause joy'. The missing balance between the commands is important for understanding the persuasive structure here. The author clearly avoids a direct command to suffer as a Christian. Instead, he uses the idea of *praising God* when suffering as a Christian, just as he mentions joy when suffering in 1.6, 8 and 4.13. These emotive factors are closely connected with readiness or willingness to suffer as a Christian.

Joy, happiness, and praise of God here serve as imminent factors, whereby the author seeks to persuade the addressees. Since he is not describing his ideology but affecting, that is, persuading, the addressees, it is natural that he does not present the structure of argumentation as a whole but allows the addressees to understand it 'between the lines'.

In 17-18 comes the explicit motivation for 16.[272] The first D in 17a is astonishing:

Fig. 4.17

D$_a$ The judgment begins
    from the House of God[273]

D$_b$ You are[274] the House of God   → **C** You shall praise God
                              (and not be criminal) (15-16)

270. For the causal ἐν see Chapter 3 §2.d.

271. The imminent motivation for 15 is implicit: On one hand, (15a) there are negative connotations of the catalogue of sins, on the other hand, (16a) '*but* if as a Christian, do not shame', implies that suffering as a criminal is shameful.

272. Against Goppelt (1978: 311) who claims that it refers to the whole section. Brox goes still further by arguing that the sentence has nothing to do with the chain of arguments here (1979: 233).

273. For the Jewish and Christian origin of the idea see Selwyn 1947: 299-303; Lohse 1954: 82-83.

274. For the causal εἰ, see above Chapter 3 §2.g.

17b identifies the addressees with the House of God in 17a and with the righteous in 18a.[275] Depending on what aspects of these elements are emphasized we obtain different structures:

Fig. 4.17-18

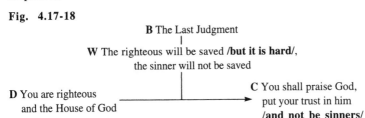

The basic structure is simple. The destiny of the ungodly and the Judgment of God should in principle only enhance the joy over the addressees' status and thus their willingness to praise God. The consolatory 19, which encourages the addressees to put their trust in God, builds upon this interpretation.[276]

The structure is however modified in a specific way, which resembles the Pauline 'indicative–imperative' scheme. The author refers to the addressees' difficult salvation[277] not only in order to show how impossible it is for the others to be saved, which in turn should add to the appreciation of the salvation. He also clearly implies that it is important for the addressees to remain on the right side of the line.[278]

---

275. The rhetorical questions in 17b and 18b can be resolved into statements: 'The end of those who are not obedient is bad'. Implied is a mysterious W, according to which the judgment will become harsher the further it goes (according to Goppelt (1978: 314) this kind of escalation is a fixed scheme in Revelation) and 'The ungodly and sinner will not be saved' (since for a sinner it is harder to be saved [W]). Here we have an *a fortiori* / *qal wachomer* (cf. also Goppelt 1978: 315 n. 58).

276. Kelly (1969: 193-94) holds this as the only possibility. Goppelt (1978: 233) calls the verse a summary, but also recognizes its function in the chain of arguments.

277. It may allude to their current sufferings; thus Selwyn 1947: 226; Goppelt 1978: 315.

278. Goppelt (1978: 314) rightly sees this warning aspect ('Er will sie vielmehr erschrecken'), but fails to recognize the alternative. Kelly (1969: 193) has the opposite opinion: those who do not obey are exclusively only the Gentiles. Kelly's argument is irresistible: 'Of course'. Only Selwyn (1947: 226) sees some ambiguity here.

Fig. 4.17-19

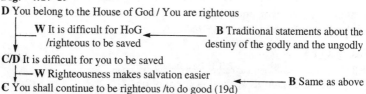

D You belong to the House of God / You are righteous

    W It is difficult for HoG   **B** Traditional statements about the
       /righteous to be saved   destiny of the godly and the ungodly

C/D It is difficult for you to be saved

    W Righteousness makes salvation easier

C You shall continue to be righteous /to do good (19d)   **B** Same as above

In the whole unit both joy over the status and fear for losing it serve as persuasive factors.[279]

Summarizing the subunit we can state that 14-19 presents the third and final version of the scheme: if the addressees have to suffer, they should do so as Christians and not as criminals. In so doing they take part in the sufferings of Christ and consequently in his glory. This should give them reason to rejoice and praise God, of which 1.3-12 speak as a fact. The joy in turn leads to endurance in the sufferings. The author thereby combines the eulogy and the paraenesis. He shows how the motivation in the paraenetic bulk of the text is built upon his statements about the addressees' joy in the midst of sufferings in 1.3-12.

The author's propagandistic repetition of the exhortation and the motivation may be criticized as a rhetorical technique. The thesis is slightly modified each time: it becomes clearer, more theological and more emotionally loaded.

c. *5.1-7—Internal Relations*

Like 5.12-14 and 1.1-2, this subunit is metacommunication: the author explains what he is saying. Although neither the form nor the contents are connected to the Gentiles, the unit also resembles the 'household code'. The exhortation and the motivating expressions are aimed not only at those who are addressed (the elders 1-4, the young men 5a) but to some extent at the whole congregation (5b-7). The peroratory aspect is clear in this unit (Thurén 1990: 157-60).

5.1   πρεσβυτέρους οὖν ἐν ὑμῖν
           παρακαλῶ
       ὁ συμπρεσβύτερος καὶ μάρτυς τῶν τοῦ Χριστοῦ παθημάτων,
       ὁ καὶ τῆς μελλούσης ἀποκαλύπτεσθαι δόξης κοινωνός·

---

279. The unit recalls 3.9-12 in this sense. The addressees are formally described as righteous and good. However, by contrasting their status and destiny with that of the ungodly the author does not simply seek to enhance their appreciation and joy of the status. More clearly than before he stresses that the addressees should avoid losing their own status.

5.2   ποιμάνατε τὸ ἐν ὑμῖν ποίμνιον τοῦ θεοῦ[280]
      μὴ ἀναγκαστῶς
ἀλλὰ ἑκουσίως <u>κατὰ</u> θεόν,
      μηδὲ αἰσχροκερδῶς
ἀλλὰ προθύμως,
5.3   μηδ' ὡς κατακυριεύοντες τῶν κλήρων
ἀλλὰ τύποι γινόμενοι τοῦ ποιμνίου·
5.4   <u>καὶ</u> φανερωθέντος τοῦ ἀρχιποίμενος κομιεῖσθε τὸν ἀμαράντινον τῆς δόξης στέφανον.
5.5   ὁμοίως νεώτεροι, ὑποτάγητε πρεσβυτέροις·
      πάντες δὲ ἀλλήλοις τὴν ταπεινοφροσύνην ἐγκομβώσασθε,
      <u>ὅτι</u> ὁ θεὸς ὑπερηφάνοις ἀντιτάσσεται, ταπεινοῖς δὲ δίδωσιν χάριν.
5.6   ταπεινώθητε <u>οὖν</u> ὑπὸ τὴν κραταιὰν χεῖρα τοῦ θεοῦ,
      <u>ἵνα</u> ὑμᾶς ὑψώσῃ ἐν καιρῷ,
5.7   πάσαν τὴν μέριμναν ὑμῶν ἐπιρίψαντες ἐπ' αὐτόν,
      <u>ὅτι</u> αὐτῷ μέλει περὶ ὑμῶν.

The basic C in 1-4 in 2a ('Be shepherds') is specified in 2-3 in several ways. As typical, each modification of the command simultaneously functions as a kind of short motivation,[281] but the clearest and most general motivation comes after all the modifications.[282]

The most interesting of these modifications is the antithesis in 2b: the elders should not be shepherds ἀναγκαστῶς but ἑκουσίως. As a command this could mean that their behaviour should not be constrained,[283] but the expression can also present the motivation for the elders' behaviour: 'not because you must, but because you are willing' (so e.g. NIV; for a Jewish background, see Goppelt 1978: 326 n. 21). This comment is important for our study of the whole motivation in the

280. Thus ℵ*, B; 𝔓[72], ℵ[2] *et al.* add ἐπισκοποῦντες.

281. Here ἑκουσίως, κατὰ θεόν, προθύμως, τύποι γενόμενοι... There are other motivating expressions, too. In v. 1 (see Chapter 3 §2.d) the author uses a technique that is actually beyond the range of this analysis of argumentation: the reference to the status of the author serves the *ethos* and *pathos* aspects in the motivation. The author's status as an apostle should give authority to his exhortation; his humble solidarity should make the addressees more willing to accept it. The author also briefly refers to the example of Christ and the relation between sufferings and glory.

282. Here in 4: καὶ φανερωθέντος... For corresponding structures, see e.g. 2.15.

283. According to a traditional but superfluous assumption, this refers to the ordination of the elders (Windisch and Preisker 1951: 75; Schelkle 1970: 129; Goppelt 1978: 326; Brox 1979: 231).

letter. If the expression is generalized to all addressees, they are not supposed to be coerced into obedience, but to obey of free will.[284]

Fig. 5.1-4

W *One will obey the person from whom one receives a valuable present*[285]

D When the Chief Shepherd appears   **C** You should be shepherds
you will receive glory (4)[286]   according to the will of God

In 5-6 the young men and everybody are told to be submissive—this time with a proper imperative (in the 'household code', an 'imperative participle' is used instead). The D in 6b is again teleological, and is resolved in the following way:

Fig. 5.5-6

B Support from the OT (5d)

W God lifts up the submissive in due time (6)

D *You want to be lifted up*   **C** You ought to be submissive (5b, c, 6a)

The motivating factor in this short structure is hard to choose, but the ground for a similar command in 7 ('because he cares for you') points toward the 'positive'—that is, the sentence is not a warning for not being lifted up, but rather a consolatory encouragement to patience.

Conclusions

In this peroratory unit a consolatory tone is clearer than before. Thus we can discern a development in the C of the author: from a narrative 'You rejoice in the midst of sufferings' (1.1-12) to an exhorting 'Be steadfast in the sufferings' (1.13–4.11) and finally to a consolatory 'You can rejoice despite the sufferings' (4.12–5.7).

The motivation is as equivocal as before. The addressees may rejoice in the midst of the sufferings, since they take part in the sufferings of

---

284. Cf. Selwyn 1947: 230 and 2 Cor. 9.7. In 3.7 the position of men is used as an example or a corresponding situation (Thurén 1990: 120). The motivating factor is theoretically ambiguous, as usual, but the positive is clearly emphasized. In principle the W could be aimed at motivating the addressees in two ways: willingness to live so that the future prize is secured, or so that joy over the prize creates willingness to thank its donor. The problem is thus the same as everywhere in the text. But this time the modifications 'not because you must but since you are willing' explicitly supports the second alternative.

285. This possible W could resemble that in Fig. 1.3-5/1.

286. καί does not here mark the purpose: see Chapter 3 §2.g. The adjective ἀμάραντον refers to the addressees' inheritance in 1.4.

Christ, which result(ed) in glory. But they are also said to rejoice in order to gain the glory. Since, however, the decisive factor is joy, as in 1.1-12, the 'positive' aspect predominates—it is difficult to visualize what a teleological, goal oriented joy could be. The eschatological motif serves primarily as consolation, but has also a warning side effect. In 5.1-7 the ethos aspect is used in the motivation, and the exhortation is applied in the addressees' internal relations. It is important for understanding the motivation that the elders are told to do their task of free will, not because they are compelled to do so.

7. The Peroratio 5.8-14[287]

5.8   νήψατε, γρηγορήσατε.
       ὁ ἀντίδικος ὑμῶν διάβολος ὡς λέων ὠρυόμενος περιπατεῖ ζητῶν
       τινα καταπιεῖν·
5.9   ᾧ ἀντίστητε στερεοὶ τῇ πίστει
       **εἰδότες τὰ αὐτὰ τῶν παθημάτων τῇ ἐν τῷ κόσμῳ ὑμῶν
       ἀδελφότητι ἐπιτελεῖσθαι.**
5.10   ὁ δὲ θεὸς πάσης χάριτος,
       ὁ καλέσας ὑμᾶς εἰς τὴν αἰώνιον αὐτοῦ δόξαν ἐν Χριστῷ,[288]
       ὀλίγον παθόντας
       αὐτὸς καταρτίσει, στηρίξει, σθενώσει, θεμελιώσει.
5.11   **αὐτῷ τὸ κράτος εἰς τοὺς αἰῶνας, ἀμήν.**

5.12   διὰ Σιλουανοῦ ὑμῖν τοῦ πιστοῦ ἀδελφοῦ, ὡς λογίζομαι, δι᾽ ὀλίγων
       ἔγραψα παρακαλῶν καὶ ἐπιμαρτυρῶν ταύτην εἶναι ἀληθῆ χάριν
       τοῦ θεοῦ εἰς ἣν στῆτε.
5.13   ἀσπάζεται ὑμᾶς ἡ ἐν Βαβυλῶνι συνεκλεκτὴ καὶ Μᾶρκος ὁ υἱός μου.
5.14   ἀσπάσασθε ἀλλήλους ἐν φιλήματι ἀγάπης.
       εἰρήνη ὑμῖν πᾶσιν τοῖς ἐν Χριστῷ.

In 5.8-9 the roaring of the lion is a dramatic picture of the addressees' difficulties (Brox 1979: 31-34, 238). The solidarity of the brethren does not go together ideologically with any other factor in the ideological structure of the motivation, but rather refers to the ethos aspect just as 5.1-2. The reasoning in 5.8-9 can be presented in the following way:[289]

---

287. This unit can be characterized as the proper *peroratio* of the text (see Thurén 1990: 160). In the formal, epistolary level we can discern a Body Closing in 12 (see Thurén 1990: 86-87) and a Letter Closing in 13-14.

288. Thus ℵ; 𝔓[72] adds Ἰησοῦ.

289. In 8-9 there is a C 'be alert and awake' which resembles 1.13 and 4.7. The D introduces a new factor in the motivation: the Devil.

Fig. 5.8

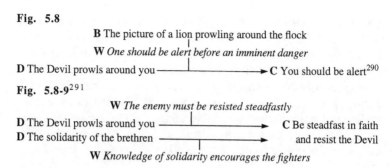

Fig. 5.8-9[291]

The short unit 5.10-11 repeats some central ideas in a peroratory manner. God is merciful and has called the addressees through Christ. The final goal of his summons is eternal glory. The expression ὀλίγον παθόντας could in principle be interpreted to be in a Grounds–Conclusion or a Means–Purpose relation to the following expressions, so that the suffering is a reason or condition for the glory. However, the statements about God's activity point toward a temporal or concessive interpretation. As in 1.1-5, God's role in the salvation, and this time even in the addressees' social and religious struggles, is emphasized. They also lead to the doxology in 11. This warm tone, the assurance of salvation and the doxology are not to be seen only as conventional or occasional phenomena, but just because they occur in the peroration they emphasize the 'positive' factor of the motivation.

The section 5.12-14 is again a metatext, where actual persuasive argumentation is not apparent. 12 as a Body Closing formula gives in a short form the reason for writing the Letter (Thurén 1990: 67). It has two sides: exhortation (παρακαλῶν) and witness to the grace (ἐπιμαρτυρῶν), which can refer to the 'positive' motivation of the exhortation, but also to the Letter's goal as a whole, that is, of intensifying the addressees' adherence to the Christian faith. The mention of

---

290. Here the B gives us a hint of the actual content of the command. The lion prowls round, seeking an animal that does not stay within the flock. Maybe the author warns the addressees not to leave their Christian community. The parallel motivation, the solidarity of the brethren, is a corresponding sociological argument.

291. In 9a the C 'resist him steadfastly' (emphasis on quality) builds upon the same D, but also on the brethren's (senders') solidarity (see above; against Kelly 1969: 210-11). In order to avoid being devoured, i.e. losing the Christian identity, the addressees should be firm in their faith.

Silvanus, Babylon (see Thurén 1990: 32-33) and the Christians there,[292] and Mark are designed to motivate the addressees by emphasizing the ethos of the text. This rhetorical function does not depend on the historical problems connected with the names.

---

292. Or 'the co-elect woman' (cf. Applegate 1992, esp. 604), which is well suited to the 'feminist' trend in 3.1-6. See above Chapter 5 §4.e.

Part III

SYNTHESIS: THE IDEOLOGICAL STRUCTURE OF THE MOTIVATION

Chapter 6

THE CLASSIFICATION OF TOPOI AND TACTICS

1. *Introduction*

The author's superb use of different techniques when combining commands and motivations is balanced on the content level by a large arsenal of motifs. Several separate motifs have been emphasized in previous research. A bourgeois and universal ethic (Grundmann 1938: 552), a reaction to God's retribution (Preisker 1949: 197, see also Michaels 1966: 401; Piper 1980: 213 n. 1, 227), a Christological-kerygmatic motif (Lohse 1954: 86, 88), and so on have been postulated by different scholars as the crux of the argumentation. This plurality originates partly from negligence of certain opposite motifs in the text (for further details see Chapter 1). Our analysis of argumentation provides us with a better basis for a comprehensive study.

It has become clear that different motivating expressions in 1 Peter seldom occur as independent. Instead, they usually constitute major logical structures, which are aimed at persuading the addressees. The author is wont to justify a command with several arguments, which are joined together into compound reasoning. In order to be effective, such a chain of arguments also requires many unexpressed factors appealing either to the reason or to the emotions. Our analysis has tried to display these factors as well. Corresponding features occur in other places in the Letter, where some previously explicit factors may in turn remain unsaid.[1] When all the particular motivating expressions—explicit and implicit—are conceptualized into motifs, and likewise the actual structures in which they occur are conceptualized into general ones, it may

---

1. See e.g. the analysis of 2.11-12 (Chapter 5 §4.a): The willingness to praise God, which is stated in the exordium, is only presumed in the motivation. On the other hand, it is not explained in the exordium how this praise is connected with obedience to God or to the author's injunctions. Such a close connection between praise and obedience appears as explicit in 2.11-12.

be possible to construct a total ideological structure of the motivation, in which all the arguments are included. Such a structure behind the text is necessary in order fully to understand the individual motivating chains of thought.

The aim of this chapter is to compile such a total structure. The study is based on the preceding analysis of argumentation, where some regular features in combining certain types of grounds, or, in other words, traces of the total structure, have already been found. Note that references to verses in 1 Peter should be seen also as references to the corresponding analyses in Chapter 5, as this chapter summarizes, and draws conclusions from, the study of argumentation.

Now, however, the scrutiny will be done on a super-textual, ideological level.[2] Even here a controlled system is needed in order to avoid overly hypothetical conclusions. The goal is not to reveal what the historical author had in mind. Instead, I want to offer a well documented alternative for understanding the text.

It is especially important to discern how the tension between the positive and the negative motivating factors is reflected in an ideological structure. This has proven to be the most difficult problem in assessing the nature of separate arguments.

First, I will classify all the explicit, and the principal implicit, motivating expressions. Then, in the following chapter, the motifs are apposed in order to reach the underlying ideological structure.

In this chapter, the motivating expressions, which have a similar content, will be collected into thematic groups, for example, utterances that refer to God's intention form one such group. The functions of the individual expressions in their argumentative structures will be compared. If they are consistent enough, the role of the theme in the ideological structure of argumentation can be determined. For practical reasons the procedure is presented in detail only in the first cases; thereafter just the results are given.

Discussion about the background of a theme is sometimes also required, since the general frame of reference, in which a certain theme

---

2.   See above Chapter 2 §4. An example: in the preceding chapter I have found in a textual unit motivating expressions a, b and c, which form a structure a–b–c. In another corresponding unit there are expressions b^1, c^1 and d, which form a structure b^1–c^1–d. Now I can state that the expressions can be generalized into themes A, B, C and D, which together build a general ideological structure A–B–C–D. This structure is useful when trying to understand the actual patterns in the text.

is to be understood, affects its interpretation. A few remarks have already been made in the preceding chapter.

In order to classify the expressions I use some general divisions. Motifs that do not imply any religious convictions on the part of the addressee are called 'non-religious'. The remainder are designated as 'religious', and will be further divided into 'anthropological', which are based on the addressees themselves, 'specifically theological', dealing with God or Christ, and 'other religious' motifs.

2. Non-Religious Motifs

a. *General Reasoning*

In 1 Peter there are many motivating expressions, whose understanding and application do not require any specific religious or Christian fore-knowledge or faith.[3] Expressions that contain specific religious components can also be included in this group, if the reasoning is understandable and effective, even if they are reduced.[4] In such cases the expressions will be discussed anew in connection with specifically religious motifs.

There are, however, many implicit Warrants, especially in *metaphors* or *similes*,[5] which appeal purely to reason or to a general custom, as for example in 1.14-17: 'a child obeys its father'. These will not be counted as non-religious motifs, if the actual argumentation has a religious content. Thus in 1.14 the appeal to the addressees becomes meaningful only if the religious component is preserved: 'As *God's* children...'

All other motivating expressions belong to religious motifs, by which I signify generalized motivating expressions whose rhetorical effectiveness requires a faith in one personal god, having thus mainly a Jewish or a Christian frame of reference.[6] Two different types of argument can be discerned: teleological and deontological (for definitions, see above Chapter 3 §1).

---

3. E.g. 2.20a ποῖον γὰρ κλέος εἰ ἁμαρτάνοντες καὶ κολαφιζόμενοι ὑπομενεῖτε;

4. E.g. 2.20b ἀλλ᾽ εἰ ἀγαθοποιοῦντες καὶ πάσχοντες ὑπομενεῖτε τοῦτο χάρις παρὰ θεῷ.

5. It is typical of 1 Peter that the distinction between these two techniques is difficult. E.g. 1.14 ὡς τέκνα can be either a simile 'like children' or a metaphor 'since you are children'. See Chapter 3 §2.e and Chapter 5 §3.b.

6. Thus e.g. 'god' in a general sense of the word as in Stoicism is not seen as a religious expression.

The first non-religious argument, or actually an explanation due to the form of the Claim, is found in 1.6-7:

> ⁶ἐν ᾧ [ἀγαλλιᾶσθε, ὀλίγον ἄρτι εἰ δέον ἐστὶν λυπηθέντες ἐν ποικίλοις πειρασμοῖς] ⁷ἵνα τὸ δοκίμιον ὑμῶν τῆς πίστεως πολυτιμότερον χρυσίου τοῦ ἀπολλυμένου διὰ πυρὸς δὲ δοκιμαζομένου, εὑρεθῇ εἰς ἔπαινον καὶ δόξαν καὶ τιμὴν [ἐν ἀποκαλύψει Ἰησοῦ Χριστοῦ]

The reasoning is sound as such, and even appealing as persuasion, although the religious factors are reduced.[7] But what is the function of the non-religious motif? The reasoning is attached to a religious idea: you rejoice, although you may have to suffer, since it is the will of God,[8] and leads to glory when Christ is revealed. Apparently the non-religious reasoning seeks to support the perhaps too simple religious motivation.

The following non-religious expression is found in 2.11-12:

> ¹¹[ἀγαπητοί, παρακαλῶ] ὡς παροίκους καὶ παρεπιδήμους [ἀπέχεσθαι τῶν σαρκικῶν ἐπιθυμιῶν] αἵτινες στρατεύονται κατὰ τῆς ψυχῆς· ¹²[τὴν ἀναστροφὴν ὑμῶν ἐν τοῖς ἔθνεσιν ἔχοντες καλήν,] ἵνα ἐν ᾧ καταλαλοῦσιν ὑμῶν ὡς κακοποιῶν ἐκ τῶν καλῶν ἔργων ἐποπτεύοντες δοξάσωσιν [τὸν θεὸν] ἐν ἡμέρᾳ ἐπισκοπῆς.

Here the non-religious motivation has, according to our survey, two distinct functions. First, since the goal is to affect the Gentiles by complying with their ethical requirements, the commands are partly motivated with thoughts which even the Gentiles could accept. Secondly, the non-religious grounds make the persuasion, which is based on God's purpose or intention, more reasonable and easier to understand. In both cases, the non-religious reasoning is thus aimed at supporting the religious one.

The non-religious grounds are used in a corresponding way in the whole unit (2.11-25): 13-15, 19-20.[9]

---

7.   See above 5.1.c, Fig. 1.6-7/b. Since standing the test results in glory, as the example of gold shows, and since the addressees want to produce glory, they are willing to stand the test, with which their current difficulties are identified. According to an alternative interpretation, the addressees rejoice despite suffering, since it does not prevent glory.

8.   If εἰ δέον ἐστίν is somewhat overinterpreted, see Selwyn 1947: 127; Goppelt 1978: 99-100. Brox (1979: 64) interprets so in the light of 3.17.

9.   E.g. the word χάρις does not necessarily have any religious content (Selwyn 1947: 89); it is typical also in Stoicism (Pohlenz 1948: 141). See the Excursus in Chapter 6.

¹³[ὑποτάγητε πάση ἀνθρωπίνη κτίσει] διὰ τὸν κύριον, ¹⁴[εἴτε βασιλεῖ] ὡς ὑπερέχοντι [εἴτε ἡγεμόσιν] ὡς δι' αὐτοῦ πεμπομένοις εἰς ἐκδίκησιν κακοποιῶν ἔπαινον δὲ ἀγαθοποιῶν ¹⁵[ὅτι οὕτως ἐστὶν τὸ θέλημα τοῦ θεοῦ] ἀγαθοποιοῦντας φιμοῦν τὴν τῶν ἀφρόνων ἀνθρώπων ἀγνωσίαν ¹⁹τοῦτο γὰρ χάρις εἰ διὰ συνείδησιν [θεοῦ] ὑποφέρει τις λύπας πάσχων ἀδίκως. ²⁰ποῖον γὰρ κλέος εἰ ἁμαρτάνοντες καὶ κολαφιζόμενοι ὑπομενεῖτε; ἀλλ' εἰ ἀγαθοποιοῦντες καὶ πάσχοντες ὑπομενεῖτε τοῦτο χάρις [παρὰ θεῷ].

In 3.1-7 the author makes a similar use of these grounds (3.1-2, 3, 4, 7). However, the short expression in 3.7b ὡς ἀσθενεστέρῳ σκεύει is not explicitly connected with any utterance about God.

¹[ὁμοίως αἱ γυναῖκες ὑποτασσόμεναι τοῖς ἰδίοις ἀνδράσιν,] ἵνα καὶ εἴ τινες ἀπειθοῦσιν τῷ λόγῳ, διὰ τῆς τῶν γυναικῶν ἀναστροφῆς ἄνευ λόγου κερδηθήσονται, ²ἐποπτεύσαντες τὴν ἐν φόβῳ ἀναστροφὴν ὑμῶν. ³[ὧν ἔστω οὐχ] ὁ ἔξωθεν ἐμπλοκῆς τριχῶν καὶ περιθέσεως χρυσίων ἢ ἐνδύσεως ἱματίων κόσμος ⁴ἀλλ' ὁ κρυπτὸς τῆς καρδίας ἄνθρωπος ἐν τῷ ἀφθάρτῳ τοῦ πραέως καὶ ἡσυχίου πνεύματος, ὅ ἐστιν [ἐνώπιον τοῦ θεοῦ] πολυτελές. ⁷οἱ ἄνδρες ὁμοίως, συνοικοῦντες κατὰ γνῶσιν, ὡς ἀσθενεστέρῳ σκεύει τῷ γυναικείῳ ἀπονέμοντες τιμήν.

In 3.10-11 comes a third function: to explain the argumentation with the judgment of God.

¹⁰ὁ γὰρ θέλων ζωὴν ἀγαπᾶν καὶ ἰδεῖν ἡμέρας ἀγαθὰς παυσάτω τὴν γλῶσσαν ἀπὸ κακοῦ καὶ χείλη τοῦ μὴ λαλῆσαι δόλον ¹¹ἐκκλινάτω δὲ ἀπὸ κακοῦ καὶ ποιησάτω ἀγαθόν ζητησάτω εἰρήνην καὶ διωξάτω αὐτήν

Deontological non-religious grounds are found also in 3.13-14, 17 and a teleological one in 3.16. They resemble the previous instances and are also connected with the addressees' relation to the Gentiles, and with God's intention with these.

¹³καὶ τίς ὁ κακώσων ὑμᾶς ἐὰν τοῦ ἀγαθοῦ ζηλωταὶ γένησθε; ¹⁴ἀλλ' εἰ καὶ πάσχοιτε διὰ δικαιοσύνην, μακάριοι. ¹⁶[ἀλλὰ μετὰ πραΰτητος καὶ φόβου, συνείδησιν ἔχοντες ἀγαθήν,] ἵνα ἐν ᾧ καταλαλεῖσθε καταισχυνθῶσιν οἱ ἐπηρεάζοντες ὑμῶν τὴν ἀγαθὴν ἐν Χριστῷ ἀναστροφήν. ¹⁷κρεῖττον γὰρ ἀγαθοποιοῦντας, [εἰ θέλοι τὸ θέλημα τοῦ θεοῦ], πάσχειν ἢ κακοποιοῦντας.

In 4.1, 8 there are two rules or Warrants that can be interpreted as non-religious grounds, but which also have a theological or a Christological content.

¹Χριστοῦ οὖν παθόντος σαρκὶ [καὶ ὑμεῖς τὴν αὐτὴν ἔννοιαν ὁπλίσασθε,] ὅτι ὁ παθὼν σαρκὶ πέπαυται ἁμαρτίας
⁸[πρὸ πάντων τὴν εἰς ἑαυτοὺς ἀγάπην ἐκτενῆ ἔχοντες], ὅτι ἀγάπη καλύπτει πλῆθος ἁμαρτιῶν.

In 4.14-16, which is the third version of the motivation (earlier in 2.19-20; 3.13-14, 17), the non-religious motif has vanished. Probably it has become unnecessary due to the modification in the rhetorical situation: the author can express himself freely in the concluding parts of the text. However, in 4.18 we can still discern a general ground, which has a context similar to the previous ones but which is now short and somewhat ambivalent: both a deontological and a teleological interpretation are possible. As Christians the addressees are identified as δίκαιοι, but it is not difficult to see an implied idea: in order to avoid the fate of the ungodly, they ought to live and act like δίκαιοι.

¹⁸καὶ εἰ ὁ δίκαιος μόλις σώζεται, ὁ ἀσεβὴς καὶ ἁμαρτωλὸς ποῦ φανεῖται;

Summarizing we can state that the non-religious expressions have rather coherent functions throughout the Letter. They are connected with theological arguments in three ways: (a) They support the argumentation based on the will of God and make it more reasonable. In this case the non-religious ground can be characterized as deontological. (b) They support the argumentation with God's intention, then in a teleological form. (c) In one case (3.10-11) the function is to explain God's judgment.

The non-religious argumentation occurs with two exceptions in the central sections of *argumentatio* (2.11–4.11), and in a context which deals with the addressees' relation to the Gentiles. Their main purpose is to show how the command to good works, καλὰ ἔργα (this is the main command in 2.11–4.11), which is motivated with God's will, is simultaneously something reasonable. Obedience to the commands corresponds to the ideal of the non-Christian people, and it is to be practiced in order to influence them. Thereby God's intention is fulfilled. Even the warning concerning God's judgment can appeal to reason.

There are thus clear signs of an ethical thinking, where not only the commands but even the heart of the ethics, the motivation, resembles the ethics of common popular philosophy (despite a possible Jewish origin; see the Excursus below). However, overly hasty conclusions should not be reached. The use of non-religious and Hellenistic ideas seems to serve a specific goal in the text. Such motivating expressions are concentrated in the section discussing relations to the non-Christians (2.11–4.11). This may well be one reason why the author shifts to a language that is understandable even in a purely Hellenistic atmosphere. When the addressees' conduct should be such as to earn the Gentiles' respect, it is far better to be καλός καὶ ἀγαθός—this is a central idea in Stoicism (Pohlenz 1948: 302, 341)—than ἅγιος.

Adding the fact that most of the expressions either have a theological aspect or are surrounded by theological and Christological statements, they can hardly be used *per se* as a proof of an unhappy development of the 'original Christian ethics' (cf. Marxsen 1989: 201).

The non-religious motifs are thus used as side-motivations which support the specifically theological one. Theological motivation itself, as appealing to authority, is typical of Early Christianity (Mack 1990: 93-102). In Greek rhetoric it is unusual and inadvisable. In Toulmin's list of *fallacies* also one category is an appeal to 'authority as the last word on a given topic' (Toulmin *et al.* 1984: 142-44). Maybe in 1 Peter non-religious reasoning is always supported by references to God, in view of the Hellenistic audience, in order to back up the motivation. Thus it is used as a good rhetorical device.

Due to the subordinate role of the non-religious argumentation no far-reaching conclusions about their importance in the author's ideology can be made. But one specific idea can be discerned: the principle of retribution. The author refers to the consequences of behaviour. If you do good you will gain credit and vice versa. Even this idea is usually placed in, for example consolatory (4.17) or explanatory (2.14) statements.

Excursus: Good Works as a Hellenistic Concept in 1 Peter

When seeking to understand the role of non-religious motivation it is useful to compare it with the surrounding culture and search for features that have parallels in Hellenistic literature.[10] The rhetorical skills in 1 Peter indicate that the author has

---

10. Since it is too arbitrary to separate Jewish material from Early Christian thinking, it is not studied here. For the Early Jewish ethical milieu as a background for 1 Peter see Prostmeier 1990: 278-318. On pp. 213-72 he offers a general view on the corresponding Hellenistic milieu.

undergone some kind of training in Hellenistic school rhetoric. Simultaneously, the text is based on a broad paraenetical tradition. These notions let us assume an influence from popular philosophy, not only in the commands but also in the motivation of the paraenesis.

W. Grundmann claims that the idea of good works in 1 Peter (and in the Pastorals) comes from Hellenistic Judaism, which in turn has been influenced by general Hellenism and Stoicism. The decisive factor in the ethics is the question of 'good' or 'right'.[11] Preisker characterizes the motivation of the paraenesis as rationalistic and moralistic; Christological and eschatological ideas have waned (1949: 217-18). Instead, he sees retribution as the crucial factor (1949: 197). Individual virtues have replaced *agape* and an ethical total view (1949: 209). All this resembles Stoicism according to Preisker.[12]

An opposite opinion is represented by van Unnik, for example, according to whom the emphasis on good works in 1 Peter comes from Jesus and the Letter displays the eschatological hope of the first generation.[13] In more general terms, the famous Stoa-scholar M. Pohlenz claims that although no direct dependence on Hellenistic philosophy can be shown in Early Christian texts, general common features may still be found (Pohlenz 1948: 406-407).

When searching for influence from Hellenistic popular philosophy, motivating expressions, which do not refer to any religious conceptions, are of great importance. Many of them resemble ethics found among popular philosophers and in Stoicism. 2.11 refers to a typical theme, the struggle between flesh and soul.[14] 2.16 (ὡς ἐλεύθεροι καὶ μὴ ὡς ἐπικάλυμμα ἔχοντες τῆς κακίας τὴν ἐλευθερίαν ἀλλ' ὡς θεοῦ δοῦλοι) recalls Seneca's maxim, for example, 'Deo parere libertas est' (*De vita beata* 15.7), or 'Philosophiae servire libertas est'.[15] The priority of inner beauty over gold and fine clothes (3.3-4) is according to Pohlenz typically Stoic.[16] The reasoning in 2.19-20 and 3.13-14, 17 (unjust suffering is not shameful) has

11. Grundmann 1938: 552-53. According to him, the paraenetical language comes from a 'Vulgärsprache' influenced by Stoicism, and this popular ethic also affected the contents of the paraenesis in 1 Peter.

12. Preisker 1949: 211. He takes up references to baptism (1.22) and the End (4.7), which are hardly typically Stoic themes.

13. Van Unnik 1954/55: 109-10; 1980: 118. According to him, the concept itself is of Greek origin. Dijkman 1987: 264-66 opposes this opinion and claims a clear Jewish origin.

14. The war between flesh and soul is also typical of Plato and the Hellenistic popular philosophy. See Selwyn 1947: 170. Kelly (1969: 104) argues that 'flesh' as such is not used in a pejorative sense. This may be partly true, but the contrast between 'soul' and 'flesh' corresponds to that of inner and outer in 3.3-4.

15. Seneca, *Epistulae morales* 1.8.7; the quotation is from Epicurus, but Seneca claims that the idea itself is common even among the Romans.

16. Pohlenz 1948: 421. However, Pohlenz presents this as an example of the Church Fathers' dependence on Stoicism and does not find it in 1 Peter.

many parallels in the philosophical texts.[17] To refer to what is good, valuable and so on is normal in a Hellenistic milieu.[18] The idea of a slave's unjust suffering (2.19) can also be found in Stoic literature.[19] The expression ἀγαθοῦ ζηλωταί and the rhetorical question in 2.20 (including the word κλέος, which is *hapax* in the New Testament), belong to the philosophical terminology.[20] The words καλός and ἀγαθός replace the Jewish ἅγιος in 2.12 (Goppelt 1978: 159; cf. Pohlenz 1948: 119-23).

Some sections in 1 Peter resemble a Jewish and an Hellenistic tradition of enumerating vices (see Wibbing 1959: 77). In 4.3 such a catalogue is explicitly used as a motivation, introduced with γάρ. Bultmann argued that this is a typical Christian custom (1953: 104), while Kamlah sees it as a Jewish custom connected with proselyte baptism.[21] At least the terminology is typical of a wide paraenetical tradition (see Wibbing 1959: 93-94). But therefore to see 4.3 as a typical example of 'jüdische... Werkheiligkeit', as Preisker does, is not plausible.[22] Other expressions resemble Hellenistic language, but do not lead to ideological inferences either: for example, φθαρτός in 1.23 sounds like a concept from popular philosophy (cf. Käsemann 1960: 137; Harder 1973: 100-103), but the author actually derives the idea from Ps. 102.12-13. In a similar way, 4.3 ἀρκετὸς γὰρ ὁ παρεληλυθὼς χρόνος... seems Hellenistic (Isocrates, Panegyricus 167: ἱκανὸς γὰρ ὁ παρεληλυθώς...), but actually only belongs to universal rhetorical devices.[23] The basic Hellenistic term ἀρετή appears in 2.9, but it is used only about God. Otherwise the term is, according to Pohlenz, superseded by ἀγάπη (Pohlenz 1948: 406). The 'household codes' are widely believed to be based on a common

17. Plato, *Gorgias* 508b: τὸ ἀδικεῖν τοῦ ἀδικεῖσθαι... κάκιον; Cicero, *Tusculanae Disputationes* 5.56: 'Accipere quam facere praestat iniuriam'. See several examples in Selwyn 1947, e.g. pp. 173-75.

18. Pohlenz 1948: 119-23. It was a typical technique in rhetoric to enumerate four or six such words. E.g. in *Missale Romanum, Praefatio*: '... gratias agamus Domino Deo nostro.—Dignum et iustum est.—Vere *dignum et iustum est, aequum et salutare*, nos tibi semper et ubique gratias agere.' Lausberg calls this way of motivation final (1960 §375). Cf. also van Unnik 1954/55: 108.

19. Seneca, *Epistulae morales* 47. See also Pohlenz 1948: 136 and Goppelt 1978: 194 n. 20.

20. E.g. Epictetus, *Dissertationes* 2.12.25. Martin (1992: 285-88), however, stresses the Jewish aspect of the expression.

21. Kamlah 1964: 179-80. He does not, however, refer to any Jewish text, and the dating of the proselyte baptism is still under discussion (see Beasley-Murray 1979: 18-31).

22. Preisker 1949: 201. It would be hard to find such a *Werkheiligkeit* even in Ancient Jewish texts, as modern studies of Judaism, especially Sanders (1977) have demonstrated. For discussion, see Laato 1991.

23. The successful campaign of the Social Democrats in Finland 1948 had a similar slogan 'Jo riittää!' (Enough!), followed by a list of the Communists' alleged faults. For further detail, see Hakalehto 1974: 31-36.

Hellenistic pattern, which however cannot be found (see Hartman 1988; Thurén 1990: 95 n. 8).

Without taking a firm stand on the question of the origin of the idea of good works in 1 Peter we can state that *per se* it has clear Hellenistic parallels and was thus easily understandable for the addressees of 1 Peter and for their neighbors. Clearly employed as a means of good communication, it is not necessarily evidence of any ideological development in the Letter.

b. *The Relation between the Author and the Addressees*
The relationship between the communicants is not used as an argument in the particular structures, except for 5.1a, where the author refers to his position as a συμπρεσβύτερος when speaking to the elders. But usually the relationship has a rather general function, enhancing the effectiveness of the argumentation and persuasion as such. To this category belong (a) the ethos or emphasis of the author's position and (b) his relation to the addressees. Expressions that belong to the first type are found in: 1.1a and 5.1, 12-13; the second type occurs in 1.1b, 2; 2.11; 4.12; and 5.9, 10-13.

Since expressions about the author are aimed at giving authority and weight to his claims,[24] utterances that refer to his relation to the addressees ought to create an emotional impact and a positive attitude toward him and his message. Therefore, following the rhetorical conventions, they are situated in the beginning and end, that is, in the *exordium* and the *peroratio* of the Letter. However, personal expressions are scarce in the text, which makes a theoretical impact. This may be partly due to its general epistolary nature and the historical situation (see Thurén 1990: 81-83, 33-38).

3. *Anthropological Motifs*

a. *Life in Sin*
Two types of motivating expression occur, referring to a way of life described pejoratively as the life in sin. In the first half of the Letter (1.1–2.10) the author refers to the *addressees' former life*: 1.14, 18, 23-24; 2.10.

> ¹⁴[μὴ συσχηματιζόμενοι] ταῖς πρότερον ἐν τῇ ἀγνοίᾳ ὑμῶν ἐπιθυμίαις

---

24. See Thurén 1990: 102. This function does not depend on the question of the origin of the Letter.

¹⁸ἐλυτρώθητε ἐκ τῆς ματαίας ὑμῶν ἀναστροφῆς πατροπαραδότου
²³ἀναγεγεννημένοι οὐκ ἐκ σπορᾶς φθαρτῆς ἀλλὰ ἀφθάρτου διὰ
λόγου ζῶντος θεοῦ καὶ μένοντος. ²⁴διότι πᾶσα σὰρξ ὡς χόρτος
καὶ πᾶσα δόξα αὐτῆς ὡς ἄνθος χόρτου· ἐξηράνθη ὁ χόρτος καὶ
τὸ ἄνθος ἐξέπεσεν·
¹⁰οἵ ποτε οὐ λαός, νῦν δὲ λαὸς θεοῦ, οἱ οὐκ ἠλεημένοι, νῦν δὲ
ἐλεηθέντες.

In the rest of the text only 2.25 can be compared with these
expressions:[25]

²⁵ἦτε γὰρ ὡς πρόβατα πλανώμενοι

In the second half of the text (2.11–5.13) the *Gentiles' current way of
life* replaces the addressees' former life: 3.12; 4.3-5 and 4.17. In the preceding text only 2.7 refers to the non-Christians so as to preface the
change of focus. In 3.19-20 the disobedient spirits are assigned a
function similar to that of the Gentiles.

3.12ὅτι ὀφθαλμοὶ κυρίου ἐπὶ δικαίους καὶ ὦτα αὐτοῦ εἰς δέησιν
αὐτῶν, πρόσωπον δὲ κυρίου ἐπὶ ποιοῦντας κακά.
4.3ἀρκετὸς γὰρ ὁ παρεληλυθὼς χρόνος τὸ βούλημα τῶν ἐθνῶν
κατειργάσθαι πεπορευμένους ἐν ἀσελγείαις, ἐπιθυμίαις,
οἰνοφλυγίαις, κώμοις, πότοις καὶ ἀθεμίτοις εἰδωλολατρίαις. ⁴ἐν ᾧ
ξενίζονται μὴ συντρεχόντων ὑμῶν εἰς τὴν αὐτὴν τῆς ἀσωτίας
ἀνάχυσιν βλασφημοῦντες, ⁵οἳ ἀποδώσουσιν λόγον τῷ ἑτοίμως
ἔχοντι κρῖναι ζῶντας καὶ νεκρούς.
¹⁷ὅτι καιρὸς τοῦ ἄρξασθαι τὸ κρίμα ἀπὸ τοῦ οἴκου τοῦ θεοῦ· εἰ
δὲ πρῶτον ἀφ' ἡμῶν, τί τὸ τέλος τῶν ἀπειθούντων τῷ τοῦ θεοῦ
εὐαγγελίῳ;

There are some characteristics of the grounds dealing with the life in sin.
It is always described as something negative. The addressees' former life
was gloomy because of its transience (1.18-25), the Gentiles' life because
of God's judgment (e.g. 4.17-18). However, when the reason for the
addressees' and the Gentiles' dreary life are identified with each other in
4.3-5, it becomes clear that the Judgment and retribution threaten the
addressees as well as the Gentiles, if they return to their former lifestyle.
Even in 4.17-18 this idea can be found, but only an implicit. Thus it is
typical of the author that the addressees are not directly threatened with
God's Judgment (so also Michaels 1966: 401).

The description of the life in sin has several functions in the text. It

25. 4.3-5 refers both to the Gentiles' and the addressees' life.

renders the commands more concrete and signifies certain ways of behaviour and thought as negative, something to be avoided (e.g. the catalogue of vices in 4.3-4).

The description seeks in each case to serve as a dark background to the addressees' new status. This is done in order to increase the addressees' appreciation of their Christian life (see e.g. the analysis of 1.14-15, Chapter 5 §3.b). The other motivating purpose is to warn the addressees. The author urges them not to begin to live again according to the old customs, which are seen as signs of their former status. He reminds them that old status means a purposeless life and God's punishment (e.g. in 1.14-17). Although this train of thought is not clearly expressed in the text, especially the use of the Gentiles and their destiny as negative examples indicate that even the addressees may meet a similar fate.

Concerning the background of the motivation with the life in sin we can state that it bears witness to a broad paraenetical tradition, but does not lead to any ideological results (see the Excursus above).

b. *Reference Groups*

The author contrasts the addressees' current status not only with the former one, or with the Gentiles' life and destiny, but also with the prophets and angels (1.10-12). The primary function of the comparison in 1.10-12 is to make the addressees appreciate their new status by showing that they have something which the prophets only could await and the angels wish to behold.

A positive reference group is found in 3.5-6. The OT women, particularly Sarah, are depicted (structurally instead of the example of Christ) to show that submissive behaviour is the right attitude for the Christian woman (and for any addressee).

c. *The Change: Baptism*

The author describes the addressees' transition to their new status in the motivation from two perspectives: as their own experience and as God's call. In the first case the references to the change are usually connected to baptism.

Seen from the addressees' perspective the transition from the old life to the new is mentioned especially in the following verses: 1.3, 22, 23; 2.1-5, 25; 3.21.

The short expressions in 3.6 and 4.10 may also belong to this category. In all the cases the author refers directly or indirectly to baptism, which thereby constitutes the most important phenomenon in the transition from the old status to the new. The author either speaks of baptismal education (e.g. 2.1) or the new birth (e.g. 1.3). Even the aorist form indicates this punctual incident (e.g. 2.3, 25). *Expressis verbis* the baptism is mentioned only in 3.1.

Because of the many expressions dealing with baptism, scholars at the beginning of the century developed a theory of 1 Peter as a baptismal homily (Perdelwitz 1911; Windisch and Preisker 1951; Cross 1954; see also above, Chapter 1 §2.a), or at least claimed that baptism is the central theme in the letter (Boismard 1961). In more modern research these theories have been commonly rejected (see Chapter 1 §2.c), but especially Hill and Kosala have attempted to discover the ways in which references to baptism are connected to the admonitions and the question about suffering.[26]

According to Hill, the baptismal references are intended to create readiness to suffer, since it is a known fact that those who are baptized have to suffer for their faith, and thus by being baptized a person expresses willingness to suffer like the other Christians do (1976: 185). Kosala claims that baptism is used as a source of power for suffering, since it is presented as giving to those who are baptized a hope of a future salvation (1985: 31-32). Baptism as such does not guarantee salvation, but it makes it easier for the Christians to live aright and thereby reach the final salvation (1985: 35-36). Kosala rebuts an interpretation, according to which those who are baptized would be children of God or his heirs (1985: 37, arguing that this interpretation is Paulinistic). According to him, the baptism is only a point of departure for the struggle toward salvation.

These solutions cause new problems. Many expressions in the text are incompatible with Kosala's interpretation: according to 1.5 God guarantees the addressees' salvation, which they are sure to attain (1.9). In 1.14, 17 they are called 'children of God', and also 1.23; 2.1-2 combines baptism, new birth, and the metaphor 'God's children'. The crucial verse is 3.21. There the author says explicitly that baptism saves the addressees. The specification οὐ ἀπόθεσις...ἀλλὰ ἐπερώτημα has in the context a meaning opposite to Kosala's interpretation. It is aimed

26. See Chapter 1 §2.4; Hill 1976; Kosala 1985. Cf. also Moule 1956/57. Hill (1976: 189) states, 'To say that the letter, or most of it, is a baptismal homily or liturgy is to treat as explicit, direct and prominent what is only implicit, presupposed and subsidiary'.

against a conviction according to which salvation would depend directly on obedience to the ethical education, which certainly has an important position in the text.

Hill's interpretation, according to which baptism is presented as an expression of the addressees' willingness to suffer for their faith (1976: 184-85), is too simple a solution. It implies that before their baptism the addressees knew people who were baptized and therefore experienced suffering, but such an implication is based on unknown historical facts. On the contrary, the Letter implies addressees to whom the connection between a life as a Christian and suffering is a new phenomenon (see e.g. 3.14; 4.12; for further details see Chapter 5 §§5.a, 6.a, and Thurén 1990: 105). The general rhetorical situation of the Letter is determined by a need to explain how this connection can be understood, and that the addressees should live as Christians even if they have to suffer—something which was either unknown to, or hardly understood by, the addressees.

My analysis of argumentation has resulted in a clear explanation of why the author uses references to baptism in the admonitions and motivating expressions.

Baptism is presented as the decisive event that has moved the addressees from the old to the new status (1.3, 23). Therefore it should be important and thus also compelling for them. The author utilizes traditional material from Early Christian baptismal education (Selwyn 1947: 393-400) in order to show the addressees that baptism means and requires a new way of life (e.g. 1.22; 2.1-5; 3.6).

Especially when referring to baptism or to baptismal terminology, the author uses ambiguous expressions, usually participles, which can be interpreted either as commands or as motivating expressions (1.22, 23; 2.1, 4, 5). This custom is intended to suit the text to different addressees (Thurén 1990: 167-76), but can also be explained on an ideological level. By using ambiguous expressions the author is trying to show how the baptism urges the addressees to a new life: just as they have begun to lead a new life after being baptized, they should now continue in the same way. This interpretation of baptism is well suited to both the 'positive' and the 'negative' lines of understanding the motivation, but especially to the 'negative'. If the addressees do not live in the way in which they are expected to do as baptized persons, they will forfeit their salvation. In order not to overemphasize this idea the author has added a reservation in 3.21, where he points out that the change in lifestyle however is not *the* factor that gives it a saving power (see the analysis of argumentation in Chapters 3–5).

The 'passive' among the implied addressees are induced to live like their neighbours in order to avoid social pressure (Thurén 1990: 112-19). Therefore one of the author's principal tasks is to show that it is impossible to be a Christian without a specific Christian way of life. With this in mind it is easy to understand why he uses the baptismal theme so much. Baptism draws the decisive borderline between the former life, which corresponds to the life of the neighbours, and the new one. This is especially emphasized in the example of Noah, who was saved through water from the corrupted society (3.19-21).[27]

Summarizing, we can say that by referring to the ethical baptismal education, with which the addressees are familiar, the author first proves that they, as being baptized, should live according to the rules of the new life. He uses a technique that resembles the Pauline imperative–indicative scheme, but in a more compact form (see Thurén 1990: 184-85). The external pressure should not prevent a specific Christian way of life.

The second purpose of the baptismal references is to describe the transition from the old to the new life from the addressees' perspective. It is a proof of God's and Christ's saving act at the personal level.

Thus the baptismal theme supports well both the commands and the motivation. It is one of the author's most conspicuous themes, but it plays only a limited role in the Letter. Therefore it is an over-interpretation to call baptism *the* central theme of the letter.

d. *The New Status*

An often repeated theme in the motivation is the reference to the new status. According to Delling the Christian existence in 1 Peter is grounded on God's act in the 'Christusgeschehen', and its goal is the *parousia*. This is why the addressees should live 'in einem neuen Handeln...' (1973: 112). Delling does not, however, explain in detail how the new way of life is actually provoked. Piper argues that this is one of the most crucial questions in the motivation in 1 Peter: How is the Christological *Kerygma* supposed to influence the addressees to

---

27. See Chapter 5 §5.b. We can see that the ideological analysis completes the basic rhetorical study and the argumentation analysis: The example of Noah, which seemed to be somewhat loose from the context, appears to carry a message that is crucial for the whole Letter.

begin to live in a new way?[28] A survey of the functions of the addressees' new status, the 'new existence', is needed in order to penetrate the solution of this problem.

We have seen that one of the central goals of the first half of the Letter (1.1–2.10) is to make the addressees appreciate their status to the degree that they become willing to act in a way which the status implies (see Chapter 5 §3, the first half, Conclusions). The life in sin, the transition, and also many other themes function in the argumentation through increasing the positive assessment of the addressees' new status: thus, for example, the addressees' former life and the Gentiles' current one serve as a dark background to the new status (1.18; 4.3-6), and the change constitutes evidence of the new relationship to God (e.g. in 2.3). Thus the description of the new status belongs without doubt to the most important motifs in the Letter.[29]

Motivating expressions that speak of the addressees' new status recur throughout in the Letter, especially in the following verses: 1.1, (5, 7, 8-9, 12,) 13, 14, 17, 21; 2.2, 4, 5, 7, 9-10, 11, 16; 3.6, 7; 4.4, 9-10, 13, 14, 17, 18; 5.3.

Even the expressions about the Spirit (1.2 and 4.14) and the warning about διάβολος (5.8) are closely connected with the addressees' new status: the first serve as consolatory statements, and the second may be aimed at aggravating the addressees' view of their problems (see the analysis, Chapter 5).

The new status is described from different perspectives. In the first part of the letter particularly it is identified with a new relation to God (e.g. in 1.14, 17) and to Christ (2.4-10). In the rest of the text (and introductory in the exordial 1.1), the author adds a new feature: alienation from the society (2.11-12) and, as a result of this, participation in Christ's sufferings (4.13).

As was the case with expressions about baptism, utterances about the new status can also be understood either as commands or as motivating expressions. The addressees' new status either urges them to be 'strangers' or ready to suffer, or it serves as a motivation: since they are strangers and people watch the behaviour of strangers, it is important to

---

28. Piper 1980: 213. Unfortunately Piper does not give any clear answer to the question.

29. Against Kosala 1985: 212: 'Daher mach 1 Petr keine indikativischen Aussagen bei die Getauften, ausser dass sie Getaufte sind. Er bringt seine Theologie, wie Jak, nur durch imperativische Aussagen zum Ausdruck.'

live ethically (2.11-12). The author also uses the new status in persuasion by showing that the sufferings the addressees as Christians have to endure are not unnatural but actually belong to the new life. Since the new life is nevertheless valuable for them, they should be ready to accept even its negative side effects.

The motivating function of the new status may be the most important, since the author never explicitly urges the addressees to suffering. As such it refers more to a Jewish background, although some striking Hellenistic traces can be found even in this type of motivation (see the Excursus, above in this chapter). The motivation can be understood, just as was the case with baptism, both in a 'positive' and in a 'negative' way: the expressions about the new life are designed to increase the joy therein and to show that sufferings should not prevent this joy, but, if a person tries to avoid the sufferings that ensue from the new life, they will lose the status.

Usually this motif is not isolated, but is connected to other grounds. Wherever it occurs its main function is to create joy and willingness to praise God (see above e.g. Chapter 5 §3, the first half, Conclusions; cf. also Nauck 1955: 76-77), which in turn should lead to willingness to obey him (e.g. 1.8-13).

e. *Hope and the Final Salvation*

One of the most impressive grounds used in order to render the addressees appreciative of their new status is the emphasis on the hope of immortality and final salvation, which belong to the new status. Such expressions are found especially in the following verses: 1.3-5, 7, 9, 13, 21; 2.2, 6; 3.7, 9; 4.(7,)13; 5.4, 5, 6. We have seen that this hope can seek to rouse the will to obey the author's admonitions in two principal ways:

First, it should produce joy over the final salvation, which the addressees have already partly obtained and certainly will obtain in full (so also Nauck 1955: 76-77). The joy should then transform into willingness to praise God and act according to his will. This is most clearly expressed in 1.3-9, where the author correspondingly emphasizes that God guarantees the salvation.

Secondly, it is aimed at producing willingness to gain, or fear of losing, the eventual salvation. The addressees are urged to behave in such way as to attain the goal into which they have been called (see e.g. the analysis of 1.17 and 3.9).[30]

---

30. This interpretation is supported to a certain degree by Michaels (1966), Piper (1980) and Kosala (1985).

The difference between the two modes lies especially in the question of the certainty of the final salvation. According to the first alternative it is assured, according to the second one it is not. The author presents the addressees as people who will be saved (e.g. 4.17), and his primary answer to the question is that the salvation is secure (1.5, 9). Therefore this interpretation is in principle to be preferred even in cases where the decision is hard to make due to syntactic or semantic ambiguity (e.g. in 3.9).

However, the second alternative should not be rejected either, since the presentation of the addressees as good Christians who will be saved is, as we have seen, partly due to the rhetorical technique used. It does not *per se* reflect the ideology behind the text. In many cases we have been able to read an implicit warning 'between the lines'. The author lets the addressees understand that they are to behave in a way that does not ruin their Christian status and final salvation (e.g. 1.17; 4.17-18). Many ambiguous expressions can also be interpreted so that good behaviour is a condition for the eventual salvation (see e.g. the interpretation of 3.9). There is even a syntactic regularity that functions in this way. When the author speaks of the final salvation, he always links it to the command with a final conjunction (2.6; 3.9; 5.6). This allows us to presume that a Means–Purpose relation is probable in these cases, and that a consecutive interpretation of words like ἵνα and εἰς τό is less plausible. In the actual reading the choice depends on the rhetorical situation, as I hope to have shown in my dissertation. But on the ideological level both possibilities remain.[31]

Piper's hypothesis about hope as the final motivating factor in 1 Peter appears to be exaggerated, since he fails to explain how hope is designed to create willingness to act according to the commands.[32]

Hope, or an 'innate and proper love of life' (1980: 231) is rather to be

31. The decisive case is 3.9, where the external structure makes both interpretations plausible. Even the Letter as a whole can be seen as a support for both readings, although the 'positive' tone is dominant. Piper rightly shows that previous research has favoured the 'positive' alternative, but in fact the 'negative' interpretation is also possible (Piper 1980). However, he cannot reject the positive alternative either. See Thurén 1990: 24-25, 150-51.

32. Piper 1980: 216-17, 230; see above Chapter 5 §4.g. In a more ideological section Piper attempts to soften his 'negative' interpretation, but arrives at a contradictory result (Piper 1980: 230-31): 'enemy-love *is* a condition of final salvation' (his italics), yet 'salvation *is* secured for all who (by God) are called...' (my italics), and God 'alone receives the glory'.

seen only as one factor or one step among the others in the argumentation; as such it is not capable of inducing the addressees to obey.

4. *Specifically Theological Motifs*

a. *God's Saving Act*
Expressions about God's call and saving act constitute a specifically theological counterpart to utterances about the addressees' own experience and baptism. Such expressions are found in

1.3	ἀναγεννήσας (15 καλέσαντα) 18 ἐλυτρώθητε (25)
2.21	ἐκλήθητε (24 ἰάθητε)
3.9	ἐκλήθητε 21
(4.6	εὐηγγελίσθη, 8)
5.10	καλέσας

The idea of God's saving act has two principal functions in the motivation. First, it serves as a proof of the addressees' new status (e.g. in 1.14). Their new position is secured by referring to the fact that God has called them. Even God's predestination (1.2) can have this function.

Secondly, it indicates *who* has caused the change in the addressees' status. When a great number of arguments are designed to guarantee that the addressees rejoice over their new status, the author utilizes expressions about God's saving act in order to transform this joy into thankfulness toward God (see e.g. 2.21, 24). In 1.3 the expression about God's saving act is used directly as a ground for the statement/command 'Praised is/be God'.

The motif 'God's saving act' is closely connected to expressions about Christ (e.g. in 1.18).

b. *God's Attitude and Being*
The text includes some utterances about God that are not directly connected to any activity but rather reflect his attitude toward the addressees: 1.(2, 3, 5); 5.7, 10(-11). 5.7 may serve as an example: αὐτῷ μέλει περὶ ὑμῶν.

Some motivating expressions refer simply to God as such (κατὰ θεόν or διὰ τὸν κύριον), without any further explanations. Such are:

1.15-16, 17	κατὰ...ἄγιον, ὅτι ἐγὼ ἄγιος
2.3, 13	χρηστὸς ὁ κύριος, διὰ τὸν κύριον
(4.11)	
5.2	κατὰ θεόν

In 4.6 the expression κατὰ θεόν is not to be seen as a motivation despite some play on words.[33]

κατὰ θεόν expressions can be understood only in their context. In 1.15-16 κατὰ θεόν refers to God's example as a counterpart to earlier desires: the author refers to God's holiness in order to give the addressees a model. However, the expression is more complex, since the explanation in 16 rather speaks of God's will or, as the ultimate ground, his being: ὅτι ἐγὼ ἅγιος. The addressees' new, valuable relation to God makes his being and example relevant and compelling for them.

In 2.13 διὰ τὸν κύριον refers (beside its general meaning) to the will of God or Christ. The continuation 2.15 speaks of God's intention as a ground for this will.

As a ground, 'God's being' is a compact, preparatory motif, which is always explicated later with references to God's example, will or intention.

c. *God's Will*

Beside the shorter expressions mentioned above, there are longer, more explicit grounds that refer to God and especially to his will: ὅτι οὕτως ἐστὶν τὸ θέλημα τοῦ θεοῦ (2.15). The references are: 1.(6,)16; 2.15, 19-20; 3.4, 12, 17; 4.2, (19).

The author follows a certain system when referring to the will of God.[34] Such expressions are attached to a general, non-religious train of thought appealing to reason: for example, in 2.20 and 3.17 God's will is combined with a general deontological reasoning, in 4.2-5 and 17-19 with the idea of retribution, and in 2.15 and 3.1-4 with a teleological motivation. Thus the author does not refer to the will of God as an abso-lute (against Brandt 1953: 13), but explains why God wants something: the will of God is always justified with ordinary rational ideas. We could also say that the motif 'God's will' serves as an extra theological addi-tion to the general motivation.

Most of the cases occur in the second half of the Letter (2.11–5.14).

---

33. See above Chapter 5 §5.b. κατὰ θεόν refers to 1.14-15 and 4.2 (θελήματι θεοῦ), but the main meaning is 'from God's perspective'.

34. A sign of this can be assumed even on the stylistic level: the preposition κατά and the substantive θέλημα are used only in connection with God. The antithesis of God's θέλημα is human ἐπιθυμία (1.14; 2.11; 4.2) or βούλημα (4.3). One reason for the choice of word is, however, the author's habit of using alliteration: here in 3.17 εἰ θέλοι τὸ θέλημα τοῦ θεοῦ, cf. 1.19; 2.21; 4.4.

This has a simple explanation. In order to function in the motivation the argument 'This is the will of God' requires of the recipients willingness to obey God. It is only after the author has created such a willingness among the implied addressees in the first part of the text, that he can use the expression 'God's will' in order to show that what he urges the addressees to do is what they actually are willing to do. The reference to the will of God can simultaneously remind the addressees of the positive and the negative basic motivation in the first part of the Letter, which is aimed at creating or intensifying the primary willingness to obey.

d. *The Judgment*

The rhetorical ambiguity in the motivation is especially prominent in grounds which refer to the final Judgment. With one important exception they occur in the two last rhetorical units: 1.17; 4.5, (7), 17-18; 5.4.

4.5 may serve as an example: οἱ ἀποδώσουσιν λόγον τῷ ἑτοίμως ἔχοντι κρῖναι ζῶντας καὶ νεκρούς.

On the one hand these grounds emphasize the extraordinarily good situation of the addressees, who will avoid the Judgment (thus especially 4.5, 7, 17-18). As such it serves as a dark background to the addressees' glorious future. Confidence on this score may add to the appreciation of the addressees' new status; see also the analysis of 1.17, alternative (a).

God's Judgment also provides the addressees with a reason to cease from repaying evil for evil. They do not need to fight against their oppressors, since they can trust in God's righteous judgment just as Christ did (see 2.23; 3.12; 4.19).[35]

On the other hand the Judgment serves as a warning. If the addressees fall from their new status by leading an unacceptable life, God's punishment threatens them—see the analysis of 1.17, alternative (b). The motivation with God's retaliation, however, means no actual ethic based on reward and punishment—the matter is more complicated (against Preisker [1949: 197] and to some extent Michaels [1966: 401]). The addressees are not persuaded with a reward, since the point of departure in the motivation is that they already are on the right side and have gained or will certainly gain the salvation (e.g. 1.9). It is also worth noticing that the negative aspect of the Judgment always remains implicit; the addressees are never directly threatened with the punishment.

35. Cf. also Osborne 1983: 397-98, according to whom God's righteous judgment is presented as opposite to human reproach and reviling.

e. *Christological Grounds*

The longest motivating sections in the letter can be characterized as Christological: 1.18-21; 2.4-8, 21-24; 3.18-19, 21-22. Shorter corresponding expressions can also, for example, be found in: 1.2, 3, 7, 11; 2.3; 4.1, 13.

The thesis about Christology as the 'ultimate and actual rationale for the ethical admonitions' in 1 Peter has after Lohse become an axiom in the research.[36] My analysis of the argumentation, however, has shown that, despite the length and importance, Christology has no dominant position in the many-sided motivation.

References to Christ have several different functions in the text.[37] They support the admonition by showing Christ's 'footsteps' (see Osborne 1983: 406-407), that is, by presenting a practical example for how Christians should meet difficult situations in their surroundings (especially 2.21-24).

Christological sections also motivate the addressees in many ways. First, expressions that emphasize the role of Christ in the salvation have a function similar to the utterances about God's saving act: they reinforce the actuality of the salvation and direct the joy over the salvation and the new relationship to God/Christ.[38] The expected result is that the addressees will begin to praise Christ and appreciate his example (especially in 1.18-21). Secondly, the example of Christ is aimed at documenting and proving that suffering really leads to glory (e.g. 1.11). Since Christ, who obeyed God, who was submissive, who did not repay evil with evil but suffered, reached the glory, this will also be the fate of the addressees, when they follow his example (see 4.13).

It is worth noticing, that the motivation with the example of Christ is usually connected to expressions about the will of God. Thus the Christological section in 2.21-25 is preceded by an utterance about the will of God in 2.15. Other similar combinations can be found elsewhere: 3.18-22 // 3.17; also 4.2, 13-14 // 4.19. Peculiarly enough, in 3.4 the will

36. Lohse 1954: 86: 'Das letzte und eigentliche Begründung'. After him Manke 1976: 74; Piper 1980: 213; Schrage 1982: 256; Richard 1986: 139.

37. Against Kosala, according to whom the meaning of Christ's saving act is not soteriological. It only enables the addressees to follow Christ's example (Kosala 1985: 137).

38. Cf. Richard (1986: 134-35), who gives only a vague explanation of the soteriological function of Christology. According to Richard, Christology is used in order to 'establish the basis for the community's unity, strength, and source of life'.

of God is attached to the example of Sarah in 3.5-6.

The Christological expressions are well suited to the central commands and the purpose of the Letter. For example, according to 2.13-14 the author argues that it is commendable to be submissive before righteous authorities, because it is reasonable, but he needs a Christological proof in order to explain why the addressees should be submissive even to wicked masters and to be ready to suffer.

First he attempts to induce the addressees to appreciate their new status. He can then show that they have obtained that status only because Christ did exactly what they are now enjoined to do. The sufferings of Christ have produced the good status that the addressees now have. Thus even their own status becomes evidence of the connection between sufferings and glory. Christ's own glory at the right hand of God (3.22) is another proof of this and indicates that the addressees will gain the same glory (4.13; cf. Richard 1986: 135-36).

It is, however, important to observe that the author does not use a semantic Reason–Result or Means–Purpose relation between the addressees' suffering and their future glory, although several expressions point in this direction (especially in 4.13). Instead, the relation between suffering and glory is concessive: the addressees can rejoice over their salvation (both the present and the imminent) *despite* the sufferings. The main requirement is the same attitude which Christ had (4.1). It can be characterized as readiness to suffer, not suffering as such.

f. *God's Intention*

Among the specifically theological motifs there are teleological expressions that refer to the purpose or intention of God: 1.(2, 7); 2.(2), 5, 9, 12, 21, 24; 3.1, 9, 16, 18; 4.(6, 11). They are often connected to expressions about the will of God, and clarify them.

The intention of God and Christ in the salvation of the addressees is that they will live aright, so that God and Christ will gain more glory. The train of thought in 2.21, 24 is, according to Deichgräber, typical of all Christian sermons: the purpose of Christ's saving act was that the saved people would begin to follow Christ and serve him or God (Deichgräber 1967: 189). The author, however, goes further: the ultimate goal is that God will be praised, not only by the Christians but also by the Gentiles (e.g. 2.9, 12-15). This goal is reached by the addressees' good behaviour (cf. Brandt 1953: 14).

The glory of God also has a counterpart: the addressees' own glory. It is attained insofar as they themselves stand steadfast in the test and do not repay evil for evil (e.g. 3.9).[39] This ambiguity in the motif 'God's intention' is evident when the idea is expressed concisely (e.g. in 1.7b, 11), where 'glory' is not determined with any genitive attribute: the author does not say whose glory he means.

The reason why God requires a specific mode of behaviour from the addressees is presented as his intention in their salvation (3.9, the 'positive' interpretation). The intention is often further explained with general appeals to reason (e.g. 2.12-15; 3.10-11). The use of this type of motif is conditional upon the so-called basic motivation: because of the salvation, the addressees have hope and thus they will praise God. Therefore (or because of fear of God) they then want to fulfil his intention.

The praise and glory of God is thus one of the most important themes in the motivation. The addressees should live aright in order to glorify God. It is his will, and it is the ultimate reason why Christ has saved the addressees. All these factors will also lead to the addressees' own eventual glory. This, however, allows of a 'negative' interpretation. If the addressees do not fulfil God's intention, they will not reach the future glory themselves.

5. *Other Religious Motifs*

a. *The Scriptures*

The author has a habit of supporting his claims with references to the Old Testament, which for is authoritative:[40] 1.16, 23-25; 2.6; 3.(5-6, 10-12), 20. Different references to the Scriptures extend, explain and exemplify what the author himself says. He will also reinforce and verify his commands and motivating expressions with quotations from the

39. The idea thus combines the 'active' and the 'passive' implied audiences (against van Unnik [1955: 108-109] and Piper [1980: 231], according to whom the addressees' own glory is not pursued in the text).

40. Against Schrage 1982: 258, according to whom OT is not normative for the author of 1 Peter. Schrage's argumentation is difficult for me to follow: 'Hier [1.15] wird nicht irgendein beliebiges Zitat angeführt, sondern ein zentrales Theologoumenon dest Alten Testaments. Also gilt nicht das ganze Alte Testament als normativ, sondern seine Grundintention wird aufgenommen...' I cannot see how the first sentence implies the second one. Schutter (1989) has shown that the way the OT is used in 1 Peter follows typically Jewish conventions.

Scriptures.[41] Sometimes the source is heavily emphasized, for example, with a phrase διότι (γέγραπται). See 1.16, 24-25; 2.6; 3.5-6, even 1.18-20 and 3.10-12.

By using this motif the author wants to prove that what he says is also the will of God. Those who proclaimed the gospel to the addressees had the same Spirit as the OT prophets (1.12, 25). Now the author claims that what he says carries a similar weight (cf. the author's statement about himself in 5.2). Since the addressees were saved by the word of God (1.25b) they ought to take account of the same word even now. The train of thought recalls the function of Christology presented above.

The references to the Scriptures are not combined with any particular motif, but rather have a general supporting function. Thus the device is similar to the reference to the relationship between the author and the addressees (6.1.b).

b. *Eschatology*
The role of eschatology in 1 Peter has often been discussed, but the argumentation has been dominated by the question as to whether the text is pseudepigraphical. Suggesting that the Letter is pseudepigraphical, and that the second generation could no longer eagerly await for the imminent end, scholars have claimed that eschatology only plays an incidental role in the Letter, appearing as a kind of formality.[42] However, a careful reading of the text shows that the need to find arguments for a late dating has distorted the picture of eschatology therein.

The motivation with the imminent end is concentrated in the beginning and end of the Letter: 1.5 (7, 12, 13); 4.(2, 5,)7, (17-18); (5.4, 10). It can be found within several motifs, especially God's Judgment (e.g. 4.17) and the addressees' hope. As independent it occurs only in 4.7: πάντων δὲ τὸ τέλος ἤγγικεν. Here the End serves as a general factor like the references to the Scriptures and the author.

The eschatological perspective is aimed at giving weight to everything the author says—it serves as a background for the whole motivation. The imminent end and the Judgment of God mean a total change, be it

---

41. Thus the author's thesis in 1.15 is verified with an OT quotation in 1.16; similarly 1.23 / 1.24-25; 2.7 / 2.6; 3.9 / 3.10-12. The latest example is discussed in greater detail by Piper (1980: 227).

42. See Brox 1979: 203; Schulz 1987: 618, 622. Parker (1994) finds new ways to undermine the explicit eschatological statements in the text.

positive or negative, in the current situation. Since the End is at hand, the addressees ought to take the author's admonition seriously.

Parker, however, rightly states that the End is not only used for emphasizing future things, but is an element of the addressees' current life and status (1994: 31).

Chapter 7

THE GENERAL IDEOLOGICAL STRUCTURE

1. *Introduction*

The analysis of the structure of argumentation on the text level has shown that single motivating expressions are almost always combined into greater logical trains of thought or structures. Furthermore, these structures often resemble each other to a great extent. The author frequently repeats a train of thought with minor modifications. The patterns can therefore be generalized so that they are seen on an ideological level. In the preceding chapter we have already identified some general motifs in the text. Particular expressions have been gathered into groups, where the function and the main contents are rather consistent.

Now, if we take the generalized motifs and appose them, it becomes possible to construct common trains of thought or *general structures* in the Letter. We have already found traces of such structures in the summaries of the argumentation analysis. In this chapter I shall argue that there are three such ideological entities in 1 Peter. Together these will yield a total picture of the motivation, or *the general ideological structure* behind the text.

2. *The Basic Motivation*

According to Burke, all persuasion is based on identification.[1] This general definition is well suited to our result, according to which the addressees' current situation and ideal identity constitute a central motif in the persuasion. The author describes their situation according to a system similar to the *narratio*[2] of ancient rhetoric, which gives a biased

1. Burke (1962: 548) defines rhetoric as persuading by identifying the author's case with the audience's interests. See also pp. 579-80.
2. Lausberg 1961 §§289-347. For a renewed insight into the importance of the narration, see O'Banion 1987.

picture. Here the author manipulates his audience by re-evaluating their difficulties (e.g. in Thurén 1990: 90-91 about the status of redefinition). He also describes them in ideal terms in order to produce a useful identification and thereby to induce them to fulfil the ideal. But the chief aim in discussing the addressees' current situation is to make them see it in a positive light despite all the difficulties; therefore the author praises the virtues of the addressees' Christian faith.

A typical technique is to present contrasts to the addressees' situation: their former life, described in a pejorative way, the Gentiles' current life, which is bound to end in catastrophe (also Noah's generation is used as an example), and the respected apostles and angels, who would envy the addressees' current status. These factors cover many of the motivating expressions in the text, and all of them are primarily used for this one goal: to make the addressees see how invaluable their position is as Christians. This function is evident whenever any of these motifs appear in the text. We have also made some tentative ideological analyses of longer sections in the text (e.g. after the analyses of 1.16, 25 and 2.20), and even there the same function can be discerned. This part of the motivating structure can be described as follows:

A life in sin, be it the addressees' former life or the Gentiles' current one (Chapter 6 §3.a), [3] serves as a negative background to the new status as Christians. This type of motif is given more power and greater weight with expressions of general transience (e.g. in 1.24). As a theological counterpart it has God's judgment (Chapter 6 §4.d. and maybe even the picture of the spirits in prison; 3.19), which confers a deeper dimension on the transience. The addressees should not only think about their death, but also God's Judgment thereafter.

But the relationship can be seen also in another way. In accordance with other non-religious motifs, the function of the description of general transience is to support the religious idea of the Last Judgment, with reference to reason so that it is not only easier to understand but also more dependable and thereby more persuasive (cf. above Chapter 6 §2.a). Thus the two references to the End support each other and strengthen the argumentation, which refers to the life in sin.

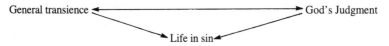

---

3.   In this chapter all references of this type relate to Part II, 'Analysis'.

Baptism is a recurrent motif in the argumentation (Chapter 6 §3.c), viz. the change from the old to the new status.[4] It has several functions: first, it is connected with the motivation, which attempts to enhance the addressees' appreciation of their new status. References to baptism serve as evidence for the actuality of the status (thus e.g. in 1.23). Secondly, the baptismal allusions are used rather directly in the admonition. This inverts the first motivating function: the appreciation of new status is aimed at making baptism, the change from the old to the new, important for the addressees. This will be discussed below.

The new status (Chapter 6 §3.d) is described in different ways. Perhaps the most distinctive is the use of the honorary titles of Israel in 2.9-10. The author wants to assure the addressees that, despite their seemingly difficult social situation, they have an admirable position as the children of God. Comparisons with prophets and angels (6 §3.b) also serve this goal. With regard to the persuasive power (above Chapter 5 §3, 'The Second Half, Conclusions'), the most significant factor in the new status is hope for immortality and final salvation (6 §3.e). From the addressees' point of view this hope makes the greatest difference compared with the counterparts (see above). Many motifs are aimed at supporting this factor: expressions about God's saving act (6 §4.a), and his positive attitude toward the addressees (6 §4.b), his foreknowledge and protection. The strongest proof may be Christ's resurrection and current glory (6 §4.e), of which the addressees are promised a share.

The emphasis on God's and Christ's role in the change from the old status to the new has a specific function: it shows whence the new status comes, which is to say, the One to whom the addressees should give credit for the positive change in their life.

The structure can be described in the following way (e.g. the prefatory analysis in Chapter 5 §3, 'The First Half, Conclusions'):

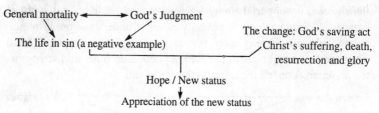

---

4.   The baptismal expressions are usually only allusions (with the exception of 3.21); baptism is implied by references to issues connected with it.

At this point a crucial question is, what part does this appreciation play in the structure of motivation, that is, what types of emotive factors is it intended to produce? Although such factors are rarely expressed in the text due to the requirements of rhetorical affectivity, we have been able to discern two types of opposite components.

According to a 'positive' line, the high value of the new status creates joy (this is expressed clearly in 1.6), and since it comes from God, this prompts gratitude to him (see above Chapter 5 §3, 'The First Half, Conclusions', and 'The Second Half, Conclusions'). The gratitude, in turn, should take its natural expression in praise of God, especially when this is presented as a commendable response to God's activity (see above Chapter 5 §4, 'The First Half, Conclusions'). In e.g. 1.14-16 this is one of the ways in which a willingness to obey God / the author, that is, to be holy, is produced among the implied addressees (see above Chapter 5 §3.b). The relation between these two factors, however, remains somewhat unclear in 1.14-16.[5]

According to a 'negative' line, the appreciation of the new life and especially the hope of the future glory, are aimed at willingness to attain, or more precisely, to preserve the promised 'inheritance' (1.4) and avoid its loss. This is evident in 1.17. Fear of losing the new status is thus also a motive for obedience. On the ideological level this motivation is easier to explain than the positive one: the addressees want to preserve their new status and reach the final salvation. Therefore they want to live according to the rules which are given them by God. They are afraid of him who as an impartial judge can take away their current or promised rewards. If they disobey, they may meet with God's punishment and all the disadvantages of the dark background, the life in sin. Thus the Gentiles' gloomy destiny serves as a warning to the addressees.

The structure can thus be continued in the following way (cf. above Chapter 5 §3, 'The Second Half, Conclusions'):

5. Cf. Deichgräber (1967: 207), who claims that thanksgiving is used in order to support the paraenesis, but nevertheless does not explain exactly how this is thought to take place.

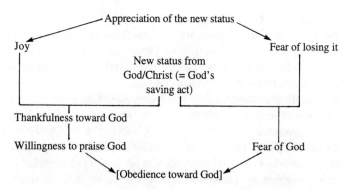

Both the positive and the negative variants of the basic motivation are found in the text side by side, or even better, interwoven. This is caused especially by the many semantically ambiguous expressions in the text, which can be interpreted in both ways. On the rhetorical level the use of such a technique is connected with the author's desire to aim the text at different types of implied addressees (Thurén 1990: 167-76), but on the ideological level it may be seen as a sign of the complex nature of the motivation, or even the theology of the author.

Another reason for the simultaneous occurrence of the two opposite motifs is that many particular motivating structures can be interpreted in both ways, since the emotive step remains implicit.[6] The positive line is far more distinct; specific signals for the priority of this interpretation have been discerned in e.g. 1.5. The negative way always remains rather implicit in the text. There is, however, discernible indication also of this interpretation, and because of its simpler ideological structure it is not to be overlooked.

Most of the expressions that have been characterized as belonging to the 'basic motivation' are concentrated in the first part of the text, 1.1–2.10. As such they serve the exordial function of the unit.[7] They are usually connected with commands that admonish the addressees to general readiness and holiness but lack specifications or a concrete, particular message. This supports the idea of the preparatory nature of this type

6. Therefore Piper (1980: 212) rightly argues that an interpretation of 1 Peter 3.9 must be built on an interaction between particular analyses of the text and a general synthesis.

7. One exception may be God's Judgment, which only in a certain rhetorical situation can function as a part of the letter's *captatio benevolentiae* (see Thurén 1990: 138, 144).

of motivation. When these motifs are used later, they usually appear in a short form or as additions, only in order to remind the addressees of the basic motivation.[8] It is thus aimed at creating a basic willingness to obey God, which means in practice the commands of the author. Once this has been achieved, and the rhetorical situation has thereby been modified, the author can proceed to more specific issues and simultaneously to more specific motivation.

The ideological progress in the rhetorical situation from 1.1–2.10 to 2.11–4.11 is supported by the simultaneous homogenization of the implied audience. This also allows the author to move into more concrete issues and greater condour.

3. *The Specific Motivation*

In 1 Peter there are themes which become understandable and persuasive first in the modified rhetorical situation produced by the basic motivation. Such are references to the will and intention of God, and the example of Christ. They are further supported by non-religious reasoning.

In accordance with the hypothesis about the ideological succession of the basic and the specific motivations, the latter appear chiefly in the second part of the Letter (2.11–4.11).[9] As was the case with the basic motivation, so also the specific grounds constitute an almost fixed model. It can be assumed to lie behind even short motivating expressions.[10] Structures that belong to the specific motivation have been presented above, for example, in connection with the summaries of 2.11-25 and 3.12.[11]

The motifs in the specific motivation are connected with more concrete issues, especially the relation to non-Christians and the idea of

---

8. Thus e.g. 2.25 is added to a merely Christological section. See further e.g. 2.16, 25; 3.15.

9. The first part of the Letter (1.1–2.10) contains some references to suffering (1.6) and motifs that belong to the specific motivation, but they remain on a preparatory level and are thus rather unclear, such as the reference to God's being in 1.16. At the end of the Letter (4.7-11; 5.1-7(-9) the exhortation is extended to the addressees' internal relations.

10. See e.g. 2.5b (...ἀνενέγκαι πνευματικὰς θυσίας), which prepares the way for these ideas in the first part of the letter.

11. See above Chapter 5 §4, the first and the second half, conclusions.

unjust suffering. The author gives many concrete examples of these ideas.

The specific motivation relies in principle on the 'positive' type of basic motivation. Whereas the aim of the basic motivation was to create or to intensify the addressees' willingness to give thanks to God and praise him, the specific motivation is designed to show that the very commands of the author constitute the application of this attitude. In other words, obedience to the author's specific admonitions is presented in the addressees' current situation as the correct way of realizing their willingness to obey God. They show how the basic willingness can be put into practice. Through this type of motivation it also becomes easier to comprehend how the 'positive' basic motivation is designed to motivate behaviour according to the admonitions. This makes the basic motivation more effective.

The addressees' obedience to the commands is presented as the will of God (Chapter 6 §4.c). This is not referred to as an absolute authority, but is given a narrower explanation: by obeying the will of God the addressees fulfil his intention (6 §4.f). This intention has a double content in the text.

First, God should obtain glory. This is achieved in a simple way: if the addressees live aright, the Gentiles will cease to blame them and their God, and begin to praise him instead. Thus God obtains praise not only from the addressees but also from the Gentiles. The logic of motivation is understandable: if the addressees want to add to the glory of God (as an effect of the basic motivation), this is the means.[12]

Secondly, God's goal in their salvation was that the addressees will obtain glory themselves. This idea can be understood also in accordance with the 'negative' basic motivation: the intention and purpose of God will be fulfilled only if the addressees obey the admonitions. This is clear especially in 3.9. However, the addressees' own glory serves also as a 'positive' factor by giving them a reason for hope and joy. After all, their glory is presented as guaranteed by God in 1.5.

The example and glorification of Christ (and even the dead Christians in 4.6) here play a major role.[13] They prove that a life according to the

12. This task resembles of the duty of Israel among the Gentiles; see McKnight 1991.

13. The motivation with the example of Christ also belongs to the basic motivation (see above): through unjust suffering he saved the addressees and gave them a reason to follow his example (2.21) The intention of Christ is presented as identical to the intention of God.

will of God (especially the attitude to unjust suffering) leads to glory[14] by showing that the way of life which the author recommends has led to a positive result also in the past.[15]

The non-religious motifs (Chapter 6 §2) appealing to reason and contemporary ethics are used in order to make the theological motivation easier to understand and more effective. The general deontological expressions show that what is said to be the will of God is simultaneously something reasonable. The general teleological expressions show that what is said to be the intention and purpose of God also functions in practice.

We can thus see a structure of the specific motivation that is designed to produce willingness to act according to the author's particular admonition. When added to the basic motivation it gives the following pattern:[16]

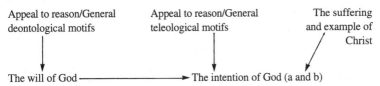

In simpler terms, when the basic motivation has made the implied addressees willing to praise God and Christ, the specific motivation informs them about God's plan, as a result of which God, Christ, and even the addressees gain praise and glory. This plan or intention is simultaneously presented as reasonable, and connected with the basic motivation also by the Christological expressions.

14. Note the play on words in 4.2, 6: Since the dead Christians have lived θελήματι θεοῦ they live even now κατὰ θεόν. See above Chapter 5 §5.c.

15. E.g. 1.11, 21; 3.21 and the corresponding analyses in Part II.

16. 2.11-16 serves as a good example of how this structure is visible in the text. As strangers (new status) the addressees should abstain from desires (command) which fight against the soul (general deontological motif) and lead a good life among the Gentiles (specification of the command) in order to make the Gentiles glorify God (general teleological motif), since it is the will of God (the will of God) since they are free (basic motivation). See the analysis of this section in Chapter 5 §4.ab. Cf. also e.g. 2.18-25, where some other factors are presented: general deontological and teleological expressions are connected with the will of God and the intention of Christ; then follows the example of Christ and his suffering, and as an addition comes a reminder of the basic motivation.

4. *The Supporting Motivation*

Beside the two large structures of motivation there are some additional factors that can be called supporting. They do not form clearly cohesive structures and are not closely connected to any other type of motivation, yet they have a common function.

To this type belong, firstly, references to the Scriptures, which are aimed at giving weight to the author's text. This goal is crucial, since both the basic and the specific motivations are designed to create willingness to obey God in the first place, not the author. By backing his commands and arguments with references to the Scriptures (Chapter 6 §5.a), and even to early Christian tradition, the author attempts to show that his claims are identical with the will of God and normal Christianity.

Secondly, the ethos or the references to the author, and the relation between the author and the addressees (6 §1.b), and third, references to the imminent end (6 §4.b) have a similar function. They have no typical connections with other types of arguments, and thus no specific position in the total structure of argumentation. Instead, they are designed to add to the reliability, importance and persuasiveness of the author's message in general.

5. *Summary: The General Ideological Structure of the Motivation*

We have seen that every particular motivating expression has a function in a larger system of motivation. Generally there are no loose *ad hoc* grounds, but a distinctive strategy by which the motivation is designed to affect the addressees. When the three major motivating factors are put together, we obtain a comprehensive ideological system of the motifs in the persuasion.

I do not claim that the historical author had this scheme as explicit in his mind—even if this were the case, the answer is beyond the limits of the method. However, as the system is presented from a careful study of the text as such, it gives a meaning for many obscure expressions and features in 1 Peter. The scheme is thus useful, because it helps us to understand the Epistle better.

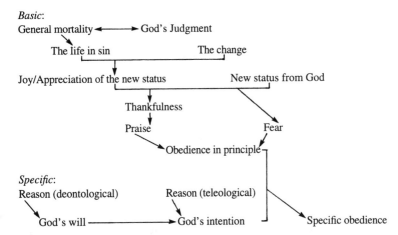

When the supporting motivation is added, the structure can be described as follows:

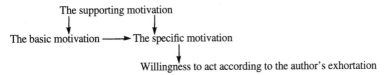

I hope to have shown that although this structure is never totally explicit, it can be found behind each section in the Letter. Every motivating expression fits into this matrix. Only then can each of them be rightly understood. A simple 'context' is not enough.

CONCLUSIONS

1. *Summary of the Method and Results*

In the search for characteristic features in Early Christian ethics we focused on the motivation of the paraenesis, and took 1 Peter as a test case. The study of the motivation in 1 Peter started from two opposite positions in the scholarship. The situation was seen as partly due to negligence of contradictory expressions in the text. Together with earlier defective analyses of the argumentation in the text, this had resulted in a biased view of the author's thinking.

The first task was to gather up all the explicit motivating expressions with a semantic method. This was necessary because of the complex way in which the commands and the motivating expressions were intertwined in the text. This semantic study in turn provided us with material for an analysis of argumentation. In this analysis, a modified form of Toulmin's model was used. It proved to be a good tool for revealing presupposed factors and for clarifying the relations between explicit statements.

The internal logic of the text became clearer, but also critical remarks about the technique of argumentation in 1 Peter were made. It was even possible to shed new light on particular verses. Thus the results may be useful in other approaches to the text. The same model may also prove useful for analyzing any other biblical text as well.

In the main analysis Toulmin's method was complemented with two aspects: with a semantical analysis of the explicit factors and with a rhetorical perspective, which puts the model in a right frame of reference. The third addition was due to our specific task. The model was enlarged so that not only argumentation but also persuasion and motivation could be taken into account.

In the study of motivation, a final step was to make a systematic classification of the results of the analysis which yield a picture of the ideological level behind the text. It became clear that 1 Peter, despite the miscellaneous background, can be seen as a coherent text, where all the ideas have well planned functions. A great number of different motifs and techniques are utilized for a single purpose, and it is a mistake to see one of these devices as the goal of the letter.

Compared with a Hellenistic environment, the paraenesis in 1 Peter had, despite clear genealogical connections, its own characteristic function described above. Compared with Judaism, especially the motivation makes the difference. The main differential is, of course, the role of Christ as a redeemer and example. But the specific character of the motivation in 1 Peter cannot be simply attributed to a 'Christology'. The motivation forms a system that consists of the whole structure described above, including the double motivating factor.

In a sense, the basic idea of the 'New ways', as a scheme for characterizing 1 Peter as a paraenetical text, is acceptable. However, the very concept has to be reconsidered, since the Letter is not aimed at giving ordinary ethical lessons (in agreement with Delling [1973: 112] and Hill [1976: 189]). The author presents many things already well-known to the addressees: the basic dogmas of Christianity, as well as a life according to the baptismal education, other ethical rules, and missionary activity. The common denominator for all these themes is that they were essential for the Christian identity. They were all used in order to intensify the addressees' religious convictions despite the various difficulties. Thereby the ultimate functions of the exhortation and its motivation come very close to each other. The gospel and the paraenesis serve the same eventual purpose.

Here the double function of the Christological statements serves as a good example of the ideology in the text. Christ is presented simultaneously as a savior and as a model for good behaviour, and neither one can be seen as more important. If the overall task of 1 Peter is to intensify the Christianity of people who are tempted to assimilate to the surrounding society in one way or another, we cannot say whether the Christ the Redeemer is ideologically[1] more central than Christ the Example and vice versa. In other words, it cannot be stated whether the emphasis on the addressees' new status, or its Christological grounds, or its eschatological goals, or the rules for practical behaviour, is the more crucial.

Although the theological expressions function semantically as arguments for the commands, we could even think from a pragmatic or

---

1. In *rhetorical* perspective, i.e. with regard to the different rhetorical situations, either one could be preferred.

rhetorical viewpoint that the paraenesis only provides the author with a traditional frame of reference for proclaiming the gospel, that is, for intensifying the religious convictions of the addressees. Behaviour then serves as indicative of faith.

2. *The 'Ultimate Factor' and its Theological Implications*

In interpreting the motivation of the paraenesis, the main (although not always the most clearly expressed) disagreement among the scholars has concerned the question of the ultimate emotive factor that is designed to motivate the addressees to think and act in a specific way. This factor eventually labels the argumentation and theology in the Letter. In most of the detailed analyses of the units in the text we have to be content with a certain duality. The more obvious 'positive' line, viz. thankfulness and praise, and the more implicit, yet veritable 'negative' line, viz. fear of deprivation of the high status and final salvation (or desire to gain it) constitute a double characteristic of the motivation. The addressees are motivated with both a certain and an uncertain salvation. Although the emphasis lies on the former, they are so neatly intertwined that a clear distinction is impossible at the ideological level.

To neglect the tension between the two ideas and to explain the ethics or theology of the author with one of the alternatives, as has been the case in studies of 1 Peter, means that violence is done to the text.

The tension between the positive and negative motivation, or the certain or uncertain final salvation, is common in many New Testament texts (and as such is not a sign of any deuteropaulinic development in 1 Peter).[2] The double motivation resembles the classical question of the relationship between good works and faith. Contrary to Paul or James, however, the author of 1 Peter does not actually discuss the question but simply utilizes it in the motivation. The ambiguity can be partly explained by appeal to the rhetorical strategy of the author.[3]

2.   Paul can also give corresponding contradictory signs within the same letter. Phil. 2.12-13 is a striking example.

3.   Different messages are aimed at different types of implied addressees. The actual situation, where the addressee receives the message, is however less confusing. Depending on the recipients' frame of reference they may receive a clear 'positive' or 'negative' message, or a suitable combination thereof. As a rhetorical device this ambiguity is useful. The addressees are both consoled and encouraged to good behaviour, but also warned of bad. A compromise or a theoretical explanation, which would solve the tension, could jeopardize the motivating power of the themes.

But there is an ideological tension behind the rhetoric in the text that is left unresolved. If the complex relation between certain and uncertain salvation, or between good works and faith, only serves as a rhetorical device, that is, if this theological ambiguity appears in the Letter only because of the requirements of the rhetorical effectiveness, one may ask whether the author neglects any deeper theological problems, as Schulz has proposed.[4] Or was the whole question, similarly to the Jewish–Christian relations (cf. Olsson 1986), not particularly interesting in the Christian tradition in which the Letter has emerged?

Here we meet the key problem of a non-theoretical text.[5] Actually, where in the New Testament Letters do we find theological discussion for the sake of theology? Even Romans or Galatians, which are often seen as presenting the doctrine of Paul, have practical and tactical goals. On the other hand, one is easily tempted to draw too hasty conclusions from the fact that most of the biblical letters relate to real situations, and are not theoretical treatises.[6] The fact that the author writes with a specific purpose and that we have an extremely limited material for studying his thoughts urges us to great hesitation when drawing conclusions about his theology or the lack of it.[7]

Even as rhetorically premeditated, the text always reflects in some way the (implied) author's ideology. In 1 Peter the way in which all the different motivating expressions seem to be embodied in a sophisticated ideological system contradicts a view according to which its theology would be purely practical and even opportunistic. Instead of simply finding a suitable argument for each command there seems to be a total theological view of the grounds for Christian behaviour, and an analysis of argumentation reveals such an implicit pattern behind each motivating

4.   Schulz 1987: 618. He claims that the opposition between faith and works is 'totally unknown' in 1 Peter.

5.   In 1 Peter we have seen how the scholars' need for dogmatic statements has distorted the interpretation of e.g. 3.21 and 4.6.

6.   Thus e.g. Doty (1977: 37) concludes that Paul was not an abstract thinker but rather a contextualist theologian, since he produced 'concrete ethical responses in each situation'. It is true, as I have tried to show, that the theology behind a New Testament text is not easy to discover. Doty's claim about Paul's *essence*, however, is a *non sequitur*.

7.   Thus also Schutter (1989: 177), who however exaggerates by saying that the way the OT is used in 1 Peter 'may not reflect in the least upon the relative development, or lack thereof, of his Christology, for example, as some kind of evidence for his stature as a theologian in the early Church'.

Argument and Theology in 1 Peter

expression. Only in this ideological 'context' can such expressions be properly understood.

In the text the ideological system serves the paraenesis. The statements about God, Christ or redemption are used in order to produce right attitudes or good behaviour. In this sense Schulz's idea of 'Moralisierung des Heils' (1987: 614-20) in 1 Peter is correct. But then, where in the New Testament do we find a 'Heil' that is not 'moralisiert'?[8] Although in different ways and on different levels, doctrinal utterances and guidance on behaviour belong intimately together throughout the New Testament.

3. *1 Peter as an Example of Early Christian Paraenesis*

This study was based on the assumption that 1 Peter as a traditional text represents a pattern of Christian thinking, instead of a personal theology. Although we have witnessed the high level of the author's rhetorical skills, the hypothesis still stands. Thus the results of this case-study may be cautiously generalized. We shall ask for the implications of this study for understanding the paraenesis as a genre.

A common opinion about the paraenesis as a genre must be made more precise (see Chapter 1 §2.b). The paraenesis does not attempt to convince the audience of new ethical rules, perhaps not any ethical rules (see Chapters 1 §2.a and 5 §3.b). For the most part, the audience is assumed to be already convinced, but not persuaded or motivated. It is supposed to know and even accept the rules, but not be willing to live according to them (see Chapter 1 §2.a). The main task of a paraenetical text is the motivation: to enhance the addressees' right attitudes, to make them more steadfast in their convictions, or in theological terms, faith.[9] This in turn leads to the action desired.

---

8. Technically the position of the paraenesis may be different. In the Pauline Letters, the exhortations often appear as a specific section after the bulk of the text. This may have led to misconceptions of Paul's view on the nature of Christian faith in the Early Church, let alone among modern interpreters: Already 2 Peter and James can be seen as a clarification of Paul in this matter. In Hebrews, the doctrinal material and the paraenesis alternate; thus the contact is much closer. In 1 Peter they appear side by side and upon each other. This alternation does not, however, mean as such that they have an ideologically different position.

9. Cf. 1 Pet. 5.12, which according to epistolographical conventions summarizes the message of the Letter (Thurén 1990: 86-87): 'I have written to you to

Our conclusions concerning the paraenesis and its motivation in 1 Peter indicate that it is not correct to describe the paraenetical interest among the first-century Christians only as caused by external influence or as a decline from an 'original' Christianity. Even if genuine Pauline texts were seen as ideal or normative Christianity—we have witnessed the scholars' habit of wearing Pauline eyeglasses throughout the study of 1 Peter—the difference is not significant. It is misleading to brand texts such as 1 Peter or the Pastoral epistles as degenerate forms of Paul only because the kerygma and the paraenesis are formally not so clearly separated. Despite structural (and genealogical) differences, ideologically the texts belong together: the basic function of the paraenesis is similar.

The paraenesis was not emphasized for its own sake or for some educational or moralistic purposes, or simply for the socialization of the addressees, although even those functions may have occurred. Its central role in the Letters points toward a more holistic picture. The paraenesis was necessary for keeping the faith of the believers alive and, at least in 1 Peter, for making missionary activity possible by enhancing the credibility of the Christians.

In other words, the ideological and practical dimensions are hard to separate in Early Christianity as reflected by 1 Peter. Like ancient Judaism, Christianity was also a way of life, a culture of its own, not only a philosophical 'religion', and the function of the paraenesis may be seen as securing adherence to that way of life.

Finally, as a practical result, the way in which the ideological structure of the motivation has now been reconstructed in 1 Peter may also have some importance for other studies of the theological thinking of the Biblical writers. I hope to have demonstrated, at least in 1 Peter, that the 'theology' cannot be described simply on the basis of separate expressions and their 'context', and their literary genre. In order to reach reliable results, one needs an analysis of the argumentation of the statements that does not proceed too quickly to the ideological level, but stays close to the text. Such a study needs to take into account the function of the expressions inside both small and large argumentative structures as they appear in the developing rhetorical situations.

exhort you and to testify that this is a true grace of God. Remain in steadfast in view of it.'

BIBLIOGRAPHY

Texts

Aristotle, *Ars rhetorica* (ed. W.D. Ross; SCBO; Oxford: Oxford University Press, 1964).

Cicero, *Tusculanae disputationes* (ed. M. Pohlenz; Stuttgart: Teubner, 1957).

Epictetus, *Dissertationes* (ed. H. Schenkl; Stuttgart: Teubner, 1965).

Isocrates, *Ad Demonicum et Panegyricus* (ed. S.E. Sandys; Greek Texts and Commentaries; New York: Arno, 1979 [repr. of 1872]).

Missale Romanum (Civitas Vaticana, 6th edn, 1970).

Nya testamentet (Bibelkommissionens utgåva; Stockholm: Norman, 1981).

Plato, *Phaedo* (ed. C. Woyte; Leipzig: Reclam, 1925).

—*Gorgias* (ed. E.R. Dodds; SCBO; Oxford: Oxford University Press, 1959).

Pyhä Raamattu (Helsinki: Suomen kirkon sisälähetysseura, 1961 [1938]).

Pyhä Raamattu (Helsinki: WSOY, 1992).

Sallust, *Catilina* (ed. L.D. Reynolds; SCBO; Oxford: Oxford University Press, 1963).

Seneca, *Epistulae morales* (ed. L.D. Reynolds; SCBO; Oxford: Oxford University Press, 1965).

—'De vita beata', in *Opera quae supersunt*, I (ed. F. Haase; Teubner: Lipsiae, 1874).

Literature

Aalen, S.

1972   'Oversettelsen av ortet ἐπερώτημα i dåpstedet 1 Petr 3:21', *TTki* 43: 161-75.

Alexandrova, D.

1987   'Rhetoric and Theory of Argumentation', in F.H. van Eemeren *et al.* (eds.), *Argumentation: Perspectives and Approaches* (Dordrecht: Foris, 1987): 266-73.

Applegate, J.

1992   'The Co-Elect Woman of 1 Peter', *NTS* 38: 587-604.

Arnold, C.C.

1986   'Implications of Perelman's Theory of Argumentation for Theory of Persuasion', in J.L. Golden and J.J. Pilotta (eds.), *Practical Reasoning in Human Affairs* (Dordrecht: Reidel).

Attridge, H.W.

1990   'Paraenesis in a Homily (λόγος παρακλήσεως): The Possible Location of, and Socialization in, the "Epistle to the Hebrews" ', *Semeia* 50: 211-26.

Austin, J.L.
1976   *How to Do Things with Words* (Oxford: Oxford University Press, 2nd
            edn).
Balch, D.
1981   '*Let Wives be Submissive': The Domestic Code in 1 Peter* (SBLMS 26;
            Chico, CA: Scholars Press).
1986   'Hellenization/Acculturation in 1 Peter', in C.H. Talbert (ed.),
            Perspectives on First Peter (NABPRSSS 9; Macon, GA: Mercer
            University Press): 79-101.
Baltz, H.
1981   'οὖν', *EWNT*, II, 1326-27.
Baltz, H. and W. Schrage
1973   *Die 'Katholischen' Briefe: Die Briefe des Jakobus, Petrus, Johannes
            und Judas* (NTD 10; Göttingen: Vandenhoeck & Ruprecht).
Barilli, R.
1989   *Rhetoric* (trans. G. Menozzi; Minneapolis: Minnesota University
            Press).
Bauer, W., K. Aland and B. Aland
1988   *Wörterbuch zum Neuen Testament* (Berlin: de Gruyter, 6th edn).
Bauernfeind, O.
1933   'ἀρετή', *ThWNT*, I, 457-61.
Beasley-Murray, G.R.
1979   *Baptism in the New Testament* (Exeter: Eerdmans, 2nd edn).
Beekman, J. and J. Callow
1974   *Translating the Word of God* (Grand Rapids: Zondervan).
Benoit, W.L. and J.J. Lindsey
1987   'Argument Fields and Forms of Argument in Natural Language', in
            F.H. van Eemeren et al. (eds.), *Argumentation: Analysis and Practices*
            (Dordrecht: Foris): 215-24.
Berger, K.
1984   *Formgeschichte des Neuen Testaments* (Heidelberg: Quelle & Meyer).
Berk, U.
1979   *Konstruktive Argumentationstheorie* (Stuttgart: Fromman–Holzboog).
Best, E.
1969–70   '1 Peter and the Gospel Tradition', *NTS* 16: 95-113.
1971   *1 Peter* (NCB; London: Oliphants).
Bitzer, L.F.
1968   'The Rhetorical Situation', *Philosophy and Rhetoric* 1: 1-14.
Bjerkelund, C.J.
1967   ΠΑΡΑΚΑΛΩ: *Studien zu Form, Funktion und Sinn der* παρακαλῶ-
            Sätze in den paulinischen Briefen (Bibliotheca Theologica Norwegica
            1; Oslo: Universitetsforlaget).
Blass, F. and A. Debrunner
1979   *Grammatik des neutestamentlichen Griechisch* (rev. F. Rehkopf;
            Göttingen: Vandenhoeck & Ruprecht, 15th edn) (= BDR).
Boismard, M.-E.
1961   *Quatre hymnes baptismales dans la première épitre de Pierre* (LD 30;
            Paris: Cerf).

Bornemann, E. and E. Risch
1978   *Griechische Grammatik* (Frankfurt am Main: Diesterweg, 2nd edn)
            (= BR).
Bornemann, W.
1919–20   'Der erste Petrusbrief—Eine Taufrede des Silvanus?', *ZNW* 19: 143-
            65.
Botha, J.
1991   *Reading Romans 13: Aspects of the Ethics of Interpretation in a
            Controversial Text* (Stellenbosch: University of Stellenbosch).
Braet, A.
1987   'The Classical Doctrine of *Status* and the Rhetorical Theory of
            Argumentation', *Philosophy and Rhetoric* 20: 79-93.
1992   'Ethos, Pathos and Logos in Aristotle's Rhetoric: A Re-Examination',
            Argumentation 6: 307-20.
Brandt, W.
1953   'Wandel als Zeugnis nach dem 1. Petrusbrief', in W. Foerster (ed.),
            Verbum Dei manet in aeternum (FS O. Schmitz; Witten-Ruhr: Luther):
            10-25.
Brooks, C. and R.P. Warren
1979   *Modern Rhetoric* (New York: Harcourt, Brace, Jovanovich, 11th edn).
Brown, R.E.
1985   *The Churches the Apostles Left Behind* (New York: Paulist Press).
Brox, N.
1986   *Der erste Petrusbrief* (EKKNT 21; Zürich: Benziger, 2nd edn [1979]).
Bühlmann, W. and K. Scherer
1973   *Stilfiguren der Bibel: Ein kleines Nachschlagewerk* (BibB 10;
            Fribourg: Schweizerisches Katholisches Bibelwerk).
Bultmann, R.
1953   *Theologie des Neuen Testaments* (Tübingen: Mohr).
Burke, K.
1962   *A Rhetoric of Motives* (New York: Prentice–Hall).
Calloud, J. and F. Genuyt
1982   *La première épître de Pierre: Analyse sémiotique* (LD 109; Paris:
            Cerf).
Carrington, P.
1940   *The Primitive Christian Catechism* (Cambridge: Cambridge University
            Press).
Carter, M.F.
1991   'The Ritual Functions of Epideictic Rhetoric: The Case of Socrates'
            Funeral Oration', *Rhetorica* 3: 209-232.
Cherniak, C.
1986   *Minimal Rationality* (Cambridge: MIT Press).
Classen, C.J.
1988   'Ars Rhetorica', *Rhetorica* 6: 7-19.
Cook, D.
1980   'I Peter iii.20: An Unnecessary Problem', *JTS* NS 31: 72-78.
Corcoran, J.
1989   'Argumentations and Logic', *Argumentation* 3: 17-44.

Cotterell, P. and M. Turner
1989   *Linguistics and Biblical Interpretation* (London: SPCK).
Coutts, J.
1956–57   'Ephesians 1.3-14 and 1 Peter 1.3-12', *NTS* 3: 115-27.
Cox, J.R. and C.A. Willard
1982   'Introduction: The Field of Argumentation', in J.R. Cox and
            C.A. Willard (eds.), *Advances in Argumentation Theory and Research*
            (Carbondale: Southern Illinois University Press): xii-xxv.
Cross, F.L.
1957   *I. Peter: A Paschal Liturgy* (London: Mowbray, 2nd edn).
Dalton, W.J.
1965   *Christ's Proclamation to the Spirits: A Study of 1 Peter 3:18–4:6*
            (AnBib 23; Rome: Pontifical Biblical Institute).
Danker, F.W.
1967   'I Peter 1,24–2,17—A Consolatory Pericope', *ZNW* 58: 93-102.
Daube, D.
1946   'Participle and Imperative in I Peter', Appended note in E.G. Selwyn,
            The First Epistle of St Peter (London: Macmillan, 2nd edn): 467-88.
Davids, P.H.
1990   *The First Epistle of Peter* (NICNT; Grand Rapids: Eerdmans).
Deichgräber, R.
1967   *Gotteshymnus und Christushymnus in der frühen Christenheit* (SUNT
            5; Göttingen: Vandenhoeck & Ruprecht).
Deissmann, A.
1923   *Licht vom Osten* (Tübingen: Mohr, 4th edn).
Delling, G.
1973   'Der Bezug der christlichen Existenz auf das Heilshandeln Gottes nach
            dem ersten Petrusbrief', in H.D. Betz (ed.), *Neues Testament und
            christliche Existenz* (FS H. Braun; Tübingen: Mohr): 94-113.
Denniston, J.D.
1954   *The Greek Particles* (Oxford: Clarendon Press, 2nd edn).
Dibelius, M.
1921   *Der Brief des Jakobus* (MeyerK 15; Göttingen: Vandenhoeck &
            Ruprecht).
1931   'Zur Formgeschichte des Neuen Testaments (ausserhalb der
            Evangelien)', *TRu* NS 3: 207-41.
Dijkman, J.H.L.
1987   '1 Peter—A Later Pastoral Stratum?', *NTS* 33: 265-71.
Donelson, L.R.
1986   *Pseudepigraphy and Ethical Argument in the Pastoral Epistles*
            (Tübingen: Mohr).
Doty, W.G.
1977   *Letters in Primitive Christianity* (Guides to Biblical Scholarship, N.T.
            Series; Philadelphia: Fortress Press).
Dressler, W.
1973   *Einführung in die Textlinguistik* (Konzepte der Sprach- und
            Literaturwissenschaft 13; Tübingen: Niemeyer, 2nd edn).

Eemeren, F.H. van
1987   'For Reason's Sake—Maximal Argumentative Analysis of Discourse',
            in F.H. van Eemeren *et al.*, *Argumentation: Across the Lines*
            (Dordrecht: Foris).
Eemeren, F.H. van and R. Grootendorst (eds.)
1984   *Speech Acts in Argumentative Discussions* (Dordrecht: Foris).
1992   *Argumentation, Communication, and Fallacies: A Pragma-Dialectical
            Perspective* (Hillsdale: Erlbaum).
Eemeren, F.H. van, R. Grootendorst and T. Kruiger (eds.)
1987   *Handbook of Argumentation Theory: A Critical Survey of Classical
            Backgrounds and Modern Studies* (Dutch original, 2nd edn, 1981;
            Pragmatics and Discourse Analysis; Dordrecht/Providence: Foris).
Eemeren, F.H. van, R. Grootendorst, J.A. Blair and Ch.A. Willard (eds.)
1987   *Argumentation: Analysis and Practices; Perspectives and Approaches;
            Across the Lines of the Discipline* (Proceedings of the Conference on
            Argumentation 1986; Dordrecht: Foris).
1991   *Proceedings of the Second International Conference on
            Argumentation* (Dordrecht: Foris).
Ehninger, D. and W. Brockriede
1966   *Decision by Debate* (New York: Dodd, Mead & Co.).
Elliger, W.
1980   'εἰς', *EWNT*, I, 965-68.
1980   'ἐν', *EWNT*, I, 1093-96.
Elliott, J.H.
1966   *The Elect and the Holy: An Exegetical Examination of 1 Peter 2:4-10
            and the Phrase* βασίλειον ἱεράτευμα (NovTSup 12, Leiden: Brill).
1976   'The Rehabilitation of an Exegetical Step-Child: 1 Peter in Recent
            Research', *JBL* 95: 243-54.
1981   *A Home for the Homeless: A Sociological Exegesis of 1 Peter, its
            Situation and Strategy* (Philadelphia: Fortress Press).
1985   'Backward and Forward "In His Steps"', in F.F. Segovia (ed.),
            Discipleship in the New Testament (Philadelphia: Fortress Press): 184-
            209.
1986   '1 Peter, its Situation and Strategy: A Discussion with David Balch', in
            C.H. Talbert (ed.), *Perspectives on First Peter* (NABPRSSS 9, Macon,
            GA: Mercer University Press): 61-78.
Ellul, D.
1990   'Un exemple de cheminement rhétorique: I Pierre', *RHPR* 70: 17-34.
Evang, M.
1989   ''Εκ καρδίας ἀλλήλους ἀγαπήσατε ἐκτενῶς. Zum Verständnis der
            Aufforderung und ihrer Begründungen in 1 Peter 1,22f', *ZNW*: 111-
            23.
Feldmeier, R.
1992   *Die Christen als Fremde* (WUNT 64, Tübingen: Mohr).
Fisher, W.R.
1987   'Technical Logic, Rhetorical Logic, and Narrative Rationality',
            Argumentation 1, 3-21.

Freeman, J.B.
1992   'Relevance, Warrants, Backing, Inductive Support', *Argumentation* 6:
            219-35.
Fuhrmann, M.
1987   *Die Antike Rhetorik: Eine Einführung* (Munich: Artemis).
Gammie, J.G.
1990   'Paraenetic Literature: Toward the Morphology of a Secondary
            Genre', *Semeia* 50: 41-77.
Geissner, H.
1987   'Rhetorical Communication as Argument', in F.H. van Eemeren *et al.*
            (eds.), *Argumentation: Accross the Lines of Discipline* (Dordrecht:
            Foris): 111-19.
Georges, K.E.
1918   *Ausführliches Lateinisch–Deutsches Handwörterbuch* (ed. H. Georges;
            Hannover: Hahnsche, 8th edn).
Golden, J.L.
1986   'The Universal Audience Revisited', in J.L. Golden and J.J. Pilotta
            (eds.), *Practical Reasoning in Human Affairs* (Dordrecht: Reidel).
Goldstein, H.
1975   *Paulinische Gemeinde im Ersten Petrusbrief* (SBS 80; Stuttgart:
            Katholisches Bibelwerk).
Goodwin, W.W. and C.B. Gulick
1981   *Greek Grammar* (W.W. Goodwin, rev. C.B. Gulick; College Classical
            Series; New Rochelle: Caratzas).
Goppelt, L.
1976   *Theologie des Neuen Testaments*, II (ed. J. Roloff; Göttingen:
            Vandenhoeck & Ruprecht).
1978   *Der Erste Petrusbrief* (ed. F. Hahn; MeyerK 12.1; Göttingen:
            Vandenhoeck & Ruprecht, 8th edn).
Göttert, K.-H.
1978   *Argumentation* (Tübingen: Niemeyer).
Green, G.L.
1990   'The Use of the Old Testament for Christian Ethics in 1 Peter', *TynBul*
            41: 276-89.
Gross, A.G.
1991   'Rhetoric of Science without Constraints', *Rhetorica* 9: 283-300.
Grundmann, W.
1938   'καλός' A-F, *ThWNT*, III, 539-53.
Gyllenberg, R.
1969   *Uuden testamentin johdanto-oppi* (Helsinki: Otava, 2nd edn).
Hakalehto, I.
1974   *Väinö Tanner—omalla linjalla* (Helsinki: Kirjayhtymä, 2nd edn).
Harder, G.
1973   'φθείρω', *ThWNT*, IX, 100-103.
Harman, G.
1986   *Change in View: Principles of Reasoning* (Cambridge: MIT Press).

Hartman, L.
1988   'Some Unorthodox Thoughts on the "Household-Code Form"', in
        J. Neusner *et al.* (eds.), *The Social World of Formative Christianity
        and Judaism* (FS H.C. Kee; Philadelphia: Fortress Press): 219-32.
Hellholm, D.
1980   *Das Visionenbuch des Hermas als Apokalypse: Formgeschichtliche
        und textteoretische Studien zu einer literarischen Gattung*, I (ConBNT
        13.1; Lund: Gleerup).
Henkemans, A.F.
1992   *Analyzing Complex Argumentation: The Reconstruction of Multiple
        and Coordinatively Compound Argumentation in a Critical Discussion*
        (Amsterdam: SICSAT).
Hess, A.J.
1980   'διά', *EWNT*, I, 712-13.
Hill, D.
1976   'On Suffering and Baptism in 1 Peter', *NovT* 18: 181-89.
Holdsworth, J.
1980   'The Sufferings in 1 Peter and "Missionary" Apocalyptic', in
        E.A. Livingstone (ed.), *Studia Biblica*, III (JSNTSup 3; Sheffield:
        JSOT Press): 225-34.
Holmer, U. and W. de Boor
1976   *Die Briefe des Petrus und der Brief des Judas* (Wuppertaler
        Studienbibel; Wuppertal: Brockhaus).
Huth, L.
1975   'Argumentationstheorie und Textanalyse', *Deutschunterricht* 27: 80-
        110.
Jewett, R.
1986   *The Thessalonian Correspondence: Pauline Rhetoric and Millinarian
        Piety* (Foundations & Facets: New Testament; Philadelphia: Fortress
        Press).
Johanson, B.C.
1987   *To All the Brethren: A Text-Linguistic and Rhetorical Approach to
        I Thessalonians* (ConBNT 16; Stockholm: Almquist & Wiksell).
Johnstone, H.W.
1989   'Argumentation and Formal Logic in Philosophy', *Argumentation* 3:
        5-16.
Jonsen, A.R. and S. Toulmin
1988   *The Abuse of Casuistry: A History of Moral Reasoning* (Berkeley:
        University of California Press).
Kamlah, E.
1964   *Die Form der katalogischen Paränese in Neuen Testament* (WUNT 7;
        Tübingen: Mohr).
Kant, I.
1961   *Critique of Pure Reason* (New York: St Martin).
Käsemann, E.
1960   *Exegetische Versuche und Besinnungen*, I (Göttingen: Vandenhoeck
        & Ruprecht, 2nd edn).

Kelly, J.N.D.
1969   *A Commentary on the Epistles of Peter and Jude* (BNTC; London: Black).
Kleine, H.
1981   'ὅτι', *EWNT*, II, 1316-17.
Knoch, O.
1990   *Der Erste und Zweite Petrusbrief. Der Judasbrief* (Regensburg: Pustet).
Köhler, W.
1981   'ἐπί', *EWNT*, II, 54-57.
1981   'κατά', *EWNT*, II, 624-27.
Kopperschmidt, J.
1981   'Argumentationstheoretische Anfragen an die Rhetorik', *Zeitschrift für Literaturwissenschaft und Linguistik* 43/44 (Göttingen): 44-65.
Kosala, K.C.P.
1985   'Taufverständnis und Theologie im Ersten Petrusbrief' (unpublished PhD thesis, University of Kiel).
Krabbe, E.C.W.
1992   Review of Informal Logic, by D.N. Walton, *Argumentation* 3: 368-73.
Kraftchick, S.J.
1985   'Ethos and Pathos Appeals in Galatians Five and Six: A Rhetorical Analysis' (unpublished PhD thesis, University of Atlanta).
Kuss, O.
1971   *Paulus* (Regensburg: Pustet).
Laato, T.
1991   *Paulus und das Judentum: Anthropologische Erwägungen* (Åbo: Abo Academy Press).
Lampe, P.
1981   'ἵνα', *EWNT*, II, 460-66.
Langsdorf, L.
1990   'On the Uses of Language in Working and Idealized Logic', *Argumentation* 4: 259-68.
Lategan, B.C.
1990   'Is Paul Developing a Specifically Christian Ethics in Galatians?', in D.L. Balch, E. Ferguson and W.A. Meeks (eds.), *Greeks, Romans, and Christians* (FS A.J. Malherbe; Minneapolis: Fortress Press).
Laub, F.
1980   *Bekenntnis und Auslegung: Die paränetische Funktion der Christologie im Hebräerbrief* (Biblische Untersuchungen 15; Regensburg: Pustet).
Lausberg, H.
1960   *Handbuch der literarischen Rhetorik* (2 vols.; Munich: Hueber).
Leaney, A.R.C.
1963–64   'I Peter and the Passover: An Interpretation', *NTS* 10: 238-51.
Liddell, H.G. and R. Scott
1978   *A Greek–English Lexicon, with a Supplement* (rev. H. Stuart Jones and R. McKenzie; E.A. Barber; Oxford: Clarendon Press, 9th edn).
Lohse, E.
1954   'Paränese und Kerygma im I. Petrusbrief', *ZNW* 45: 68-89.

236   *Argument and Theology in 1 Peter*

Louw, J.P. and E. Nida (eds.)
1988   *Greek–English Lexicon of the New Testament Based on Semantic Domains* (2 vols.; New York: United Bible Society).
Lüdemann, G.
1980   'εἰ', *EWNT*, I, 931-33.
Luther, M.
1891   *Werke* (Kritische Gesamtausgabe 12; Weimar: Böhlau).
Mack, B.
1990   *Rhetoric and the New Testament* (Minneapolis: Fortress Press).
Makau, J.M.
1987   Review of J.D. Moss, 'Rhetoric and Praxis', *Rhetorica*.
Malherbe, A.
1986   *Moral Exhortation: A Greco-Roman Source Book* (Philadelphia: Fortress Press).
Manke, H.
1976   'Leiden und Herrlichkeit: Eine Studie zur Christologie des 1. Petrusbriefes', Münster (unpublished).
Marshall, I.H.
1991   *1 Peter* (IVP NT Commentary Series; Leicester: InterVarsity).
1991   'Rhetoric in 1 Peter', *ExpTim* 102: 317.
Martin, T.
1992a   *Metaphor and Composition in 1 Peter* (SBLDS 131; Atlanta: Scholars Press).
1992b   'The Present Indicative in the Eschatological Statements of 1 Pet 1.6, 8', *JBL* 111: 307-12.
Marxsen, W.
1989   *'Christliche' und cristliche Ethik im Neuen Testament* (Gütersloh: Mohn).
McCartney, D.
1991   'λογικός in 1 Peter 2,2', *ZNW* 82: 128-32.
McKnight, S.
1991   *A Light among the Gentiles—Jewish Missionary Activity in the Second Temple Period* (Minneapolis: Fortress Press).
Meiland, J.W.
1987   'Argument as Inquiry and Argument as Persuasion', *Argumentation* 1: 185-96.
Melanchthon, P.
1925   *Die Loci communes* (ed. G.L. Plitt and T. Kolde; Leipzig: Deichert, 4th edn).
Michaels, J.R.
1966   'Eschatology in I Peter III.17', *NTS* 13: 394-401.
1988   *1 Peter* (WBC 49; Waco, TX: Word Books).
Miller, J.H.
1989   'Is There an Ethics of Reading?', in J. Phelan (ed.), *Reading Narrative: Form, Ethics, Ideology* (Columbus: Ohio State University Press).

Mitchell, M.M.
1991   *Paul and the Rhetoric of Reconciliation* (Hermeneutische
            Untersuchungen zur Theologie 28; Tübingen: Mohr).
Moss, J.D.
1986   'The Revival of Practical Reasoning', in J.D. Moss (ed.), *Rhetoric and
            Praxis* (Washington: Catholic University of America Press): 1-21.
Moule, C.F.D.
1956-57   'The Nature and Purpose of 1 Peter', *NTS* 3: 1-11.
Nauck, W.
1955   'Freude im Leiden. Zum Problem einer urchristlichen
            Verfolgungstradition', *ZNW* 46: 68-80.
1958   'Das οὐκ-paräneticum', *ZNW* 49: 134-35.
Neugebauer, F.
1979   'Zur Deutung und Bedeutung des 1. Petrusbriefes', *NTS* 26: 61-86.
Nida, E.A.
1975   *Exploring Semantic Structures* (Munich: Fink).
Nieder, L.
1956   *Die Motive der religiös-sittlichen Paränese in den Paulinischen
            Gemeindebriefen* (Münchener Theologische Studien 12; Munich).
Nissilä, K.
1979   *Das Hohepriestermotiv im Hebräerbrief: Eine exegetische
            Untersuchung* (Schriften der Finnischen exegetischen Gesellschaft 33;
            Helsinki: Finnish Exegetical Society).
Nuchelmans, G.
1991   *Dilemmatic Arguments: Towards a History of their Logic and Rhetoric*
            (Amsterdam: North-Holland).
Nygren, A.
1944   *Pauli brev till romarna*, Tolkning av Nya testamentet 6 (Stockholm:
            Svenska kyrkans diakonistiftelsens bokförlag).
O'Banion, J.D.
1987   'Narration and Argumentation: Quintilian on *Narratio* as the Heart of
            Rhetorical Thinking', *Rhetorica*, 325-51.
Oepke, A.
1935   'διά', *ThWNT*, II, 64-69.
Olsson, B.
1982   *Första Petrusbrevet* (Kommentar till Nya Testamentet 17; Stockholm:
            EFS).
1986   'Den petrinska traditionen och judarna', in B. Gerhardsson *et al.*
            (eds.), *Judendom och kristendom under de första århundradena*
            (Nordiskt patristikerprojekt 1982–1985; Stavanger/Oslo/Bergen/
            Tromsø: Universitetsforlaget): 215-36.
Osborne, T.P.
1983   'Guide Lines for Christian Suffering: A Source-Critical and
            Theological Study of 1 Peter 2,21-25', *Bib* 64, 3: 381-408.
Parker, D.
1994   'The Eschatology of 1 Peter', *BTB* 24: 27-32.

Perdelwitz, R.
1911   *Die Mysterienreligionen und das Problem des I. Petrusbriefes: Ein
            literarischer und religionsgeschichtlicher Versuch* (Religions-
            geschichtliche Versuche und Vorarbeiten 11.3; Giessen: Töpelmann).
Perdue, L.G.
1990   'The Social Character of Paraenesis and Paraenetic Literature', *Semeia*
            50: 5-39.
Perelman, C.
1982   *The Realm of Rhetoric* (trans. from French; Notre Dame: University of
            Notre Dame Press).
Perelman, C. and L. Olbrechts-Tyteca
1969   *The New Rhetoric: A Treatise on Argumentation* (French original
            1958; Notre Dame: University of Notre Dame Press).
Piper, J.
1979   *'Love your Enemies': Jesus' Love Command in the Synoptic Gospels
            and in the Early Christian Paraenesis* (SNTSS 38; Cambridge:
            Cambridge University Press).
1980   'Hope as the Motivation of Love: 1 Peter 3.9-12', *NTS* 26: 221-31.
Pohlenz, M.
1948   *Die Stoa* (Göttingen: Vandenhoeck & Ruprecht).
Porter, S.
1994   *Idioms of the Greek New Testament* (Biblical Languages: Greek 2;
            Sheffield: JSOT Press, 2nd edn with corrections,).
Preisker, H.
1949   *Das Ethos des Urchristentums* (Gütersloh: Mohn, 2nd edn).
Pridik, K.-H.
1980   'γάρ', *EWNT*, I, 571-72.
1981   'καί', *EWNT*, II, 557-60.
Prostmeier, F.-R.
1990   *Handlungsmodelle im Ersten Petrusbrief* (Forschung zur Bibel 63,
            Würzburg: Echter).
Quinn, J.D.
1990   'Paraenesis and the Pastoral Epistles', *Semeia* 50: 189-210.
Radermacher, L.
1926   'Der erste Petrusbrief und Silvanus', *ZNW* 25: 287-99.
Reichert, A.
1989   *Eine urchristliche Praeparatio ad martyrium: Studien zur
            Komposition, Traditionsgeschichte und Theologie des 1 Petrusbriefes*
            (Frankfurt: Lang).
Reicke, B.
1964   *The Epistles of James, Peter, and Jude* (AB 37; New York: Doubleday,
            2nd edn).
Rensburg, J.J.J. van
1990   'The Use of Intersentence Relational Particles and Asyndeton in First
            Peter', *Neot* 24: 283-300.

Richard, E.
1986   'The Functional Christology of First Peter', in C.H. Talbert (ed.),
             Perspectives on First Peter (NABPRSSS 9; Macon, GA: Mercer
             University Press): 121-39.
Robbins, V.K.
1990   'A Socio-Rhetorical Response', *Semeia* 50: 261-71.
Rousseau, J.
1986   'A Multidimensional Approach Towards the Communication of an
             Ancient Canonized Text: Towards Determining the Thrust, Perspective
             and Strategy of 1 Peter' (Pretoria) (unpublished).
Sanders, E.P.
1977   *Paul and Palestinian Judaism: A Comparison of Patterns of Religion*
             (London: SCM Press).
Sanders, J.T.
1986   *Ethics in the New Testament* (London: SCM Press).
Schelkle, K.H.
1970   *Die Petrusbriefe: Der Judasbrief* (HTKNT 13.2; Freiburg: Herder, 2nd
             edn).
Schnackenburg, R.
1991   *The Epistle to the Ephesians: A Commentary* (trans. H. Heron;
             Edinburgh: T. & T. Clark).
Schneider, G.
1980   'διό', *EWNT*, I, 811.
1980   'διότι', *EWNT*, I, 812-13.
Schrage, W.
1961   *Die konkreten Einzelgebote in der paulinischen Paränese: Ein Beitrag
             zur neutestamentlichen Ethik* (Gütersloh: Mohn).
1982   *Ethik des Neuen Testaments* (Grundrisse zum Neuen Testament, NTD
             4.4; Göttingen: Vandenhoeck & Ruprecht).
Schulz, S.
1987   *Neutestamentliche Ethik* (Zürich: Theologischer Verlag).
Schutter, W.L.
1989   *Hermeneutic and Composition in I Peter* (WUNT 2; Reihe 30,
             Tübingen: Mohr).
Schwyzer, E.
1953–71   *Griechische Grammatik*, I-IV (ed. A. Debrunner, D.J. Georgacas and
             S. Radt; Handbuch der Altertumswissenschaft; Munich: Beck, 1950,
             2nd edn).
Searle, J.R.
1970   *Speech Acts* (Cambridge: Cambridge University Press, 2nd edn).
Seeberg, A.
1966   *Der Katechismus der Urchristenheit* (Munich: Kaiser Verlag, 1903).
Selwyn, E.G.
1947   *The First Epistle of St Peter* (London: Macmillan, 2nd edn).
Siegert, F.
1985   *Argumentation bei Paulus gezeigt an Röm 9–11* (WUNT 34;
             Tübingen: Mohr).

240   *Argument and Theology in 1 Peter*

Simons, H.W.
1976   *Persuasion* (Reading: Addison–Wesley).
1990   *The Rhetorical Turn* (Chicago: University of California Press).
Snyder, S.
1991   '1 Peter 2:17: A Reconsideration', *Filología Neotestamentaria* 4: 211-
            15.
Spicq, C.
1966   *Les épîtres de Saint Pierre* (SB; Paris: Gabalda).
Stowers, S.
1986   *Letter-Writing in Greco-Roman Antiquity* (Philadelphia: Westminster
            Press).
Strobel, A.
1956   'Zum Verständnis von Röm 13', *ZNW* 47: 80-85.
Sutton, J.
1986   'The Death of Rhetoric and its Rebirth in Philosophy', *Rhetorica* 4:
            203-26.
Sylva, D.
1982   'A 1 Peter Bibliography', *JETS* 25: 75-89.
Thiede, C.P.
1986   'Babylon, der andere Ort: Anmerkungen zu 1 Petr 5,13 und Apg
            12,17', *Bib* 67: 532-38.
Thornton, T.C.G.
1961   '1 Peter—A Paschal Liturgy?', *JTS* NS 12: 14-26.
Thurén, L.
1988a   'Parenesens motivering i Första Petrusbrevet' (Licentiate thesis,
            unpublished, Åbo).
1988b   *Ensimmäinen ja toinen Pietarinkirje* (Helsinki: SLEY-kirjat).
1990   *The Rhetorical Strategy of 1 Peter* (Åbo: Abo Academy Press).
1991   'Vad är retorisk kritik?', *Teologinen Aikakauskirja* 1: 41-45.
Toulmin, S.
1958   *The Uses of Argument* (Cambridge: Cambridge University Press).
Toulmin,S., R. Rieke and A. Janik
1984   *An Introduction to Reasoning* (New York: Macmillan, 2nd edn).
Turner, N.
1976   *J.H. Moulton: A Grammar of New Testament Greek.* III. *Syntax*
            (Edinburgh: T. & T. Clark).
Unnik, W.C. van
1954–55   'The Teaching of Good Works in 1 Peter', *NTS* 1: 198-202.
Vanhoye, A.
1979   '1 Pierre au carrefour des théologies du Noveau Testament', in *Etudes
            sur la première lettre de Pierre: Congrès de l'ACFEB* (Paris: Cerf): 97-
            128.
Varga, A.K.
1987   'Some Questions about the Rhetorical Analysis of Literary Texts', in
            van Eemeren, Grootendorst, Blair and Willard 1987: 289-94.
Vickers, B.
1988   *In Defense of Rhetoric* (Oxford: Clarendon University Press).

Viertel, W.
1976   'The Hermeneutics of Paul' (unpublished PhD thesis, University of
            Waco).
Wallace, W.A.
1986   '*Aitia*: Causal Reasoning in Composition and Rhetoric', in J.D. Moss
            (ed.), *Rhetoric and Praxis* (Washington: Catholic University of
            America Press): 107-33.
Walton, D.N.
1989   *Informal Logic: A Handbook for Critical Argumentation* (Cambridge:
            Cambridge University Press).
Warnick, B.
1989   'Judgment, Probability, and Aristotle's Rhetoric', *Quarterly Journal of
            Speech*: 299-311.
Weinstein, M.
1990   'Toward an Account of Argumentation in Science', *Argumentation* 4:
            269-98.
Wendland, H.-D.
1970   *Ethik des Neuen Testaments* (NTD 4; Göttingen: Vandenhoeck &
            Ruprecht).
Wenzel, J.W.
1987a   'The Rhetorical View on Argumentation: Exploring a Paradigm',
            Argumentation 1: 73-89.
1987b   'The Rhetorical Perspective on Argument', in van Eemeren,
            Grootendorst, Blair and Willard 1987: 101-109.
Wibbing, S.
1959   *Die Tugend- und Lasterkataloge im NT* (Berlin: Töpelmann).
Williams, D.C. and M.D. Hazen (eds.)
1990   *Argumentation Theory and the Rhetoric of Assent* (Tuscaloosa:
            University of Alabama Press).
Windisch, H.
1951   *Die katholischen Briefe* (HNT 15; 3rd edn rev. H. Preisker; Tübingen:
            Mohr [1911]).
Wire, A.C.
1990   *The Corinthian Women Prophets: A Reconstruction through Paul's
            Rhetoric* (Minneapolis: Fortress Press).
Wohlrapp, H.
1987   'Toulmin's Theory and the Dynamics of Argumentation', in
            van Eemeren, Grootendorst, Blair and Willard 1987: 327-35.
Wonneberger, R.
1976   'Ansätze zu einer textlinguistischen Beschreibung der Argumentation
            bei Paulus', in W. Meid and K. Heller (eds.), *Textlinguistik und
            Semantik* (Innsbruck: Innsbruck Institut für Sprachwissenschaft).
Wuellner, W.
1979   'Greek Rhetoric and Pauline Argumentation', in W.R. Schoedel and
            R.L. Wilken (eds.), *Early Christian Literature and the Classical
            Intellectual Tradition* (FS R.M. Grant; Théologie historique 53; Paris:
            Beauchesne): 177-88.

Zappel, K.
1987   'Argumentation and Literary Texts', in van Eemeren, Grootendorst, Blair and Willard 1987: 217-24.

Zerwick, M.
1963   *Biblical Greek* (trans. J. Smith; Rome: Scripta Pontifici instituti biblici).

INDEXES

INDEX OF REFERENCES

INDEX OF AUTHORS

JOURNAL FOR THE STUDY OF THE NEW TESTAMENT

Supplement Series